Publications of the Texas Folklore Society Number XLIII

LEGENDARY LADIES OF TEXAS

LEGENDARY LADIES
OF TEXAS

Edited by Francis Edward Abernethy

1994 / University of North Texas Press / Denton

© 1981, 1994 Texas Folklore Society / Nacogdoches, Texas

Originally published by E-Heart Press, Dallas, Texas
Original design by Eje Wray

Second Edition 1994

10 9 8 7 6 5 4 3 2 1

Requests for permission to reproduce material from this work should be sent
to:

Texas Folklore Society
Post Office Box 13007, SFA Station
Nacogdoches, Texas 75962

Library of Congress Cataloging-in-Publication Data

Legendary ladies of Texas / edited by Francis Edward Abernethy
    p.   cm. — (Publications of the Texas Folklore Society ; no. 43)
                    Includes index.
                    ISBN 0-929398-75-0 (pbk.)
    1. Women—Texas—History. 2. Women—Texas—Biography. 3. Women—
Texas—Folklore. 4. Legends—Texas. I. Abernethy, Francis Edward. I. Series.
                    GR1.T4 no. 43, 1994
                    [HQ1438.T4]
                    390 s—de20
        [305.4'09764   94-16318
                    CIP

CONTENTS

In which the editor searches his soul, encounters the need for an agonizing reappraisal, and finally realizes that he is living in sin—and likes it.

PREFACE

When the women's liberation movement began to gather steam and national publicity, I took a quick glance at myself, perceived a more than generous sense of liberality where the sexes were concerned, and considered that I was a viable part of the new equalities. I was indignant and incensed at the laws that discriminated against women, at administrators who would not pay equal wages for equal labors, and at bankers and businesses that failed to deal with single women on terms equal to men. I paraded my new-found virtue with ostentation.

I continually found myself working in close association with women, especially literary women, and I had not the least difficulty. They were kind enough never to threaten my manhood, and I responded in the same spirit. I quit buying *Playboy* because of its flagrant exploitation of sexuality and indignantly left the room during the television airings of the Miss America Pageant.

My wife never doubted the concept of female equality and, in fact, frequently voiced a firm confidence in female superiority—mentally, physically, and morally. I seldom question her judgment. This, in fact, was my downfall. I did truly believe that women were cut out of a finer piece of cloth than men. I believed that they existed on a higher plane, were purer and more refined than men. I lived in the "damsel syndrome," where knights put their ladies on pedestals and sang sad songs to them, and sighed longingly in fourteen-line, iambic pentameter poems. I felt that men were put on earth to rescue women from dragons and to protect them from robber barons. I enjoyed lighting their cigarettes, opening doors, helping them with their coats, walking on the outside, tipping my hat. I truly believed that all this was my show of respect in the equality game and that ladies should reciprocate by graciously accepting these gestures and smiling warmly in approval.

Then I was told in no uncertain terms that in spite of my attitude toward the legalities of women's rights these other actions were glaring indicators of the grossest sort of male chauvinism and that they reflected my real feelings of macho superiority. It was a traumatic moment.

This recognition scene occurred at coffee one morning when several faculty members, male and female, were discussing whether or not women should be drafted. In spite of the pronouncements of Rosalyn Carter, I asserted—in a very moderate tone, really, and doubting not but that all present would readily agree—that women were the rocks of the family hearth, the carriers of the seeds of man's survival, that they were celestial beings who should be shielded from harshness, protected, loved, and cherished—never drafted!

Well, you won't believe this, but the women at the table pounced on me as if I had just pronounced their doomdom in outer darkness. The kindest remark they made was, "Now, if that's not a piece of (commonly used four-letter word deleted)!" In the following thirty minutes the ladies completely disabused me of my liberal self image. They argued that true sexual equality meant that women would bear the same martial responsibilities as men. Furthermore, they pointed out that my type of hat tipping, door opening, male prancing and pluming was a Victorian anachronism and a male chauvinistic display that modern women were well rid of.

It took some while to get over this upbraiding. I was plagued by doubts and disbelief and some guilt. I sat at coffee with men's P.E. teachers or my friends from the schools of forestry and agriculture. I attempted to follow that dictum of Greek classicism, "Know thyself," and tried to develop a more positive self image, meanwhile skulking shamedly when approached by women and knowing that they discussed my transgressions and were probably plotting some horrible revenge. During this time I tipped no hats, lit no cigarettes, bought no coffee, walked on no outsides.

Then one day I chanced into an experience that had a profound effect on my life. I learned that I was truly a male chauvinist—according to the modern women's liberation definition—and that I had always been and would always be, in spite of my liberal caterwaulings. And with this knowledge I put on wisdom and accepted my condition.

It happened like this.

I was leaving my building and I happened to arrive at the door at the same time as a lady of very noticeable qualities. She was just about half a notch past prime, obviously a woman of generosity and understanding. My chauvinistic conditioning completely took over, and I opened the door with a flourish and just a hint of a bow. She passed through, pausing almost imperceptibly, and then smiled, looking directly into my eyes.

My ingrained inclination was to rush after her, furiously tipping my hat, offering a cigarette that I might light it, spreading my J. C. Penney corduroy coat on the asphalt to protect her dainty feet. I could have passed a dozen amusing pleasantries had I merely walked down the steps with her, bon mots that would have brightened her day to hear them and mine to have said them. As it was, I responded as I usually do in such situations: I lost my power of speech and went into static shock and stood with my hand on the door until she had faded forever into the traffic.

When I recovered my composure my first thought was of lost opportunity. Then, more importantly, I realized that though I had lost the moment I had gained an education. I had shown my true Victorian male colors. My previous liberalism was a sham only slightly covering my real chauvinistic nature. I think that educationists would refer to this experience as a positive reinforcement of a latent conditioned response. Whatever the case, I therewith accepted my destiny as I have accepted the other warts and moles of my character. I have since decided to wear my scarlet MC as a badge of honor, recognizing also that if I acted otherwise I would stress my nervous system by going against my nature. And I have found peace.

Well, almost.

I have been having considerable difficulty with terminology. I early on accepted the Ms. tag, mainly on pragmatic, not philosophic grounds. Also, in my part of the country "Miz" and "Mizzes" are standard pronunciations, usually referring to a Mrs. I found *Ms.*, however, to be useful in correspondence when marital status was unknown, so I use it without qualm.

I find myself on less solid ground with other words that refer to the feminine gender. My eldest daughter once showered down on me during one of our shouting matches for referring to her as a woman. She was sixteen at the time and somehow or other felt that there was a coarseness implicit in that appelation. I proceeded to give her an extended lecture on the strength of womanhood and forgot the topic of our original argument.

I have been challenged on the use of *girls*, a term I increasingly use as I grow older and find that most females I deal with are my daughters' ages or younger. Also, I frequently call ladies "girls" to imply that I recognize and appreciate the youthful charm that I still recognize in them. There are some who do not understand this subtle implication.

I have been informed that the use of the word *female* divests them of their sexuality so I placed that word on the Index. I think that there are times when they want their sexuality to be recognized and times when they don't. One can't always be sure which time applies. Then to completely abort my vocabulary I received a strong paragraph from a ♀

criticizing my use of *ladies* in the title of this book. Her case was that *ladies* was a term used in condescension, as in "ladies' teas," and had as of late fallen into the illest sort of repute.

The terms *broads, frails, chicks, skirts,* and *quail* have long been forbidden figures of speech, and one is always careful of his usage of *madam*. I had a rakish uncle who in Old Testament humor referred to his sweeties as "ribs," a practice I imitated in my youth but no more. I won't even discuss the prevailing feminist attitudes toward *sugar, honey, babe, doll,* and *sweet thing,* all of which I once fondly thought expressed my feeling of warmth and love for the sex that I am not ("Opposite sex" can also be faulted on the basis of why and who is "opposite."). These new adjustments to the vocabulary of the women's liberation movement are making life and language increasingly complex.

In spite of which, I still thought it necessary that the Texas Folklore Society produce this book.

Several things sighted me in on the legendary ladies topic. It was very timely, for one thing, and the women's liberation movement is a modern social phenomenon that needs this sort of contemporary documentation by the Texas Folklore Society. Also, the East Texas Historical Society in September, 1976, presented a program on historical and legendary ladies that indicated what a wide and fascinating field this was.

I think, though, that what really inspired me to do this was remembering Frank Dobie's story about Pamelia Mann in that great Centennial puff, *The Flavor of Texas*. I had read Dobie's story years back and at first had only the vaguest sort of outline in my head. But what I did have was the core of folklore and legend; I had forgotten the facts but I remembered the spirit. I remembered Sam Houston talking Pamelia out of a team of oxen during the Runaway Scrape. She said that taking her team was all right as long as he was staying on the road to Nacogdoches. He said he was, and he hooked the yoke to a wagon carrying the Twin Sisters and began hauling. At the Harrisburg road, however, he turned off and was several miles down the road before Pamelia caught up with him.

Mrs. Mann blued the air with her denunciation of the General, cut loose her oxen, and headed them toward Nacogdoches with her black snake popping. One of Houston's officers set off in pursuit of her with the warning from the General that the woman would bite. When the officer returned late into the night he showed all the signs of having been bitten, bruised, and scratched and his shirt was torn half way off of him. One of the soldiers remarked that Mrs. Mann must have needed the shirt cloth for baby rags.

I liked that woman and that story from the first time I read it. Whether the story is fact or folklore never really entered my mind. It certainly is based on some facts because there were eye witness accounts of the episode, but there were also variations of the account. It is a good legend. I liked the woman. Whether I would have liked her in real life is something else. In the story she is a real person, but she stands for qualities that are bigger than real. She is the strong individual battling a strong system and winning and making the system look silly.

The great folklore of the world—that which has proved its value to society by surviving many generations of selecting—is definitely not a bunch of old lies, even though the stories and songs and traditions and beliefs might not bear the close scrutiny of the cold and scientific eye. Mankind's emotional perception of his experiences cannot be evaluated with a plumb line, square, and level. And this thing called Truth that the seekers and philosophers have so hotly pursued through the centuries comes in many shy and shifting shapes. The ultimate truths are those that man finds in his gods and in his heavens, and in those rare and holy moments when he briefly but completely comprehends the awesome beauty of life and living, and in his straining and spine-wracking striving for perfections that his plumb line tells him are far beyond his worldly dimensions. The heroes of legend—the Joshuas and Judiths, the Hectors and Hecubas, the Molly Pitchers and George Washingtons, and Pamelia Mann and The Babe—all of these men and women are forms of the ultimate truths, because out of the color and the vitality and the humanity of their lives they have become symbols for some of our highest and most enduring values. In the bare-boned truth of their own times they might have been strung on the same strings of raw nerves and sinews as all the rest of their fellows, and like the rest of us frail mortals they surely suffered the agonies of not knowing their right hands from their left—but the legends that grew from the seed of their deeds transcended their times and became larger than their times as we invested them with some aspect of our culture's chief values. We made them our heroes, and we let them stand for what we wished we could be when we wanted to be our best. And we would be a petty people without them.

So that's what *Legendary Ladies* is. It's a book about Texas women whose deeds have so struck the public imagination that they have become archetypes, representing the virtues and values that people have found interesting and admirable, characteristics that have survival value. The fact that the stories of these ladies have not been adequately documented down through the years is an error of omission that the Texas Folklore Society would like to do its part to correct.

The Society is proud to be doing this volume in cooperation with the Texas Foundation for Women's Resources, more specifically with the Foundation's Women in Texas History Project, under the directorship of Mary Beth Rogers of Austin. Mrs. Rogers runs a tight ship with a sharp crew, and her researchers, many of whom have contributed to this volume, have amassed an impressive collection of histories of Texas women. Their major work at this time is their 350 page *Texas Women's History Project Bibliography*, edited by Ruthe Winegarten and published this past year in 1979. In 1981 the Foundation will present a major exhibit featuring women in Texas history at the Institute of Texan Cultures in San Antonio. After the Institute show, the exhibit will go on tour for two years.

The point that the History Project makes is that women have been an active, energetic, and influential part of Texas history since the first one crossed its borders. And all this activity and involvement did not begin with Carrie Nations (who busted up her share of bars in Texas) or the suffragettes or women's liberation or the ERA movement. It began with Lilith and Eve. It's just that the wheel has really started squeaking now and the media is finally giving it the grease that it has always deserved. The Texas Folklore Society is pleased to be pulling in tandem with the Texas Foundation and doing its bit in belated but heartfelt recognition.

I usually end the preface with a flourish and an out-of-space to the Society's main benefactors, President of the University William R. Johnson and Head of the English Department Roy E. Cain. I always thank them for their moral and financial support, comment on their fine posture and high academic qualities, and hope that the good will that presently exists between the Society and the university continues. I thank Martha Dickson, the Society's secretary and assistant editor, who ably manages the manuscripts for these volumes until it is time to turn them over to other hands. And I give special thanks to the contributors, without whom . . . *etc.* Consider these formalities happily attended to.

This preface shall have an extra paragraph. Will all the male members of the Society please stand and raise high their glasses of bourbon and branch water.

This forty-third volume of the publications of the Texas Folklore Society is dedicated to all the great women who touch a man's life and make it worth living: to our grandmothers, those great old snuff-dipping pioneers and settler sisters who were Texans when the range grass was stirrup high; to the mothers who raised us and are still convinced that someday we're going to grow up and be responsible citizens; to the wives who have blessed us and baned us beyond description and analysis and who are convinced that they will eventually make us better men; and to our dear daughters who have loved us more than we can possibly expect or deserve.

To the mothers and the others—the paragons, quintessences, the most exciting and beautiful parts of our lives, who have saved us from as many idiocies as they have driven us to—God bless them!

Francis Edward Abernethy
Nacogdoches, Texas
October 16, 1980

LEGENDARY LADIES OF TEXAS

WOMEN IN TEXAS HISTORY AND LEGEND

Mary Beth Rogers

Project Director
Texas Women's History Project
Texas Foundation for Women's Resources

Texas women and the conflicting images and myths that have grown up about them! We all know some of the stories about the saints on those proverbial pedestals and the sinners wallowing in the gritty Texas dust—grand tales of adventure and excitement. Now some of the best of these are presented by the Texas Folklore Society in this most welcome publication, *Legendary Ladies of Texas*.

The Texas Women's History Project of the Foundation for Women's Resources has been collecting stories like these, and others, based on scraps of historical facts, documents, records, letters and journals. For the first time this information is being organized to illustrate the nature of the female experience, a distinct and largely ignored part of our social and political heritage as Texans.

The Foundation for Women's Resources, working with the Institute of Texan Cultures, is also sponsoring a major exhibit about Texas women which will be touring the state in 1981 and 1982. Five "sampler" exhibits are available to small museums, libraries, public schools and other public institutions.

These exhibits use historical materials to show that Texas women were influential in the development of the state. They focus on the

Texas women who were gun runners, cotton pickers, politicians, mothers, ranchers, bridge builders, do-gooders, capitalists, telephone operators, labor organizers, institutional fundraisers, community leaders, military pilots, physicians, rodeo queens, rock stars and more.

The facts about these women are just as interesting as the legends about our better known saints and sinners.

Texas women were activists. They ran ranches, branded cattle, lobbied the halls of the Texas Legislature with the most hardened "good ole boys," wrote books, invented products, made big money, negotiated treaties, led strikes, ran hospitals, preached the gospel, got elected to public office and built major institutions.

Women brought civilized life to hundreds of Texas towns by organizing libraries, museums, parks, symphony orchestras, Sunday schools, literary clubs and charitable organizations.

Some Texas women were even quite outrageous. Many were outlaws in spirit, if not always in fact. The artist Elizabet Ney scandalized her neighbors with her unorthodox behavior. Janis Joplin scandalized the nation while she captivated a whole generation of rock music fans. Socialist leader Lucy Gonzalez Parsons and her husband Albert Parsons, the Chicago Haymarket Square martyr, had to leave Texas to fight for their unpopular causes.

Other Texas women expanded the range of allowable experiences for women by proving their own extraordinary capabilities. Babe Didrikson's athletic successes forty years ago have set a precedent for women's sports programs today. Her achievement made it illogical (and now it is illegal) to deny young women opportunities to develop their athletic potential in the public schools. Much of this information about Texas women has been overlooked or discounted by historians who may have been unaware of its significance. Their omissions are no longer excusable or acceptable.

The Texas Women's History Project has identified certain patterns arising from the female experience which have made a difference to Texas.

Here are some of the facts:

There is a tradition of effective organized political activity among women dating from the 1880's. It began with the Temperance Movement, led largely by women. Many Temperance leaders also moved into the Texas Woman's Suffrage Movement in the period from 1903 to 1920. Both movements achieved their goals, and their leaders moved on again. Hundreds of Texas women held elective office in the 1920's and 30's. Governor Miriam A. Ferguson is perhaps the state's most notable female politician. State School Superintendent Annie Webb Blanton and Secretary of State Jane Y. McCallum might have been the most effective. The influence of these women and others working in the "Petticoat Lobby" in the 1920's shaped the state's modern education and penal systems, child labor laws, and social service legislation.

There is a tradition of community service in Texas, largely initiated by women. Women's Clubs organized eighty-five percent of Texas' libraries. Garden Clubs established parks. Mothers' Clubs set up public kindergartens and provided equipment for public schools. Women started and staffed major charities in every city in the state. Texas' great women philanthropists, including Ima Hogg and Mary Moody Northen, are part of this tradition.

There is a tradition of entrepreneurial involvement in Texas business. Women have carved their own niche by inventing or developing products that arose out of their experiences as women. Bette Graham invented Liquid Paper and liberated secretaries all over the world. Elsie Frankfurt Pollock designed an attractive maternity dress for her sister and her Page Boy Maternity Wear changed the way pregnant women looked in America. Lucille Bishop Smith invented the first hot biscuit mix and led the way for a new food industry. Ninfa Laurenzo transferred her culinary skills from home to work and built a successful chain of Mexican-food restaurants.

There is a tradition of preserving what is valuable in our heritage. Clara Driscoll and the Daughters of the Republic of Texas saved the Alamo. Other Texas women in hundreds of local communities preserve historical buildings and records for future generations. Women serve as the unofficial guardians of Texas history.

There is a tradition of domestic arts and crafts that is passed from generation to generation by women. The lives of many Texas women center around preserving the traditions of food making, needle work, quilting, family rituals, religious customs, and ethnic celebrations. They have provided a richness to the lives of individual Texans through their careful cultivation of a domestic or "women's" culture. And their activities may spring from a set of values that is quite different from those of men. It is important to understand the impact of these female values on Texas institutions.

This last tradition is one that should be of particular interest to the state's folklorists. The whole story of the female experience in Texas cannot really be understood until we know more about the cultural context of most female beliefs and behavior. This means that we have to look at the values, customs and beliefs that women teach each other, including the traditions that move from grandmother to daughter to grand-daughter. Folklore studies about women would help to complete the story of the Texas female experience.

If research into the history of Texas women can provide a guide to the study of folklore of Texas women, it is this: There is a richness of available material and objects about women or used by women. After conducting a statewide survey, we have identified and compiled much of it. The results were published in 1979 in the *Texas Women's History Project Bibliography*. We found that many materials exist in unpacked boxes in museums, or that they are hidden away with collections of famous men, or that they remain in the attics and basements of tradition-minded individuals who have preserved their own family histories.

The material is there to be examined and interpreted. The Texas Women's History Project is finding and using some of it to arrive at a factual understanding about women's lives. Texas folklorists can also use it to round out the diverse folk culture of Texas.

We salute the Texas Folklore Society for beginning the process. This collection of articles about some of Texas' *Legendary Ladies* is most welcome and needed. It captures the spirit of real women who were so unique or adventurous that they simply could not be forgotten or overlooked. Some of their stories have been so embroidered and elaborated with the passage of time that they have become archetypal tales. It is as if people have to tell and retell the stories to discharge some of the energy unleashed by the activities of these women. So they become legends—larger than life. As such, they tell us as much about ourselves as they do about the women whose lives have invaded our fantasies. The legends fulfill real human needs to idealize, objectify, humorize, or glorify those activities that we simply can't fit into the normal day-to-day pattern of our lives.

There should be no conflict between the legends that have grown up about some Texas women, and the actual facts about the lives of most Texas women—as long as we know what is factual and what is legendary. Facts inform us; legends enrich us. Together they provide human balance.

With the collection of historical data, the Texas Women's History project is showing that women made a difference in the history of this state.

With the publication of *Legendary Ladies of Texas* the Texas Folklore Society is showing that Texas women have also made a difference in the imagination of a people.

EARLY DAYS

The Venerable María de Jesus de Agreda, The Lady in Blue,
preaching to the Indians.

MARÍA DE AGREDA
The Lady in Blue

Francis Edward Abernethy

There were women of legend in the Americas long before the Europeans arrived, even though we don't know who they were. But we do know that all cultures, the American Indian included, recognized the great ones among themselves by elevating their status into the realm of legend or myth. The legendary ones always have some touch with reality and real time and space and history. The creatures of myth are from the early dawn of time or from other worlds.

The first woman of Texas legend after the coming of Church and chains and armored horse and rider was a fair and loving figure somewhere between the world of legend and myth. She was The Lady in Blue and her story in the earliest history of Texas is as that of the bringer of a soft and generous Christianity to the tribes of the Southwest and East Texas.

The story of The Lady in Blue probably started with the Franciscan Friar Juan de Salas who ministered to the Indians of south and west Texas in the 1620s. Father de Salas was a strong and loving man who had traveled widely and earned the affection of those Indians among whom he moved. Particularly did the Jumanos admire him, and they begged that he come to visit them on their ground on the Río Concho, near present-day San Angelo. In 1629 Father de Salas was able to go.

In 1629 the Custodian of the New Mexican area, Father Alonzo de Benavides, received from Spain thirty Franciscan friars to send out from San Antonio de Ysleta (near El Paso) to minister to the Indians. He sent

Father Juan de Salas and Father Diego López to the Jumanos of the Río Concho, who had long been requesting missionaries. Father Benavides questioned the Indians who came to guide the padres. This is his account in his *Memorials* published in 1630: "Before they went, we asked the Indians to tell us the reasons why they were with so much concern petitioning us for baptism, and for Religious to go to indoctrinate them. They replied that a woman like that one whom we had there painted— which was a picture of the Mother Luisa de Carrion—used to preach to each one of them in their own tongue, telling them that they should come to summon the Fathers to instruct and baptize them, and that they should not be slothful about it. And that the woman who preached to them was dressed precisely like her who was painted there; but that the face was not like that one, but that she, their visitant, was young and beautiful. And always whenever Indians came newly from those nations, looking upon the picture and comparing it among themselves, they said that the clothing was the same but the face was not, because the face of the woman who preached to them was that of a young and beautiful girl." In describing the clothing the Indians pointed out the regular nun's habit but emphasized the cloak of blue which the saintly visitant wore. She came to be referred to by the fathers and the Indians as The Lady in Blue.

The friars de Salas and López who went to the Jumanos found much to their surprise that the Indians were already well instructed in the doctrines of the Church. They attributed this to the visitations of The Lady in Blue, so without further teaching they baptized the chief and the entire tribe of ten thousand people. Before they left the encampment, according to Benavides' later report, the sick came by to be healed by the power of their new religion. The healing lasted from three o'clock one afternoon until ten o'clock the next morning: and "instantly they rose up well of all their infirmities, the blind, lame, dropsied, and of all their pains."[1]

Father Benavides soon returned to Mexico City, where he received orders to return to Spain and report the progress of the Church in the New World to his superiors. His *Memorials* of 1630 is the result and the report of his work, and it was received with high favor among his superiors. Of course, the report of the miraculous conversion of the Jumanos was a part of this report and was the occasion of much comment. The result was that he was sent on April 29, 1631, to the town of Agreda, on the border of Aragon and Castille, where Mother María de Jesús had earlier declared that by the miracle of bilocation, being in two places at one time, she had been visiting the Indians of the New World over the past ten years.

Father Benavides arrived in Agreda on the last day of April in 1631 and said in a report, "Mother María de Jesús, Abbess now of the Convent of the Immaculate Conception, is about twenty-nine years of age, not quite that, handsome of face, very fair in color, with a rosy tinge and large black eyes. The style of her habit, as well as that of all the nuns of that convent, who are twenty-nine in all, is the same as ours;

that is, it is of brown (pardo) sackcloth, very coarse, worn next to the body without a tunic, undershirt, or skirt. Over this brown habit is worn a white one of coarse sackcloth with a scapulary of the same material and the cord of our Father Saint Francis. Over the scapulary they carry the rosary. They wear no shoes or sandals other than boards tied to the feet. The cloak is of blue cloth, coarse, with a black veil."[2]

María Fernández Coronel, or Mother María de Jesús de Agreda, was born into a very devout Catholic family in Agreda in Castille in 1602. She took the vow of chastity when she was eight, and when she was sixteen she persuaded her parents to convert their house into a convent and take the vows themselves. As a nun in this convent María wore no shoes but sandals made of wood or straw. She wore a cassock of coarse brown sackcloth next to the skin, covered by a white habit tied by the knotted cord of St. Francis, and over all this she wore a mantle of blue for the Virgin Mary.

María was deeply and mystically contemplative from her youth, and in 1621 when she was eighteen her contemplations became miracles. She began going into trances, and in this state she was transported to the New World in a wild and primitive country and moved among savages, who, when she spoke, understood her even though she spoke in Spanish. And when they spoke she understood them even though they spoke in their own language. She visited different tribes during the period between 1620 and 1631, making around five hundred trips, sometimes completing as many as four visitations a day, and she told them about Christ and the Mother and God's wounds and Mary's tears for the suffering of mankind. She was martyred on one visit, receiving many wounds and a crown from God for her suffering. This visitation occurred, she said, in the Indian kingdom of the Ticlas, or Theas, or Techas (manuscript spelling was confused), in the northeastern part of New Spain, in the part of the New World that they would call Tejas.[3]

Benavides had written the report of his visit to the Jumanos in 1630. Although Mother María did not have any more trances in which she was transported to the New World after 1631 and we have no reports of a Lady in Blue appearing among the Indians, the story continued in its circulation both in the Old and New Worlds.

In Spain the story was familiar to Father Damien Massanet, one of Mother María's adherents who went to the New World to pursue this inspiration along with his professional pursuit of souls for the Mother Church. Father Damien in his studies of the legend concluded that the Theas, Ticlas, or Techas Indians of which Maria spoke were the Tejas Indians, the name then popularly attributed to the Hasinai Caddoes of East Texas. In order to continue this line of investigation he obtained a station at Mission Caldera in Coahuila. His chance to meet the Tejas came in 1689, when he accompanied Alonzo de Leon on an expedition to search out and destroy all Frenchmen in New Spain. They found the burnt remains of La Salle's fort, and they made their first contact with the Tejas. De Leon wrote the following account of the latter episode in a letter of May, 1689: "They [the Tejas] are very familiar with the fact that there is only one true God, that he is in Heaven, and that he was born of the Holy Virgin. They perform many Christian rites, and the Indian Governor asked me for missionaries to instruct them, saying that many years ago a woman went inland to instruct them, but that she has not been there for a long time; and certainly it is a pity that people so rational, who plant crops and know there is a God, should have no one to teach them the Gospel, especially when the province of Texas is so large and so fertile and has so fine a climate."[4]

In another note de Leon says of these Indians, referring to María: "They are very fond of blue because of the mantle of the venerable mother."[5]

The woman who came to the Tejas was certainly no one sent by the Church, so this was accepted as further indication of María's supernatural presence. The result of Damien Massanet's meeting with the Tejas in 1689 was that he promised them that he would come to them in the following year "when the corn was ripe." He went to East Texas in 1690, founding the missions San Francisco de los Tejas and Santísimo Nombre de María before returning to New Spain (probably either Monclova or his College at Querétero) and writing an account of his journey. He concludes this account with what he calls "the most noteworthy thing of all, namely this: While we were at the Tejas Hasinai village, after we had distributed clothing to the Indians and to the governor of the Tejas, that governor asked me for a piece of blue baize in which to bury his mother when she died; I told him that cloth would be more suitable, and he answered that he did not want any other color than blue. I then asked him what mysterious reason he had for preferring the blue color, and in reply he said they were very fond of that color, particularly for burial clothes, because in times past they had been visited frequently by a beautiful woman, who used to come down from the hills, dressed in blue garments, and that they wished to do as that woman had done. On my asking whether that had been long since, the governor said that it had been before his time, but his mother, who was aged, had seen that woman, as had also other old people. From this it is easily to be seen that they referred to the Madre María de Jesús de Agreda, who was frequently in those regions, as she herself acknowledged to the Father Custodian of New Mexico, her last visit being in 1631, the last fact being evident from her own statement, made to the Father Custodian of New Mexico."[6]

The end of this part of the legend occurred with the abandonment of the East Texas missions in 1693. Father Damien, on his return to East Texas in 1691, found that although the memory of The Lady in Blue remained in Indian stories, her precepts were poorly attended. The Indians became openly hostile toward the Spanish and indifferent to Catholic teaching. Completely disillusioned, Father Damien and the friars left the Tejas in 1693, and San Francisco moldered back into the red dirt on which it was built.

The Lady in Blue legend continued to circulate among the Indians and Spanish of East Texas, and in later years, according to later stories, she returned to bring comfort to other East Texas settlers. In the early 1840s, during the late winter and early spring, the Sabine overflowed and isolated many of the river-bottom settlers. The black-tongue plague, or malaria, struck, and whole families sickened and many died. In the midst of the plague a mysterious lady in blue appeared to look after the sick. She stayed and cheered and healed the sick until the plague abated; then she disappeared as mysteriously as she came.[7]

According to other stories the ghost nun still wanders the Camino del Caballo, the old Smugglers Road that skirted the customs and out-posts at Nacogdoches. She cries sadly from time to time, perhaps in mourning for the vanished Tejas whom she came to save.[8]

So what happened? Were The Lady in Blue's appearances examples of mass hysteria among Indians, psycho-phenomena similar to our fly-ing-saucer sightings? Or was it the ultimate con game played by the Indians on the Spanish in order to get the gifts the priests handed out along with their more abstract blessings? *Or*, are there stranger things in heaven and earth than we and Horatio ever dreamed of in our phi-losophies—and is this a prime example of the miracle of bilocation? If it is a miracle, as her adherents believed, was she transported in body or in spirit, a point of contention among Agredistas of that time? She said that in some of her transportations she took crosses with her which she evidently left with Indians, because she could never find them there-after, which would seem to indicate corporeal bilocation. Those who faltered on the threshold of belief in corporeal bilocation were reminded of the power of God in the manipulation of miracles and told of the numberless angels who could dance on the head of a pin.

Interestingly, in *The Catholic Encyclopedia* and in *The New Catholic Encyclopedia*, to mention only two standard reference works on Catholic faith and practices, nothing is said about María's miraculous trips to the New World. She is discussed as the friend and advisor of Philip IV, and she is much discussed as the author of the very controversial *The Mysti-cal City of God and the Divine History of the Virgin Mother of God* (3 vols. Madrid 1670), which was periodically on and off the Inquisitional Index. María claimed that she was transported in 1627, this time to the Celes-tial City, where God commanded her to write the definitive biography of the Virgin. Not to be unreasonable, he gave her eight angels as assistants and then showed her all the stages of the Virgin's life. Very disturbing to some of her readers—especially French readers who, her supporters said, read Spanish poorly—was the description of the Vir-gin's nine months in her mother's womb. More interesting but equally disturbing was the chapter on the Immaculate Conception, which *The New Catholic Encyclopedia* evaluates as "though perhaps crude, was not, as was alleged, immoral."

Mother María and Father Margil and the marvelous Texas legends that went with them were the last flickerings of the Medieval Age of Faith and were, in a sense, anachronisms. Erasmus from his lofty Re-naissance perch had already surveyed the superstitions of the Church and the folly of its people and its pieties—and he had laughed to scorn that part of the institution that proliferated Franciscan anti-intellectualism and he had stood agape at the outrageously miraculous saints legends. Erasmus spoke for most men of enlightment of the Renaissance.

But who can tell what dreams there are that men must have, what miracles and madnesses, what inspirations and insanities that they *must* have to guide their ways into strange new worlds. The Lord provided the Jews a pillar of cloud by day and a pillar of fire by night. He just might have given the Spanish The Lady in Blue.

NOTES

1. The episode with the Jumanos is a paraphrase of *The Memorial of Fray Alonso de Benavides*, 1630, Mrs. Edward E. Ayer, trans. (Albuquerque: Horn and Wallace, Publ., 1965), pp. 57–63.

2. Carlos Castañeda, "The Mission Era: The Finding of Texas, 1519–1693," *Our Catholic Heritage in Texas, 1519–1936* (Austin: Von Boeckmann-Jones, 1936), I, 197.

3. José Antonio Pichardo, *Limits of Louisiana and Texas* (c. 1810), Charles Hackett, trans. (Austin: University of Texas Press, 1934), II, 480 ff.

4. Charles Heimsath, "The Mysterious Woman in Blue," *Legends of Texas*, PTFS III, J. Frank Dobie, ed. (Hatboro, Pa.: Folklore Associates, Inc., 1964/1924 c.), 134.

5. Pichardo, II, 144.

6. Letter of Fray Damien Massanet to Don Carlos de Siguenza, 1690," in *Spanish Exploration in the Southwest, 1542–1706*, Herbert E. Bolton, ed. (New York: Barnes and Noble, Inc., 1967/1908 c.), p. 387.

7. Joe F. Combs, *Legends of the Pineys* (San Antonio: The Naylor Co., 1965), pp. 76–89.

8. Harry G. Pettey, "Names and Creeks Along Historic Road are Stories in Themselves," *The Daily Sentinel*, Nacogdoches, Texas, July 9, 1963, II, 1.

ANGELINA

Diane H. Corbin

The figure of Angelina, the "Texas" Indian woman who mysteriously spoke Spanish, appears in the early period of Texas history. Tradition has turned the little which is really known of her into a romantic legend bearing little resemblance to the facts. For example, with no indication of the basis for the statement, the East Texas historian R. B. Blake, says of her, ". . . the Indian maiden Angelina, first native missionary to the East Texas Indians, guided the spiritual lives of her people."[1]

What is the truth about the "famous Angelina,"[2] or can we know the truth?

Tradition has the first appearance of Angelina in 1690, when Alonso DeLeon, accompanied by Father Massanet, journeyed to the easternmost area of Spain's possessions of Coahuila and Texas with the purpose of founding four missions, primarily with an eye to keeping out French intruders. According to the *Lufkin News*, at the site of Nuestro Padre San Francisco de los Texas, Massanet is supposed to have met an "Indian maiden with a bright intellect and possessing striking personal appearance" who "expressed a desire to learn the Father's language. . . . She soon became a favorite and was given the name 'Little Angel' or Angelina."[3] Unfortunately for tradition, Massanet was not sufficiently impressed by the maiden to mention her in his extensive account of the voyage,[4] nor did the devoted Father Casañas, who remained at nearby Nuestra Señora de la Purísima Concepción and reported extensively on his findings.[5]

The first documented appearance of Angelina comes in 1712. Pénicaut, accompanying St. Denis on one of his many voyages into Texas,
recounts:

> *In this village we found a woman named Angélique, who has been baptized*
> *by Spanish priests on a mission to their village. She spoke Spanish, and as M.*
> *de St. Denis too spoke that language fairly well, he made use of her to tell the*
> *Assinais chiefs to let us have some guides for hire.*[6]

Spanish activity in East Texas resembles the tides: effort ebbed and
flowed, principally in reaction to French intrusions. The next mention
of Angelina comes four years later, during one of the sporadic Spanish
missionizing expeditions, the Ramón expedition of 1716. Although Captain Ramón's own diary[7] fails to mention Angelina, Father Espinosa,
who accompanied Ramón, writes that the expedition had "recourse to a
learned Indian woman of this Assinai tribe, reared in Coahuila."[8] Three
years later we find another reference to a nameless learned Indian
woman. Fray Francisco Celíz, diarist of the Alarcón expedition of
1718–19, writes:

> *Later the governor [Alarcón] proceeded to distribute clothing to all of the*
> *family of those baptized, among whom is found the sagacious Indian woman*
> *interpreter who at the persuasion of the said governor came to live with her*
> *entire family near the village.*[9]

The next appearance of Angelina, this time by name, is in 1720, and
conforms to the romantic tradition. A young French officer, Simars de
Belle-Isle, found himself abandoned (or he may have deserted) on the
Texas coast in 1720. After much cruel treatment by the coastal Indians,
he fell into the hands of the Assinais, especially those of a Spanish-
speaking woman who "served me all the best she had, and she had as
much love for me as if I had been her child."[10] Belle-Isle remained
among the Assinais for some time, recuperating from his ill-treatment,
but began at last to pine for his country. The woman noticed his sorrow
and offered to send him to the French, guided by two of her children.
He mentions finally that "this Indian woman, called Angelica, had lived
with the Spaniards since her childhood. That is why we understood
each other so well."[11]

The final appearance of Angelina is in 1721, during the expedition
of the Marquis de Aguayo, at the "village where the mission of La
Purísima Concepción was founded."[12] Once again serving as interpreter
was "one Angelina who had been raised on the Rio Grande and spoke
both Spanish and the Texas languages."[13]

We must note two problems concerning Angelina. The first is her
age; if she was a "maiden" in 1690, it is hardly likely that she would be a
matron with children thirty years later, young enough to be attractive to
a young French officer, given the hardships of life in the early eigh-

teenth century, as well as the probable lifespan of the Texas Indian. Since there is no documentation of Angelina's existence in 1690, only tradition, it is perhaps best to place her existence a bit later and call her a young woman in 1712 and later. Bossu (see note 11) calls her an "old widow" but does not say where he obtains this information, as Belle-Isle calls her only a "sauvagesse," i.e., a female savage. Belle-Isle's tale could confirm her age, perhaps, for she seems to treat him as a child, and she has children of an age to serve him as guides.

The second problem concerns Angelina's acquisition of Spanish. Pénicaut and tradition have her learning Spanish locally: "In their village we found a woman named Angélique, *who had been baptized by Spanish priests on a mission to their village.*"[14] More sources, however, have her learning Spanish, and, indeed, being reared, elsewhere. Espinosa says she was "reared in Coahuila"; Aguayo's diarist, Peña, has her "raised on the Rio Grande"; Morfi, writing much later, in the *Memorias*, says she "had been baptized and reared in the Mission of San Juan Bautista [Eagle Pass] on the Rio Grande in Coahuila."[15] Belle-Isle, who knew her, does not really resolve the problem, although his statement that she "had lived with the Spaniards since her childhood" seems to indicate a mission upbringing. That she learned Spanish in Coahuila is certainly possible, despite the distance and difficulty of travel involved. Ethnographers indicate a high degree of mobility among the Indians generally in Texas. Massanet[16] speaks of "an Indian [un Yndio] who was then with the Tejas but came from the country beyond—from Coahuila—and who spoke Mexican." Espinosa, in his *Crónica*, adds to his earlier statement concerning the Indian woman that "she had been reared in Coahuila, since her parents had been there a long time when the Spaniards left Texas in 1693." Of course, this last poses several more questions: How long is a "long time"? Was she born yet? Or were there perhaps *two* Spanish-speaking Indian women?

There is probably no doubt that the river was named for Angelina. She must have had a strong personality, sufficient at least for someone to attach her name to a geographical feature; contemporary chroniclers call her "famous," "learned," and "sagacious." Morfi definitely associates the two in his *History*, written between 1778–1783. De Mézières speaks of the Angelina River in 1779,[18] and Lafora's map of 1771 clearly shows the Angelina River. Solís' diary for 1768[19] pushes the date of association back even farther, but we cannot know the first date the name was given to the river.

What conclusions can we draw from the available data? There was indeed an Indian woman named Angelina who spoke Spanish at least as early as 1712, and seems to have been of great use and greatly appreciated by the Spanish, although we do not know where she learned the explorers' tongue. She might have accompanied her family to Coahuila; she might have been traded from the area as a slave and returned; or her origins might be elsewhere and her appearance in this area the result of chance. Unless evidence can be found to prove her presence at a mission in Coahuila we can probably not answer the question of where she learned Spanish, but it is gratifying to know that an Indian woman had an early hand in shaping the fate of Texas.

NOTES

1. R. B. Blake, "Locations of the Early Spanish Missions and Presidio in Nacogdoches County," *Southwestern Historical Quarterly*, XLI, No. 3 (1938), 220.
2. J. A. Pichardo, *Treatise on the Limits of Louisiana and Texas*, C. W. Hackett, C. C. Shelby, and M. R. Splawn, trans., C. W. Hackett, ed., (Austin: University of Texas Press, 1931–49), IV, 163.
3. "Angelina History Rich," *Lufkin News*, n.d., n.p.
4. Father Damián Massanet, "Letter to Don Carlos de Siguenza relative to the Discovery of the Bay of Espíritu Santo," *Texas State Historical Association Quarterly*, II, No. 4 (1898–99), 281–312.
5. Mattie Austin Hatcher, "Descriptions of the Tejas or Asinai Indians, 1691–1722," Fray Casañas and Father Espinosa, trans., *Southwestern Historical Quarterly*, XXX, No. 3 (1926–27), 206–218, No. 4, 283–304; XXXI, No. 1 (1927–28), 50–63, No. 2, 150–180.
6. R. G. McWilliams, ed., *Fleur de Lys and Calumet, Being the Pénicaut Narrative of the French Adventure in Louisiana* (Baton Rouge: Louisiana State University Press, 1953), pp. 150–151.
7. Paul J. Foik, ed., *Captain Don Domingo Ramón's Diary of his Expedition into Texas in 1716*, Preliminary Studies of the Texas Catholic Historical Society, II, No. 5 (April 1933).
8. Gabriel Tous, ed., *The Ramón Expedition: Espinosa's Diary of 1716*. Preliminary Studies of the Texas Catholic Historical Society, I, No. 4 (April 1930).
9. Fray Francisco Celíz, *Diary of the Alarcón Expedition into Texas, 1718–19*, Fritz Leo Hoffman, trans., Publications of the Quivira Society, V (1935).
10. Henri Folmer, "De Bellisle on the Texas Coast," *Southwestern Historical Quarterly*, XLIV, No. 2 (1946), 223–24.
11. Folmer, p. 225. There is another version of Belle-Isle's story (somewhat less romantic) which says he became "the dog [i.e., slave] of an old widow" (J. B. Bossu, *Travels through that part of North America formerly called Louisiana*, John Reinhold Forster, trans., London: T. Davies, 1771, I, 338.) and was rescued due to the efforts of a young Indian who took Belle-Isle's commission and a letter to St. Denis. At his departure "the woman who had adopted M. de Belle-Isle shed tears (Bossu, I, 343)." Or perhaps Belle-Isle was simply more fortunate than most lost travelers in falling into the hands of sympathetic women.
12. Fray Juan Augustín Morfi, *History of Texas 1673–1779*, Carlos Castañeda, trans. Publications of the Quivira Society, VI (1935), 74–75, note 75. See also Eleanor Claire Buckley, "The Aguayo Expedition into Texas and Louisiana, 1719–22," *Texas State Historical Association Quarterly*, XV, No. 1 (1911–12), 1–65.
13. Morfi, *loc. cit.*
14. Emphasis mine.
15. Fray Juan Augustín Morfi, *Memorias for the History of Texas*, quoted in Carlos E. Castañeda, *The Mission Era: The Winning of Texas*, Vol. II of *Our Catholic Heritage in Texas*, 1519–1936, Paul J. Foik, ed., (Austin: Von-Boeckmann-Jones, 1936), II, 58; see also Morfi, *History*, p. 203. It is interesting to note that San Juan Bautista was not founded until 1699.
16. Massanet, p. 306.
17. Quoted in Pichardo, IV, 172.
18. Herbert E. Bolton, ed., *Athanase de Mézières and the Louisiana-Texas Frontier*,

1768–1780; documents published for the first time (Cleveland: Arthur H. Clark, 1914), II, 262–63.

19. Fray Gaspar José de Solís, "Diary of a Visit of Inspection of the Texas Missions, 1767–68," Margaret Kenney Kress, trans., *Southern Historical Quarterly*, XXXV, No. 1 (1931–32), 62.

The Yellow Rose Of Texas

Traditional

"The Yellow Rose of Texas" is believed to have been inspired by Emily Morgan.

EMILY MORGAN
Yellow Rose of Texas

Martha Anne Turner

An old myth insists that on each recurring April 21, the anniversary of the Battle of San Jacinto, the specter of a golden-skinned girl returns to Texas from the East to preside over the famous battlesite. The ghost is that of the long-haired, twenty-year-old mulatto slave girl, Emily Morgan—"The Yellow Rose of Texas"—whose role in the quarters of General Antonio Lopez de Santa Anna at San Jacinto is approaching international legend. Stripped of illusion, the comely mulatto occupies her rightful—but long-disputed—place in history as a heroine of the Texas Revolution.

Intelligent as well as beautiful, Emily Morgan was a member of the household of Colonel James Morgan. When Santa Anna captured her at Morgan's Point, her master was stationed at Galveston guarding Texas refugees and the fugitive government officials. The wealthy Morgan, a staunch patriot, erected the fortification on the island as he contributed the use of his ships to the Texas cause and provisioned the army.

In 1835 Morgan, in partnership with Lorenzo de Zavala and several New York financiers, laid out the town of New Washington on the point later named for him. In order to circumvent the law prohibiting slavery in the Mexican province, he converted his sixteen slaves into indentured servants for ninety-nine years. To populate the colony Morgan imported Scotch highlanders, blacks from Bermuda, and other indentured servants, among them Emily Morgan of New York.

At forty-two the Mexican commander Santa Anna considered himself a connoisseur of women. His arrogance, lust for power, and handsome looks made him attractive to them. A man of fastidious tastes with a penchant for expensive attire, Santa Anna was likewise addicted to such luxuries as silk sheets, exquisite crystal stemware, silver serving dishes, and a mounted sterling chamberpot. When he invaded Texas in 1836 he brought with him an octagonal-shaped, carpeted marquee to serve as headquarters. In 1836 the self-styled "Napoleon of the West" was a prestigious figure at the height of his career.

Near Harrisburg on April 15 the main body of the Mexican army waited for stragglers. Santa Anna, accompanied by an adjutant and fifteen dragoons, had walked a mile to the town, where he learned that the Texas government officials had left the morning before, intent upon reaching the safety of Galveston Island. At three o'clock on April 17, after ordering his men to put Harrisburg to the torch, Santa Anna began the march toward New Washington in pursuit of the officers.

Meanwhile, on the opposite side of the bayou Mexican soldiers had discovered houses containing women's apparel, fine furniture, a magnificent piano, jars of preserves, chocolates, and fruits, all of which they appropriated for the pleasure of their commander.

A storm delayed the progress of Santa Anna's contingent, but Colonel Juan N. Almonte and a detachment arrived at New Washington on April 17 just as the fleeing Texas officials embarked successfully for Galveston on a ship moored in the bay.

Santa Anna, with his contingent of 1,000 infantrymen and equipment, arrived at New Washington at noon of April 18. Except for the soldiers looting the place and Morgan's indentured servants, who remained to take care of the plantation, the settlement—perhaps the richest in Texas—was deserted. The Mexican general first observed the graceful movements of the mulatto beauty at the wharf as she assisted others in loading a flatboat with supplies for the Texas army. Santa Anna decided immediately that Emily would be an integral part of the loot.

On April 19, after sacking and burning New Washington, Santa Anna took as captives Emily and a yellow boy named Turner. He tried to bribe the youth, a printer's apprentice of above average intelligence, to ascertain the position of Houston for him. Accordingly, he sent Turner, who was also an excellent horseman, ahead, with a small detail of dragoons, to reconnoiter the Texas army's location. Before Turner and the detail left the Mexican general's entourage, Emily managed to inform him covertly that Houston was encamped near Lynchburg on the bayou and instructed him to warn the Texas general of the enemy's approach if he could do so without divulging his position.

Turner, taking advantage of the speed of his mount, escaped Mexican surveillance and warned Houston on the morning of the twentieth. Thus Emily Morgan, loyal to the Texans, conveyed her warning to Houston before she reached the battlesite herself.

It was not until eight o'clock on the morning of April 20, when the Mexicans were ready to move out, that Santa Anna received news of

Houston's position from one of his own scouts. In the meantime, to delay the Mexican commander's advance, Turner had tried to mislead him into thinking that Houston was encamped on the Trinity River with his rag-tag and disgruntled little army.

When Santa Anna discovered Emily at New Washington he had been deprived of feminine companionship for two weeks. Emily was a replacement for the "bride" of his mock marriage in San Antonio before the final assault on the Alamo—lovely seventeen-year-old Melchora Iniega Barrera. Santa Anna and his lady had left San Antonio on March 31 in his royal coach drawn by six resplendent white mules and escorted by fifty elegantly uniformed dragoons. His tent and carpeting, huge supply of champagne, his opium cabinet, and crates of fighting cocks were transported by a train of pack mules. When the royal contingent reached the Guadalupe River at Gonzales, on April 2, it was impossible to ford the turgid stream with the heavy carriage. As the commander expected to rejoin Melchora in a short time, he sent her the next day in the heavy vehicle with a trunk full of silver under escort to Mexico City.

Because of the weight of their additional plunder, the heavy ordnance cases, and cumbersome brass twelve-pound field piece, the Mexican army inched across the rutted, boggy Texas marshlands at less than a mile an hour. To reduce their baggage, soldiers were forced to abandon their knapsacks on the outskirts of New Washington. At approximately two o'clock in the afternoon of April 20 the aggregation reached the perimeter of a large wooded area where a few of Houston's pickets were stationed. Houston's main force, which had made camp on the east side of Buffalo Bayou, was completely obscured by trees and undergrowth. Hastily, then, Santa Anna chose a position on the plains of San Jacinto, approximately a mile from Houston's, and ordered his men to encamp. The worst possible location, the site violated all military rules. Officers of the Mexican general's staff opposed the choice openly. But Santa Anna, traveling with his dusky prize, was impatient of further movement.

And, if he chose the general campsite for his soldiers injudiciously, Santa Anna selected the spot for himself and Emily to occupy with extreme care. Like a man on his honeymoon, he had the gaudy marquee set up on a rise with a romantic view overlooking San Jacinto Bay.

The few Texas soldiers and the two six-pound cannon—the Twin Sisters—Santa Anna saw upon arrival failed to excite admiration. More interested in what awaited him in the red-striped tent, cocky and confident, Santa Anna, nevertheless, ordered Delgado to engage the Texans in a skirmish in a grove of trees between the two campsites. He displayed further contempt for the Texans by having his musicians play "Deguello," the old throat-cutting song of no quarter, to the sinister notes of which the Alamo defenders had fallen. Nor could he resist at least a token appearance after sending his aide to convey the twelve-pound cannon—the Gold Standard—to the island of timber separating the two military positions. Bedecked with medals and wearing his jaunty Napoleon-style headpiece, he appeared grandiloquently on a big bay foolishly exposing himself to the Texans' fire. It was an act designed to attract the attention of his gorgeous captive as well as to impress the enemy.

As if under a spell, Santa Anna continued to make mistakes. At this point he ordered Delgado to unload the powder and ammunition for the cannon and to relinquish twenty pack mules laden with the ordnance stores to Captain Barragan. Barragan was to take the mules and retrieve the knapsacks left at the edge of New Washington. Realizing the danger of executing such an order, Delgado released only fourteen of the mules. Wisely he retained six so as to transport the ordnance supplies to camp.

After issuing his erratic order, Santa Anna again paraded his elegance in full view of the Texans before making his dramatic exit. When the Texans saw the artillery and ammunition stores unprotected, they pounded away. Their fire made a direct hit on the Mexicans' cannon, disabling it somewhat, scattered ordnance boxes, and killed two of the six mules.

A lull of approximately two hours ensued—an interlude that left Santa Anna's liaison with Emily uninterrupted. History does not record exactly how the Mexican commander spent it in his sumptuous three-room tent with its eight-by-eleven-foot central section and silken partitions. One wonders if he had Emily model the dresses his soldiers took at Harrisburg or sample the chocolates and other delicacies comprising the spoils. Or did he tempt the graceful mulatto with the fine piano? Whether Emily was musically inclined, such a splendid instrument could not fail to impress her.

Hostilities resumed at four o'clock when Colonel Sidney Sherman obtained Houston's reluctant permission to try to take the unguarded Mexican cannon. He and seventy volunteers, including Secretary of State Thomas J. Rusk and privates Mirabeau B. Lamar and Walter P. Lane, were badly defeated. While Santa Anna sent in reinforcements, Houston, believing that Sherman had incited a major action in disobedience to his orders, refused to honor his request for infantry support. Consequently, even though the Texans had won the first charge, they were forced to retreat.

The men in camp resented Houston's refusal to support Sherman, and on the evening of April 20 solicited volunteers to fight the next day whether the general was ready or not. Morale was exceedingly high. As they watched Houston's raft being built for possible further retreat, they were of one accord: they would not follow further orders to run. Secretary of State Rusk had informed Houston that the men were prepared to follow another leader if he did not order the charge the next day.

Meanwhile, as cautious Houston maintained his reserve, across the grassy plain there was a veritable symphony of silence unmarred by the popping of champagne corks.

By April 21 Santa Anna was confident of victory. According to his intelligence, the entire Texan force numbered fewer than 800 disheveled men. His equipment was superior to Houston's, his soldiers better disciplined, and esprit de corps impeccable. In addition, General Martin Perfecto de Cos arrived at nine o'clock on the morning of April 21 with reinforcements of 300 recruits. Since the reinforcements had not slept, Santa Anna directed them to stack their guns and withdraw to an adjoining grove to rest. With no threat from the opposite camp and with more intriguing activity awaiting him, Santa Anna, enormously pleased with himself, returned to his rococo quarters overlooking beautiful San Jacinto Bay.

As early as eight o'clock Houston's scouts informed him of the approach of the Mexican reinforcements. For that matter, on April 18 Deaf Smith, his most capable scout, had intercepted Miguel Bachiller with General Filisola's reply to Santa Anna's request for support.

Whether Houston slept on the night preceding the battle is doubtful. Certainly he was aware of the increasing insubordination in camp. He was equally aware that the men were spoiling for a fight. Schooled in the military tactics of his patron Andrew Jackson, Houston remained circumspect.

Early on the morning of April 21 Houston ordered Deaf Smith to destroy Vince's Bridge, the only means of exit to the Brazos, where Santa Anna's second-in-command General Filisola was encamped. The bridge, over which Cos and his men had traveled, was only eight miles from camp. Its destruction would prohibit further reinforcements from reaching the enemy and remove any means of escape for either side.

But before Smith and his assistants undertook to remove the bridge, Houston instructed the scout to proceed to the San Jacinto River and, from an elevation between the two positions, count tent tops to estimate Mexican troop strength. Smith trained his spyglass on the camp from a position so close that he could observe everything taking place. His estimate of Mexican troop strength at approximately 1500 men was accurate.

But Smith reported more than numbers to Houston. He reported the stacked guns and the Mexican officers and soldiers partying with their women in their tents. Houston was aware of the presence of the *soldaderas* and knew of Santa Anna's capture of Emily. Before she had sent him the warning, his expert espionage and reconnaissance units had kept him informed of what had happened at New Washington. Indeed, he himself had climbed a tree and watched the slave girl serve breakfast to Santa Anna wearing his bright red silk robe.

However, Houston did not know that the revelry had begun so early in the day. Nor did he know the extent of it until Smith informed him. Undoubtedly Smith's report influenced Houston's decision to act almost at once and even dictated strategy. "I hope that slave girl makes Santa Anna neglect his business," Houston told Smith, "and keeps him in bed all day." Houston held his council of war from twelve noon until two o'clock, had Lieutenant Colonel Joseph Bennett poll the men, arranged for the music to accompany the charge, and paraded and aligned his men in battle formation.

When Houston got the Texans in position to fight at four o'clock that afternoon, not a single Mexican was in view. Waving his famous hat so that the flank commanders could see it, he led the charge on his white stallion, Saracen. Screened by the trees and rising ground, the Texans in a formation two men deep, advanced on the run. Later the line stretched out across the prairie. Twenty paces from the enemy barricade Houston shouted the order: "Kneel! Shoot low! Fire!" He continued to caution his men to hold their fire and to aim low. Why did he keep insisting that the men fire only at extremly close range and order them to kneel and shoot low? The answer is obvious: Houston knew that the Mexican targets were *horizontal*, not *vertical*.

Caught by total surprise in the midst of their day-long dissipation, the Mexicans offered only semi-resistance. Pandemonium ensued. Most of the enemy tried to escape to the safety of Vince's Bridge. At the site of the burned bridge the bayou was wide and deep and, therefore, difficult to ford. As a result, many of the Santanistas, attempting to escape through the boggy marshes, made prime targets for the pursuing Texans. Shouting their battle cry, "Remember the Alamo! Remember Goliad!," Texans scattered Mexican corpses across the eight miles of prairie between the campsite and Vince's Bayou. Within the fewest minutes the assault had deteriorated into an orgy of wanton slaughter with the Texans resorting to the use of knives, pistols, shotguns, and the butts of their rifles for clubs.

Among the first to attempt to escape was Santa Anna. He ran out of the marquee completely disoriented and an aide offered him Old Whip, the magnificent stallion commandeered from the Allen Vince ranch the day before. Santa Anna jumped on the animal and fled at breakneck speed. He was wearing only red morocco house slippers, a linen shirt with diamond studs, and white silk drawers. In his flight he managed to take along a fine gray vest with gold buttons, a bed sheet, a box of the Harrisburg chocolates, and a gourd water-bottle half filled.

The bloodbath persisted despite Houston's efforts to stop it. When Houston, who sustained a severe ankle wound and was later forced to retire, gave the order to "parade," General Rusk countermanded it. Replacing Houston in command then, Rusk restored order and brought in 250 Mexican prisoners.

To the spirited tempo of two nineteenth-century love songs—Thomas Moore's "Will You Come To The Bower?" and the old folksong "The Girl I Left Behind"—Texans certified their independence from Mexico. The musicians consisted of three fifers—Frederick Lemsky, John Beebe, and Luke Bust—and a drummer—Hendrick Arnold, the free black man, who also served as a spy with Deaf Smith.

At the end of the eighteen-minute orgy, evidence remained to confirm that the party in Santa Anna's quarters had been in full swing. George Bernard Erath, the Texan who later guarded the Mexican commander's baggage, was one of the first to confirm the fact. He discovered gourmet food left uneaten and large quantities of champagne. Lucy A. Erath, who edited the *Memoirs of George Bernard Erath*, quotes him as stating that Santa Anna's personal effects included such luxuries "as a European prince might have taken with him in the field." Erath also concluded that much of the victory at San Jacinto was traceable to "Santa Anna's voluptousness."

That evening, when the captive Santanistas surrounded huge fires, under guard in the absence of a stockade, Texans compiled statistics: 630 Mexicans killed, 208 wounded, and 730 taken prisoner. Houston cited his strength at 783. Rusk's estimate was 750. Only two Texans were killed while seven others succumbed later from injuries.

When Santa Anna was captured the next day between the charred bridge and the Lynchburg ferry, he was wearing a foul smelling cap, a faded blue cotton jacket, over his diamond-studded shirt, and coarse white domestic pants. He was carrying a bundle made of his sheet, his wet underwear, and his water bottle. Around his shoulders he had draped a blanket serape-fashion. His feet were bare and bleeding from brambles. Although the six-man patrol suspected their captive was an officer because of his fine shirt, Santa Anna did not disclose his identity.

Only when Santa Anna's men disclosed his identity in the presence of Houston did he acknowledge it and request courtesies of war commensurate with his rank. As soon as the Texans learned of Santa Anna's identity, they had to be restrained from attacking him. Apprehensive of the hostility demonstrated and unaware of Houston's intention to spare his life, Santa Anna gave the Masonic distress signal. The signal was honored, and before the Mexican commander could engage in the two-hour interview with Houston he had to chew plugs of opium to regain his composure.

And what became of Emily? The slave girl survived the Battle of San Jacinto and related the details of her role in it to Colonel Morgan. How she returned to the plantation—a distance of seven or eight miles from the battlesite—is not of record. It is logical, however, to think that a member of the spying unit may have given her safe escort. Deaf Smith and Hendrick Arnold knew her as they had obtained intelligence from the indentured servants of New Washington.

Emily related her story to Colonel Morgan on April 23 when he and Vice President de Zavala stopped at New Washington en route to the battlesite with reinforcements and supplies for Houston's army. Unaware that the battle had been fought on April 21, the two men anchored the *Cayuga*, on which they had come from Galveston, in the bay and obtained their first news of the victory from the servants at the plantation.

For the mulatto's participation in the Battle of San Jacinto Colonel Morgan granted her her freedom. Legend has it that he also bought her a home in a community of free Negroes in Houston. Later Emily was issued a passport and returned to New York. At the auction after the battle Morgan purchased the candy-striped marquee and presented it to Samuel Swartwout, customs collector of New York.

Morgan transmitted the story of Emily to others, including his English friend William Bollaert, to whom he quoted the slave girl's account verbatim. Bollaert, an ethnologist who frequently visited Texas, was among the first to report the incident. He kept diaries of his experiences from December, 1841, to April 11, 1844. However, for some obscure reason the extensive Bollaert Papers did not attract attention in America until 1902. Not until 1956 did a major portion of the material appear in *William Bollaert's Texas*, edited by W. Eugene Hollon and Ruth Lapham Butler.

Long before the ethnologist's material was published, the story of Emily Morgan was widely circulated as an aspect of Texas folklore. Furthermore, Mexican historians have verified Emily Morgan's presence at San Jacinto for years. Generally they categorize her as Santa Anna's "quadroon mistress during the Texas Campaign."

Was the lovely mulatto infatuated with the emperor of Mexico? Despite any hypothetical attraction she might have felt for Santa Anna, Emily Morgan was a captive and was familiar with the status quo. Increasingly, the belief that she performed her service for her adopted home of Texas out of loyalty is gaining credence.

What is the significance of the Texas heroine's contribution? The results of Emily Morgan's performance at San Jacinto are without precedent. Not only did her dalliance with Santa Anna keep him occupied and cement the victory of the sixteenth decisive battle of the world, it validated an empire—the Republic of Texas—that flourished for a decade. Moreover, the victory at San Jacinto not only brought Texas into the United States but also added eventually the future states of New Mexico, Arizona, California, Utah, Colorado, Wyoming, Kansas, and Oklahoma—a million square miles of territory that more than doubled the size of the American nation at the time.

Even for a most generous ladies' man, this real estate, in terms of intrinsic nineteenth-century values, had to be an all-time record as a fee for the companionship of Emily for a period of less than two days and nights. As payment by the hour for that brief time, the fee approximated a world-shattering record. The fortunes paid by the crowned heads of Europe for the favors of Madame de Pompadour and her successor, the Comtesse Dú Barry, become paltry sums by comparison.

Before people knew of Emily Morgan's role at San Jacinto, they were familiar with the song she is credited to have inspired. Perhaps no song in the history of music has made a greater bid for immortality than "The Yellow Rose of Texas." Originating as a Negro folksong after 1836, the music has achieved its one hundred and forty-third milestone.

During its long evolution "The Yellow Rose of Texas" has been converted into a popular standard with no loss of appeal. Played and sung everywhere, it has evolved into innumerable variants. Two notable twentieth-century redactions are an operatic transcription by David Guion, composed in the 1930's, and a popular version recorded by bandleader Mitch Miller and featured on his Sing-Along television show in the 1960's.

First copyrighted in 1858, with the musical arrangement attributed to the enigmatic J. K., "The Yellow Rose of Texas" has provided marching music for three wars. The armed forces of both world wars adopted it—the song that salutes a Texas heroine—music that has the quality lacking in similar melodies, long since forgotten . . . that intangible something that inspires the world to sing.

One tale links La Llorona's water haunting with the 1925 Rio Grande flood, in which she is supposed to have drowned her children.

*In other stories, crazed by mistreatment from her man,
she kills their children.*

THE WEEPING WOMAN
La Llorona

John O. West

Among Texas' most fascinating women is La Llorona, the focus of a migratory legend to be found in many cultures. Not a historical character like some heroes and heroines—say Davy Crockett, or the Babe of the Alamo—nonetheless La Llorona is real to many people. She fits a pattern—in her behavior, when and where she appears, and such—and she fills a need, much like defeated Southerners needed a don't-fence-me-in model like Jesse James. The Weeping Woman teaches a lesson—thou shalt not fool around outside your social class—or provides a scarecrow to keep wayward children (or even erring husbands) on the straight and narrow. Although the legend of Llorona travels from place to place, she often acquires local characteristics to make her even more horrible—or like the flame that attracts the moth, even more fascinating.

Like many other dwellers in the Southwest, La Llorona is not native-born. In fact, the weeping woman garbed in white who haunts particular places—especially water—is found in many parts of the world. In Germany, for example, she appears in Cologne as *Die Weisse Frau*. She is the spirit of a peasant girl, led astray and deserted by a naughty young nobleman; in a mad rage she killed their child, stabbed the father to death with his own sword, and later hanged herself—but she comes back regularly to haunt the scene of the double murder, and woe betide anyone who speaks to her.[1] Another girl led astray was reported in the Philippines after World War II. In this case the girl, of Spanish heritage, became the prey of Japanese occupation troops—and the mother of several children. After the liberation she wanted to return to her native village, but the children were evidence of her shame, so she killed them—then went mad and sought in vain for her babies.[2]

These two stories, albeit far in scene from the Hispanic Southwest, contain most of the essential details of the La Llorona story. In both stories there is a cultural or racial difference between the lovers, the girl kills the offspring, and madness results. And the typical Mexican relative of La Llorona follows much the same pattern: a Spanish nobleman and a low-born maiden fall in love and have children; when he goes to Spain on business, he's encouraged by his parents to marry an eligible lady of his own class. On his return to Mexico, he breaks the news to his mistress, who goes mad and drowns the children and kills herself— but her soul cannot rest. She must search for her children forever until she finds them.[3] Here the element of water occurs—and the basic pattern of La Llorona in the Southwest is completed.

In the El Paso area stories of the woman in white are plentiful, especially among the Hispanic population of low economic status. Told by children, they are simply horror stories; told by parents, they become obedience tales, intended to warn daughters, especially, against liaisons outside one's own social level. The pickings are rich indeed. Witness the following, collected in the El Paso area:

> Late one night my uncle and one of his friends were coming home late from the cantina. They always took too much tequila, you know, and so it was pretty late. All at once they saw this lady, about a block away, walking toward the canal. She really had a good figure.
>
> Well, you know how guys are when they've had too much tequila—they get interested in the ladies. So they hurried to catch up, and they even called to her, but she didn't wait. She walked on down by the canal.
>
> Finally they were just a few yards away, and they called to her to wait. Slowly, she turned around—and she didn't have any face! She lifted up her hands toward them, and she had shiny claws, like tin! And she was coming toward them, like she was going to get them, you know!
>
> Well, they turned and ran, with the woman right behind them, 'til they got to a bright street light, where she disappeared. My uncle never went to the cantina after that—he didn't want to meet La Llorona again.[4]

A story collected locally by Norma Herrera, a student of folklore at the University of Texas at El Paso, has an interesting twist:

> When she was born, she was a twin. She and her sister were so identical, that when they were baptized, the other one was baptized twice. La Llorona was never baptized. She married when she was nineteen and had a son and a daughter. But she did not love them, so she drowned them in a ditch. When she died and went before God, He punished her by having her cry and search throughout the world for her children, until the day the world ends. Then she

will be pardoned. They say that she appears where there are lakes and ditches, and her weeping and wailing can be heard.

As has been noted, La Llorona is usually found near water, and often the location is related to the crime that condemned her, like the Wandering Jew, to wander the earth searching for peace. One little old lady told the author about La Llorona, linking her sorrowful deed of drowning her children with the 1925 flood of the Rio Grande, providing believability with the detail of date—as well as making available enough water to drown any number of children.

In an occasional story told on the border, the rejected lover, crazed by the way she has been treated by her mate, kills their children and serves them as a meal to their father and his new love. Medea stopped short of making dinner of them, but not so "The Wicked Stepmother" of our Southern mountains who made the little boy into "rabbit stew."[5] And many stories have as their theme La Llorona's hatred of men, luring them to their deaths or driving them mad, much like Lilith of Hebrew tradition.[6] Kirtley finds reason to believe that although there are apparent connections between La Llorona and the Aztec goddess Civacoatl, there is much more evidence of European origin for the basic story, with local variants occurring, as is common in oral transmission, wherever a similar sort of tragedy has reportedly taken place.[7]

Along the Texas-Mexico border, where a blend of Hispanic and Indian culture has dominated the scene for most of the last four centuries, it would be quite unlikely not to find the same sort of blending and variety as elsewhere in this world-wide narrative. The Lilith strain was found (with an interesting twist) by Ray Green and Federico Aguilar, Jr., in the following:

La Llorona hated men, especially men who have two or more women. She appears to them dressed in a white robe and makes a pass and when they follow her they are always found drowned, sometimes in the canal, but sometimes they will be in the street. They always die with their eyes open like they were looking up at something and couldn't stop.

They also found that the death of La Llorona's children is not always deliberate, although the result is somewhat standard:

There was a woman who had gone out into the fields one day to help her husband with the crop. She left her children unattended. When she came home that evening, she found all of her children dead. Somehow they had poisoned themselves. When she saw this, she went out of her mind and killed herself. Since a suicide cannot be admitted to heaven, the Llorona was condemned to wander the earth.

William Campion found a lady of seventy-two who never forgot the lesson she learned many years ago:

As a young lady I often met José in the grove of trees near the river. Much kissing and loving took place but I was always careful to leave the area well before midnight. One night shortly before my engagement, time got away from me and I failed to leave before 12:00. A cold chilling wind came up suddenly from the north with a furious intensity. A cat screamed, and a plaintive wailing sound came to my ears. It grew louder and louder until a blast of wind caused a white-robed figure to whisk past me. As the figure darted by, I saw that it had no face. I fell to my knees and sought God's help. Before long the wind stopped, and I could no longer hear the mournful cries. To this day, I have not returned to that cursed spot.

A youngster interviewed by Mary Lee Wight got her story straight from *mamá*:

My mother said to never go to the Rio Grande because if I do there will be this lady and her name will be La Llorona. My mother said if I went there the lady might drown me. She is always crying every time because she drowned her children. If you go she will drown you too.

But another girl, who told her experience to Ralph Montelongo years later, had to learn her lesson the hard way—she got a life-long affliction of asthma from being out too late:

I stayed outside because it was too hot inside. Then I heard a howl like a coyote and I thought it was a dog. Then I heard a woman's voice scream: "Quiero mis hijos! Donde están?" [I want my children. Where are they?]. Then a white shawl, or scarf, fell on my face and it made me take a very deep breath. The scarf smelled so bad that when I breathed in, all the odor went to my lungs. This caused me to have asthma ever since. Then it started to rain very hard and all I could do was stand there and cry. When my mother came home a few minutes later, she found me lying on the ground, all wet and cold, with the scarf next to me. Next day it was very sunny and my mother washed the scarf and set it to dry on the tendedero *[clothesline]. When she sent for it about noon, it was gone! I think that La Llorona took it back.*

Ignacio Escandon recalls from his own childhood in El Paso that children were told *"La Llorona te llevará si no te portas bien!"* [La Llorona will carry you off if you don't behave!] His memory was that

she had lost her sons and that if she did not find her children she would take other children. She was called by other names—Chamuco, Roba-chicos, La Llorona, and La Malinche. Chamuco is only a name for bogey-man; Roba-chicos literally means stealer of children; and La Malinche I used to equate with the idea of mal—*evil, from* mal *in* malinche.

And Cathy Skender collected a differently motivated one from a boy raised in Cd. Juarez, Chihuahua:

A long time ago, an Indian couple was to be married, another ordinary marriage as it may appear. But as time went on, the economic status of the family went from fair to very poor. When the couple had its first baby, a boy, the father knew he couldn't feed him so after thinking about what was best for the child, he went to the river, and after asking God for forgiveness, he dropped the child in the river. The husband believed he was doing the right thing and repeated his feat as each child was born. Each time the town's people heard the wife screaming, "Ay, my hijo" [Oh, my son] in an eerie tone.

When her last son was born [all previous ones were boys], she was determined to have him live. She went down to the river, and after her husband dropped the boy, she went after him. Since she wasn't skilled in the art of swimming, she drowned along with her son.

Nobody thought much of it after the death, but one foggy night, one of the farm workers saw the ghostly figure of a woman and child in the river. The woman screamed in her high pitched voice, "Oh, my son." After that night, the ghost appeared on the water and the nearby land. The husband couldn't sleep because he heard these eerie sounds. Finally the husband, knife in hand, jumped into the river and tried to kill the woman. After his unsuccessful try, his body was never found.

After the story was spread around, people reported seeing her in different places. But the local people said that she appeared only on rainy, foggy nights.

Rainy nights provoke another Llorona to appear, Miss Skender reports:

Well, my friends told me there once lived this lady who had a bunch of kids. Well you see, she couldn't feed these kids. So she decided to kill them. She took them to the river and told them they were going to go swimming. They believed her. She drowned them. And God punished her for this. So He said, "You will always cry when a person puts a broom in the corner and it's raining." She regretted what she had done. But every time someone puts a broom in the corner when it rains at night, she has to go out and kill someone.

In the dark of night, if one has been told often of La Llorona since early childhood, shapes and sounds bring back memories, and goose bumps go up one's neck. La Llorona wants to get even with those who are happy; this is why men—the cause of her trouble—often are driven mad by the sight of her in the night.

What does La Llorona look like? Stories vary, but generally she looks beautiful—even enticing men closer—until one can see either the face of a horse or a blank, empty one. She dresses in long flowing robes—white or black—and her long, shiny fingernails are like knives by starlight.[8]

Several years ago, people in one of the local *barrios* kept hearing La Llorona cry about eight at night, every night. They began to group together for comfort and protection—and whoever was making the sounds of La Llorona robbed the houses people had left in fear. Such is the power of the tales of La Llorona.

But whether you think La Llorona is only a legend or not, when you are out walking late at night, you'd better beware! She may appear to you, entice you and leave you mad. As our Mexican friends would say, *"Cuídate! La Llorona!"*

NOTES

1. Johann G. T. Grässe, *Sagenbuch des Preussischen Staats*, cited in Bacil F. Kirtley, "'La Llorona' and Related Themes," *WF*, XIX No. 3 (July 1960), 158. Kirtley's 14 page article is packed with world-wide echoes of La Llorona.

2. Richard L. Hayden, then a Radioman third class in the U. S. Navy, collected this local legend at San Miguel, P.I., in 1968 or 1969.

3. Soledad Pérez, "Mexican Folklore from Austin, Texas," *The Healer of Los Olmos, PTFS*, XXIV (1951), 73–76, brings together several variants of the Llorona story. I have synthesized the essential story from her work as well as from others collected around El Paso.

4. A student (whose name I have forgotten) at what was then Texas Western College gave me this jewel in 1963. Student-collected materials will be cited hereafter in text. They form an important part of the University of Texas at El Paso Folklore Archive.

5. Richard Chase, *American Folk Tales and Songs* (1956; rpt. New York: Dover Books, c. 1971), pp. 47–50.

6. Lilith, according to Nathan Ausubel, *A Treasury of Jewish Folklore* (New York: Crown, c. 1948), pp. 592–594, was—or is—a female demon, seductress, and man-hater, sometimes called "The Howling One"—not too far from "The Weeping Woman"; in addition, she kills the children she bears after seducing unwary men. Lilly Rivlin in "Lilith," *Ms.*, I (Dec. 1972), 96, says "In medieval Europe (especially in Germany), Lilith became a popular man-devouring creature . . . who covets other women's children, and threatens to steal them. . . . [Also] she becomes in the Middle Ages a scraggy-toothed hag. . . . Though ugly and malformed she still prevails, however, as the seductress of sleeping men."

7. Kirtley, pp. 159–162.

8. Pérez, pp. 73–74.

SETTLERS

Belle Starr in her favorite velvet gown with her pistols.

BELLE STARR
The Bandit Queen of Dallas

Ruthe Winegarten

Texas Foundation for Women's Resources

Of all women of the Cleopatra type, since the days of the Egyptian queen herself, the universe has produced none more remarkable than Bella Starr, the Bandit Queen. Her character was a combination of the very worst as well as some of the very best traits of her sex. She was more amorous than Anthony's mistress; more relentless than Pharaoh's daughter, and braver than Joan of Arc. Of her it may well be said that Mother Nature was indulging in one of her rarest freaks, when she produced such a novel specimen of womankind. Bella was not only well educated, but gifted with uncommon musical and literary talents, which were almost thrown away through the bias of her nomadic and lawless disposition, which early isolated her from civilized life, except at intervals, when in a strange country, and under an assumed name, she brightened the social circle for a week or a month, and then was, perhaps, lost forever.[1]

Bella Starr, the Bandit Queen or The Female Jesse James, a twenty-five cent paperback novel, was rushed into print by Richard Fox, publisher of the *National Police Gazette*, a few months after Belle's death in 1889. Unique without "a single essential fact correct,"[2] and consisting primarily of highly imaginative fiction, this biography was the source, nevertheless, of most later accounts of Belle's life. Because Fox's book, like his other sensational publications, commanded a circulation "that reached into every self-respecting barbershop, billiard parlor, barroom, and bagnio throughout the Republic,"[3] it packed a powerful punch in

creating the legends about Belle in which she and her guntotin' comrades were transformed into glamorous heroes and heroines.

Belle has continued to be an irresistible heroine to the American public for a hundred years. Still a popular standby in western lore, her saga triggered fifty books, a lengthy 1939 Broadway run of *Missouri Legend*, a 1941 Twentieth Century Fox movie with Gene Tierney, and a 1969 London musical with Betty Grable. In 1975, a successful off-Broadway play, *Jesse and the Bandit Queen*, was produced, based on a mythical love affair between Jesse James and Belle, and in 1980, a TV special featured Elizabeth Montgomery as Belle.

Although the facts about her life are hard to establish, the real Belle Starr was a fascinating woman in her own right, needing no fictional embellishments. Even her most reliable biographer, Burton Rascoe, could locate only a few primary sources—a handful of court records, newspaper articles, letters, and reminiscences of old-timers. Rascoe, unfortunately, used no footnotes and in addition confused his narrative with fabrications and inconsistencies. Rascoe, too, succumbed to "the legendary Belle Starr, . . . a more enticing person than the one who emerges from recital of the cold facts."[4]

Belle Starr was a sexually liberated, unconventional nineteenth century woman. Unfettered by social mores and with a mind of her own, Belle refused to be locked into the traditional female roles of her society. Her life paralleled in many ways that of another outrageous contemporary woman, the notorious French writer, George Sand (Aurore Dudivant). They both moved in and out of polite society, defying it at will, determined to make their own way in the world. They often dressed as men and enjoyed the free camaraderie of male society. Belle complained that all women discuss are pumpkins and babies. Belle and George were small women, olive-skinned, with strong but rather homely faces. Belle hated mirrors: "I have a face like a hatchet." They each ran through a long string of lovers, usually younger men, were excellent horsewomen, piano players, and conversationalists. When their personal lives became complicated, they packed their children off to relatives or boarding school. Both their daughters became prostitutes, George's Solange, the highest paid courtesan in Europe, and Belle's Pearl, the madam of Ft. Smith's finest Bawdy House.

At fifteen, Belle eloped against her father's will to "marry" an outlaw in a mock horseback ceremony. By the age of twenty-three she had two illegitimate children, and had joined a band of horse thieves. After ostracism from family and "polite" Dallas society (which was not much more high-toned than she), and with a second outlaw-lover in hiding, Belle was now on her own. She supported herself by singing in Dallas dance halls, dealing poker as a professional gambler, and running a livery stable which trafficked in stolen horses. Belle dressed flamboyantly in black velvet, long flowing skirts, white chiffon waists, and a man's Stetson hat decorated with an ostrich plume. *The Dallas News* of June 7, 1886, said, "She was a dashing horsewoman, and exceedingly graceful in the saddle," with two revolvers suspended in holsters from a cartridge belt around her waist. Apparently unprejudiced, she had a succession of Indian lovers—Jack Spaniard, Jim French, Choctaw Charlie, Blue Duck, and Jim July—finally wedding Oklahoma Cherokee Sam Starr in the only official marriage which has been verified. She forced her last lover, Jim July, to switch his name to hers, and he became Jim Starr. "I changed my name the first time. After that the men change," she boasted.

The Cleopatra of the Plains was born Myra Belle Shirley on February 5, 1848, near Carthage, Missouri. The youngest child of John and Elizabeth Shirley, stock-raising Ozark farmers, she had two brothers— Ed, eight, and Preston, ten. This was wild, dreary country, recently vacated by Osage Indians who frequently returned to scalp the white settlers and burn their homes. In 1856, when Belle was eight, the Shirleys moved to Carthage (population 100) where Shirley opened a hotel and stable with horses and hacks for hire. Belle must have learned to ride and handle horses quite young as she was a superb horse-woman. First attending a private school in the local Masonic Hall, she was remembered by a classmate as a small and dark ten year old, "a bright, intelligent girl but was of a fierce nature and would fight any-one, boy or girl, that she quarreled with."[5] Later Belle probably at-tended the Carthage Female Academy, a typical frontier finishing school, where the young ladies learned a smattering of Greek, Latin, Hebrew, and French, needlework, and good manners. Belle must have also taken advantage of the optional $50-a-year piano lessons as later legends tout her musical talents.

During this period before the Civil War, the area was shattered by an undeclared border war between Missouri and Kansas over the ques-tion of slavery. Missouri, settled primarily by Southerners, was a pro-slavery state, sending advocates into Kansas to be met by New England abolitionists led by John Brown. After the outbreak of the Civil War, local citizens feared not only the regular Federal and Rebel forces, but the bands of irregular guerrilla gangs on both sides who "preyed upon the defenseless without regard to political belief or sympathies."[6] The most notorious of all the bushwhacker bands was led by the bloody William Quantrill under whose tutelage the James and Younger broth-ers received their training in pillage and murder. The careers of the Jameses and Youngers were later to be linked with Belle's.

Belle's family were Confederate sympathizers. At sixteen, already with a reputation for daring horsemanship, Belle is supposed to have rescued her brother Ed, possibly a member of Quantrill's gang, from the clutches of the "Feds" by out-riding a Union Cavalry unit sent to arrest him. This oft-repeated story is considered false by Rascoe. Ed was later killed by Federal militia in 1863. The avenging of Ed's death is often given as the motive for Belle's later bandit career, his murder having enlivened "all the animosity of which her untrammeled nature was capable. . . ."[7]

In October, 1863, Carthage was burned by Confederate guerrillas. Now homeless, Belle and her parents, along with hordes of other

border state emigrants, headed for Texas. They passed through Ft. Smith, Arkansas, a wild and tough town where Belle would later stand trial before "Hanging" Judge Parker.

Upon arrival in the Dallas area, the Shirleys moved into a dug-out with Belle's brother Preston, who had settled several years earlier in Scyene, ten miles east of downtown. At that time, Dallas had a population of 2000 and one main street, alternately a mud-hole and a dust bowl. The county had its water problems even then, and the clannish Shirleys made themselves unpopular with their neighbors by draining the communal well dry. John Shirley again turned to raising crops and horses. And Belle? An official Texas Historical Marker has been placed on the site of the Scyene Meeting Place where, it is alleged, Belle was a pupil.[8] Dallas historian A. C. Greene, on the other hand, claims that Belle taught school there. Whether student or school marm, Belle, now about sixteen, and a survivor of the Missouri frontier, must have found life dull in Scyene.

Historians disagree as to whether Belle's first lover and father of her daughter Pearl was Cole Younger or Jim Reed. Belle herself could have cleared up the mystery, but chose not to do so. In 1886, she granted interviews to correspondents with the *Dallas Morning News* (June 7) and the *Ft. Smith Elevator* (May 30), in which she said that the first man she ever fell in love with and married was a noted guerrilla, but she declined to give his name. No record of this marriage has been found. The *News* story read:

After the surrender (end of the Civil War), Quantrill's men came to the locality and were at all times welcome guests at her father's home [John Shirley in Scyene]. When less than fifteen years of age she fell in love with one of the dashing guerrillas, whose name she said it was not necessary for her to give. Her father objected to her marriage and she ran away with her lover, being married on horseback in the presence of about twenty of her husband's companions. John Fisher, one of the most noted outlaws in the State of Texas, held her horse while the ceremony was being performed, her wedding attire being a black velvet riding habit.

Both Rascoe and Glenn Shirley believe that Cole Younger was Belle's first lover. According to Shirley:

. . . dark, handsome, twenty-four-year-old Cole Younger rode into the Shirley ranch with his three brothers and Frank and Jesse James, fresh from their first bank job at Liberty, Missouri, and Myra Belle fell in love with Cole. When the outlaw rode back with his gang to Missouri in 1867, he left her pregnant with a child.

Myra Belle never saw Cole Younger again. The gang startled the nation with its daring bank and train robberies. Sheriffs and Pinkerton detectives were hot on their trail. At Northfield, Minnesota, the gang was nearly annihilated; only

Frank and Jesse escaped; Cole and Bob were wounded and captured and sentenced to life terms in the state prison at Stillwater. Meanwhile, Myra Belle's scandal swept the Texas country-side. Scyene society ostracized her.[9]

Rascoe and Glenn Shirley are probably correct in believing that Cole Younger was Belle's first lover, primarily because she named her first child, born around 1868, Pearl Younger. Belle was too honest a woman to have given this cherished child a false name. Also, Pearl was born four years before court records indicate that Jim Reed came to Dallas. In addition, Belle romantically named her last home "Younger's Bend." Assuming that Cole Younger was her first lover, he did not stay around long. He either deserted her, as Rascoe claims, or he asked Belle to "become a kitchen slavey to his outfit. He had to abandon the project under the eloquent cussing-out she gave him."[10] Belle, already suffering from family and local rejection for having borne Younger's child, broke finally with Dallas society and its conventions. Leaving Pearl with her parents, she entered the saloon life of Dallas as a woman on a man's terms, but asking no quarter from men. She supported herself as a singer or an entertainer in a Dallas dance hall, dealt poker and faro as a professional gambler, and did very well financially.

After awhile, Belle became known as the wife of Jim Reed, a two-bit Scyene desperado, also originally from Missouri, and served as the fence for a large band of horse thieves who preyed on Texas herds and ran them north. Belle and Jim soon had a son whom they named Ed Reed.

The options for women at that time, particularly single women with illegitimate children, were severely limited. Less than ten percent of all Texas women, married or single, were employed. Teaching was the only occupation available for a woman with any education. The other major sources of employment were as agricultural laborers or farmers, domestics, personal servants, launderesses, and dress-makers.[11] It is hardly surprising that Belle, excluded from teaching because of her illegitimate child, and considering the other job opportunities, would have turned bandit.

On November 20, 1873, the first robbery in which Belle herself (along with Reed) is supposed to have participated was that perpetrated upon a wealthy Oklahoma Creek Indian named Watt Grayson, tortured and robbed of $30,000 in gold by a gang, one of whom was a woman dressed as a man. Labeled a criminal by every chronicle, Reed went into hiding, but Belle brazenly established herself at the Planter's Hotel in Dallas.

Belle dressed and behaved in a spectacular manner. She purchased a horse and buggy, a riding horse and a stud which she kept in the stables back of the hotel, hiring a Negro as her special hostler and groom. She dressed in black velvet, with long flowing skirts when she rode side-saddle, and wore white chiffon waists, a tight black jacket, high-topped boots and a man's Stetson hat turned up

in front and decorated with an ostrich plume . . . around her waist she wore a cartridge belt from which two revolvers were suspended in holsters. She attended the races, the circus and the county fair. She would enter bars and drink like a man or take her place at gaming tables for a try of her luck at dice, cards or roulette.

When the mood struck her, she shocked the women and more respectable citizens of Dallas by changing into beaded and fringed buckskin costumes like those worn by Buffalo Bill, and riding at breakneck speed through the streets of the town, scattering everyone to the sidewalk. The constabulary and the whole town was afraid of her; and she gloried in being pointed out as the Bandit Queen. She had nothing to fear as long as there was no warrant out for her arrest. Not even the knowledge that her husband had a price of $1,500 on his head was any legal reason for molesting her.[12]

Belle opened a livery stable on Camp Street, dealing in stolen horses, near the present location of the *Dallas Times Herald*. Flush from the Grayson robbery, she invested in a string of handsome race horses, including a black stud named Venus who was to become her favorite.

The crossing of two railroads in 1873 had catapulted Dallas, already the world's largest buffalo hide center, into a spectacular boom town, and Belle was in her element. The teeming town was noisy and disorderly, jammed with a scruffy pack of frontier riffraff squared off in an uneasy truce with a tiny group of civic-minded, law-abiding members of the establishment. The population, now 7000, had doubled in the last three years, and Dallas boasted the state's best bawdy houses, casinos, and taverns. Every general store had a whiskey barrel serving free drinks to the customers until the saloon keepers, who outnumbered the merchants, stopped the practice with a city ordinance. Herds of longhorns forded the Trinity River across from Dealey Plaza, and Elm Street was a sea of tall white cotton bales.[13]

Belle and Jim were soon implicated in another sensational crime: a hold-up at gunpoint of the San Antonio-Austin stagecoach on April 7, 1874. Local newspapers followed the incident with great interest and were soon pleased to announce the arrest of Jim Reed.[14] Reed was released for insufficient evidence, nor was Belle indicted. Later that year Reed was killed trying to escape the custody of a deputy sheriff.[15]

After Reed's death, Belle seems to have lived quietly for a while and then she decided to give Pearl music and dancing lessons, hoping to launch her daughter in a theatrical career. Belle described her ambitions for Pearl in a letter to Reed's family in Missouri:

. . . she has the reputation of being the prettiest girl in Dallas. She is learning very fast. She has been playing on the stage here in the Dallas theatre and gained a world-wide reputation for her prize performance. My people were very much opposed to it but I wanted her to be able to make a living of her own without depending on anyone.[16]

Belle no doubt was remembering her own economic vulnerability. But Pearl's budding theatrical career was short-circuited by a serious illness, probably a brain hemorrhage.

Restless again, Belle took Ed to his Missouri grandmother and packed Pearl off to Arkansas relatives. Belle returned to Dallas and "began to exhibit her former roving disposition, right into an arson charge."[17] Out on a reckless ride with a girl friend, the two set fire to a small general store. Emma, the friend, snitched, and Belle was brought to trial for arson. A generous stockman named Patterson posted Belle's $2400 bond, but we don't know what he got in the bargain.

About 1876, Belle began branching out from Dallas. Because she was the only literate member of the gang, she became the brains of a band of rustlers operating across the Texas-Oklahoma border. They stole horses. Constantly on the run, they stuck to Indian trails, spending days and nights in the saddle. Belle was their "fix." She fenced the stolen property and kept them out of jail. Horse stealing was big business in Texas during the 1870's. "The editor of the *Frontier Echo* in Jacksboro estimated that there had been 100,000 horses stolen in the state during the three years preceding March 8, 1878, that 750 men were regularly engaged in the business, and that not more than one in ten was ever caught and brought to Justice."[18] Before we judge Belle and her friends too harshly, consider the following explanation by Rupert Richardson: "The Northwest Texas Stock Association . . . organized at Graham in 1877, devoted considerable effort toward suppressing cattle theft, but for several years the results were discouraging because men of wealth and influence were doing a considerable part of the stealing."[19]

Sometime around 1880, Belle acquired dower rights to a share in Indian communal land by marrying Sam Starr, an Oklahoma Cherokee. The couple and Belle's children Pearl and Ed settled in a log cabin overlooking a curve of the Canadian River. Belle romantically named their new home "Younger's Bend," a sentimental reference to her first lover, Cole Younger. Belle soon turned the area into a haven for outlaws. The *Dallas News* of June 7, 1886, continues with Belle's story "as told by the lady herself":

After a more adventurous life than generally falls to the lot of women, I settled permanently in the Indian territory, selecting a place of picturesque beauty on the Canadian River. There, far from society, I hoped to pass the remainder of my life in peace and quietude. So long had I been estranged from the society of women, whom I thoroughly detest, that I thought I would find it irksome to live in their midst. So I selected a place that but few had ever had the gratification of gossiping around.

For a time I lived very happily in the society of my little girl and husband, a Cherokee Indian, son of the noted Tom Starr. But it soon became noised around

that I was a woman of some notoriety from Texas, and from that time on my home and actions have been severely criticized.

My home became famous as an outlaw's ranch long before it was visited by any of the boys who were friends of mine in times past. Indeed, I never corresponded with any of my old associates, and was desirous my whereabouts should be unknown to them. Through rumor they learned of it. Jesse James first came in and remained several weeks. He was unknown to my husband, who never knew until long afterward that our home had been honored by Jesse's presence. . . . But few outlaws have visited my home, notwithstanding so much has been said. The best people in the country are my friends. I have considerable ignorance to cope with, consequently my troubles originate mostly in that quarter. Surrounded by a low down class of shoddy whites, who have made the Indian country their home to evade paying tax on their dogs, and who I will not permit to hunt on my premises, I am the constant theme of their slanderous tongues. In all the world there is no woman more peaceably inclined than I.

From 1880 to 1882 Belle limited herself to managing the affairs of her outlaw gangs, using Younger's Bend as a headquarters. In February, 1883, she and Sam Starr were brought before "Hanging" Judge Parker's Federal Court in Ft. Smith on charges of stealing two horses. The trial created a sensation. This was the first time a woman had been brought before the bench there, indicted as the leader of a band of horse thieves. Fame had at last reached Belle Starr. The Petticoat Terror, as the papers called her, participated in her own defense, handing frequent notes to her attorneys who paid strict attention to their contents.

A devil-may-care expression rested on her countenance during the entire trial, and at no time did she give sign of weakening before the mass of testimony that was raised against her. Once, when allusion was made to Jim Reed, her former husband and the father of her child, tears welled up in her eyes and trickled down her cheeks, but they were quickly wiped away and the countenance resumed its wonted appearance.

As an equestrienne, Belle Starr is without rival, is said to be an expert marksman with the pistol, and it is claimed that she was at one time the wife of Bruce [sic] Younger, the notorious horse thief and desperado, and while she could not be considered even a good-looking woman, her appearance is of that kind as would be sure to attract attention of wild and desperate characters.[20]

Belle and Sam were sentenced to a year in the Detroit penitentiary, the only prison term Belle ever served. While behind bars, she is said to have worked on a book and tutored the warden's children in music and French. With time off for good behavior, she and Sam returned to their Oklahoma home. In 1885, Belle ran off with a wanted murderer, John Middleton. Middleton was drowned under mysterious circumstances, perhaps killed by a jealous Sam to whom Belle then returned. In 1886,

Sam and Belle were arrested once more—this time for robbing an Indian and his three sons. Belle posted bond and spent the week in Ft. Smith, shopping and sight-seeing. The June 7, 1886, *Dallas News* ran this spicy account:

For the past week the noted Belle Starr has been quite an attraction on the streets of this city. She came to answer two indictments in the Federal Court . . . first for being implicated in the stealing of a fine mare, the one ridden by the notorious John Middleton when he was drowned in the Poteau River, twenty-five miles above this city, in May, 1885; and second, on a charge of robbery, in which it is claimed that Belle, dressed in male attire, led a party of three men who robbed an old man named Ferrell and his three sons. . . .

Monday night Belle swung her Winchester to her saddle, buckled her revolver around her, and mounting her horses, set out for her home on the Canadian. Before leaving, she purchased a fine pair of 45-calibre revolvers. . . Belle says she anticipates no trouble in establishing her innocence in the cases against her, but thinks it terribly annoying to have to spend her time and money coming down here to court five and six times a year.

Belle attracts considerable attention wherever she goes, being a dashing horsewoman, and exceedingly graceful in the saddle. She dresses plainly, and wears a broad-brimmed white man's hat, surmounted by a wide black plush band, with feathers and ornaments, which is very becoming to her. She is of medium size, well formed, a dark brunette, with bright and intelligent black eyes. . . .

Belle is a crack shot, and handles her pistols with as much dexterity as any frontiersman. No man enters Younger's Bend without first giving a thorough account of himself before he gets out.

Belle related many incidents of her life that would be of interest, and says she has been offered big money by publishers for a complete history of it, but she does not desire to have it published yet. She has a complete manuscript record, and when she dies she will give it to the public. She spends most of her time writing when at home.

'You can just say that I am a friend to any brave and gallant outlaw, but have no use for that sneaking coward class of thieves who can be found in every locality, and who would betray a friend or comrade for the sake of their own gain. . . .

A few months after their court appearance, Sam was killed in a blazing gunbattle with a deputy.

Belle's last lover was Jim July, a handsome twenty-four-year-old Creek Indian, who moved in with her after Sam's death, and changed his name to Jim Starr. Two years later, at the age of forty-one, on February 3, 1889, Belle was murdered by an unknown assailant, blasted

from behind with four buckshot in her back, as she rode near nightfall on a lonely path by her cabin. Some said she was killed by a neighbor whose advances she had rejected. But local gossip insisted that her own son Ed Reed had killed her,[21] that they had had incestuous relations complicated by Belle's extreme sadism. The real murderer was never caught.

Belle was buried in her front yard, dressed in black silk skirt and white waist, clasping her favorite six-shooter. In an ancient tribal ritual, each Cherokee passing by for a last look dropped pinches of cornmeal into the coffin.[22] Pearl commissioned the following tombstone inscription:

Shed not for her the bitter tear,
Nor give the heart to vain regret;
Tis but the casket that lies here,
The gem that filled it sparkles yet.

The mistaken legends about Belle, based on the Fox book, began a few months after her death. The most remarkable woman in the history of border outlawry had captured the imagination of the American people and become a folk heroine.

Belle's son Ed came to a bad end, as she had often predicted. After a bootlegging conviction, he turned policeman and died in a drunken brawl in 1896. Pearl recovered from her illness and first entered a Ft. Smith bawdy house, but she soon opened her own business and prospered with the magnificent Pea Green House, the pride of the Southwest. She married several times, had four children, retired from "show business" in 1918, and died in 1925.

Tales of buried gold still linger about Younger's Bend, twenty miles east of Eufaula, Oklahoma. Eager treasure hunters have repeatedly and unsuccessfully dug up the ground, searching for money and jewels believed hidden there by the bandits. The treasure and the truth have been equally elusive.

NOTES

1. *Bella Starr, the Bandit Queen, or The Female Jesse James*, anonymous (Austin: The Steck Company, 1960. Based on the original edition: New York: Richard K. Fox Publisher, 1889).

2. Burton Rascoe, *Belle Starr* (New York: Random House, 1941), p. 14. Basic sources for this paper were William Y. Shackleford, *Belle Starr, the Bandit Queen* (Girard, Kansas: Haldeman-Julius Pubs., 1943); S. W. Harmon, *Belle Starr, the Female Desperado* (Houston: Frontier Press of Texas, 1954; originally published in 1898 at Ft. Smith, Arkansas in *Hell on the Border*); A. C. Greene, *A Place Called Dallas* (Dallas County Heritage Society, 1975); Glenn Shirley, *Law West of Fort Smith: Frontier Justice in the Indian Territory, 1834–1896* (New York: Collier Books, 1961); Lon Tinkle, "Belle Starr," in *Notable American Women* (Cambridge: Harvard University Press, 1974); and John William Rogers, *The Lusty Texans of Dallas* (New York: E. P. Dutton, 1951).

3. Peter Lyon, "The Wild Wild West," *American Heritage*, August, 1960, p. 35.

4. Rascoe, pp. 40–41.

5. *Carthage, Missouri Press*, Sept. 7, 1922. Interview with Mrs. James Brummett.

6. Rascoe, p. 76.

7. Harman, p. 10.

8. *Dallas Times Herald*, December 16, 1976.

9. Shirley, p. 118.

10. Rascoe, p. 154.

11. *Tenth Census Population—1880* (Washington: Government Printing Office, 1883), Table XXXIV—"Persons Engaged in Each Selected Occupation, etc.: 1880, Texas," p. 847.

12. Rascoe, pp. 177–178.

13. Rogers, pp. 140–146.

14. *Dallas Times Herald*, April 28, 1874.

15. *Dallas Times Herald*, August 7, 1874.

16. Rascoe, pp. 186–187.

17. Harmon, pp. 21–22.

18. Rupert N. Richardson, *Texas, the Lone Star State* (Englewood Cliffs, N.J., 2nd edition, 1958), p. 233.

19. *Idem.*

20. *Ft. Smith Arkansas New Era*, February 22, 1883.

21. Tinkle, p. 350.

22. Shackleford, p. 22.

Guilty consciences in San Patricio about the treatment of Chipita Rodriguez have produced many stories about her arrest, trial, hanging, and accusing ghost.

THE GHOST OF CHIPITA

The Crying Woman of San Patricio

Marylyn Underwood

When execution of a woman is pending in Texas, the ghost of Chipita Rodriguez stirs. She walked when a Fayette County woman was to be hanged after World War I but returned to the grave when the woman died in a cell before her execution. She moaned among the mesquites that line the Nueces River bottom when, in the 1940's, Mrs. Emma Oliver was condemned to die; but she ceased her cries of anguish when Mrs. Oliver's sentence was commuted. Again, she was visible among the gnarled mesquites at the proposed electrocution of Mrs. Maggie Morgan in 1959. But with that commuted sentence, Chipita's ghost once again withdrew. Presumably, she came forth yet another time when, as recent as 1978, Mary Lou Anderson was tried for murder; then her sentence was reduced for testifying against her accomplice. Perhaps Chipita, disturbed by the circumstances of her own trial and execution, sees the awfulness of another woman's death in a way that causes Chipita's spectre to come forward. Or perhaps, until her name is cleared, Chipita bemoans her fate.

Chipita Rodriguez is San Patricio's best-known historical figure around whom has spread almost as many stories as there have been years since her hanging. One of these stories obviously deals with her ghost. Others pertain to her trial and subsequent conviction and the hanging itself. Still another concerns the Irish Catholic village's guilt, from the youngest who brought her cookies, to the oldest who criticized the wake Chipita never had. Also contributing to their feeling of

guilt was the motive for murder being eliminated; the trial considered unorthodox; the hanging too speedy an execution. The stories have been perpetuated since the event by San Patricio locals, by news media, and by writers and historians. All have helped to create the legend of Chipita Rodriguez.

Chipita was found guilty of murdering a horse trader named John Savage for the $600 in gold he carried in his saddlebags. Six hundred dollars in gold is substantial motive for murder—and was in 1863—but the gold was found before the trial got underway. Nonetheless, this discovery didn't slow down the trial proceedings. Chipita had given Savage a cot on her lean-to porch, as she had done for many weary Cotton Road travelers in those days, for she operated a humble inn on the Aransas River a few miles north of San Patricio. Savage had last been seen there. Whether the next day, or two days later, his hacked body was supposedly discovered by two Negro women who worked on the Welder Ranch. They found it floating in a burlap sack in the Aransas. Suspicion pointed to the withered, very old Chipita whose cabin was near the location of the sighting of the body.

Chipita was arrested in August, 1863, by Sheriff William Means of San Patricio for the ax slaying of John Savage. On Friday the 13th, November 1863, she was hanged for that murder. None can deny that Chipita received a speedy trial by jury. But the trial's proceedings were quite unorthodox. For example, the man who had arrested her later served as foreman for the jury. Not only that, the same man, Sheriff Means, selected the other men who served on the jury. Four of these had served on the grand jury that had indicted Chipita. Several were courthouse officials and county employees, and at least three individuals were on the court docket for crimes which they had allegedly committed. The sheriff had been instructed to obtain qualified men by Circuit Judge Benjamin Neal, for the previous July there had been no names drawn to serve on the jury for the coming session. When Judge Neal arrived, therefore, for the week of October 5–10 to call the Fourteenth District Court of Texas into session, there were no jurors. Circumstances were not favorable for Chipita in her trial for life. The jury found her guilty of first degree murder; an accomplice, Juan Silvera, who the court agreed helped her dispose of the body, was found guilty of second degree murder.

Judge Neal refused clemency asked by the jury on account of Chipita's old age (she was apparently around ninety years old). Instead, he assessed her punishment to be, according to court records, "hanging by the neck until . . . dead." The speed with which the indictment, trial, and execution were carried out is curious to the reviewer of the scant court records when he reads of the number of those individuals whose cases had been in continuance for several years. Chipita also seemed to have little in the way of defense counsel as there was no motion in arrest of judgment. A motion for a new trial was withdrawn with no reason given for its withdrawal. The only words Chipita uttered in her defense were "Not guilty."

So it was on a dreary, misty November 13, 1863, that Chipita could be seen chained to the back wall of the San Patricio frame courthouse, in which position she had been placed since Judge Neal's pronouncement of execution the month before. On this fatal day, John Gilpin, the hangman, went to the home of Betty McCumber to obtain her new wagon for the hanging of the old Mexican murderess. But Betty Mc-Cumber drove him off with a stick. Eventually, however, she was forced to turn it over, probably to one of the sheriff's deputies, but there is some disagreement among present San Patricio locals as to who had that duty.

While Gilpin was getting the wagon, school children looked kindly upon the poor woman bound in irons and shared their lunches with her, giving her cookies. Travis Moreman, reporter for the Corpus Christi *Caller-Times* at one time and one who has delved into the legends surrounding Chipita, writes that he could "never come up with one bit of evidence supporting . . . that school children would come by the jail and share their lunches with her." Besides the cookies, the children allegedly brought Chipita corn shucks for cigarettes. A local San Pat historian, Pat Conlan, reports that the grandmother of Hugh McCown (who used to own the Old San Pat Store) gave Chipita "cigarette makings when she was in jail."

Soon, though, Chipita's time had come. Gilpin returned with Betty McCumber's new wagon; he unlatched the irons binding her to the courthouse wall, but he unmercifully left the iron leggings around her ankles. Painfully, unaided, she lifted her frail body onto the wagon and sat down on the newly-made cypress coffin, calmly smoking a cigarette—and so she is described by Mrs. Rachel Bluntzer Hebert in her narrative poem, *Shadows on the Nueces.* Mrs. Hebert's greataunt Josephine Sullivan purported to have "seen her in jail and saw her riding down the street sitting on her coffin."

Some San Patricio townspeople followed the wagon at a discreet distance to the hanging tree on the Weir property bordering the Nueces River. There, according to legend, she was hanged from a big mesquite. But Garrett Klatt, a descendant of the Weir family, and Pat Conlan, both agree that there were no mesquite trees in 1863. States Mr. Klatt: "There were no mesquites here then. It was all flat and level. The only trees were on the river." Pat Conlan adds the story of a surveyor who had come once to San Patricio and asked to see the hanging tree. He was taken to a mesquite tree thought to be the right one, but the surveyor pointed out that that tree was too young. "He could tell by the bark," says Pat Conlan, and concludes, "When they started the cattle drives from King Ranch, they started mesquite trees then." To further undermine the idea of Chipita's hanging from a mesquite tree, Mrs. Hebert quotes her aunt Lida Dougherty (1873–1945) as saying that the hanging tree "even in her time . . . was lost."

Regardless of the kind of tree from which Chipita was hanged, there is no doubt as to the skillfulness with which Hangman Gilpin threw his rope over a jutting branch, slipped his notch over the head of

the old Mexican woman standing in the wagon, and methodically drove the oxen forward. Chipita's face, the horrors of her choking and strangulation uncovered, gave those villagers watching a gruesome sight. One woman fainted; a young boy ran all the way home—a mile or more away—at full speed.

None went forward to help Gilpin remove the form dangling from the tree limb. None helped him lower the body into the waiting, opened coffin; and none helped him dig the shallow grave just beneath the hanging tree to drop the coffin therein. In fact, none were too friendly to Gilpin thereafter. Legend maintains that he was forced to leave town.

Many of the inhabitants thought Chipita was innocent. They thought she had been shielding someone else. Stories are related even today that she sacrificed her life for her son's. Those who perpetuate this tale confuse Juan Silvera with her illegitimate son whose father was an American trader who took him from Chipita when he was just a boy. According to legend, though, Chipita covered up for Juan Silvera, protecting him from hanging, only to come back from the dead to haunt him and to accuse him with her eyes.

That which upset most of the Irish Catholics in the community, however, was the fact that Chipita had had no wake. About this Lida Dougherty once asked, "Could a more unholy or unnatural thing have happened to an Irish village?"

Would that we could find the infamous hanging tree, if only to place a simple plaque or monument marking the place of the only woman ever legally hanged in the state of Texas. But the tree is gone: hit by lightning and cut up for firewood. The exact location is a mystery. At one time, a depression marked the place and two sisters, Mrs. Hugh McCown and Mrs. Kate Bluntzer, placed wildflowers on it daily when they were girls. Now both Mrs. McCown and Mrs. Bluntzer are gone and the knowledge of that possible site lies with them.

Accounts of Chipita's ghost have been perpetuated largely via the news media. Travis Moreman, for instance, admits that anything found in the *Caller-Times* files before 1960 on the subject could not be considered factual because "about that time, we indicted our newspaper as being the chief organ of perpetuating fanciful myths about the history of South Texas and in historical stories and special editions thereafter, we relied on interviews only if they could be substantiated."

But substantiation is not the stuff that legends are made of. Rather, legends are the stuff of the minds of the folk who believe or want to believe them. Few of the residents of San Patricio today claim to have heard the cries or to have seen the ghost of Chipita (whom the media prior to 1960 described as having a frayed noose around her neck). However, they know the legend and share it excitedly with one eager to hear it. Mrs. Petra Alaniz, for example, reports having heard a woman crying—"It came from the river!"—at the early hour of two or three in the morning. Mrs. Eugene McCown, who maintains a thick scrapbook of San Patricio news clippings, states that she had heard the story of

Chipita when she first married and moved to San Patricio in 1939. Later, she told her teen-age daughter the stories she had heard, and these stories insured her daughter and her boyfriends' getting into the safety of the house rather than sitting in the car our front. John L. Norris, former editor of *The Mathis News*, asserts that San Patricio after dark still poses some fright for its teen population who, after a school event, hasten home.

Any older resident of San Patricio can rattle off a story relating to Chipita upon request, for stories surrounding the event abound. Pat Conlan relays, for example, that "G. W. McCown said that Joe Wall's grandmother told him [Joe] that the Sunday afternoon after the hanging the sheriff was on his way to church. He saw the devil sittin' on the church fence. He turned around and went home."

My father, Woodrow Hicks, Sr., told me the story of Chipita. He would point to the brushy mesquites on the side of the road going through San Patricio from our home in Mathis and say, "That's where the crying woman was hung."

The true account of Chipita's death is shrouded, yet the people of San Patricio will not or cannot forget the event of Chipita's hanging. Every time a woman is convicted of murder in Texas, another news item appears in a paper somewhere, ticking off those women who have met similar sentencings but who, for sundry reasons, did not meet the same fate. Many believe that the circumstances surrounding Chipita's trial and subsequent death acted as a curse upon the town, for never again did it thrive as before, and in 1893 the county seat was moved to nearby Sinton.

Vagaries are abundant regarding Chipita's stories; the truth perhaps will never be known because of the lack of evidence; but, as Mrs. Hebert succinctly put it, "the material was so conducive to the supernatural that a ghost story just had to spring from it."

BIBLIOGRAPHY

Blackburn, Cliff. "Hanging Tree: Ghost of Texas' Only Executed Woman Walks." *Houston Post*, 15 May, 1960, p. 9, Sec. 1.

Hebert, Rachel Bluntzer. *Shadows on the Nueces*. Georgia: Banner Press, 1942.

McDaniel, Ruel. "The Day They Hanged Chipita." *Texas Parade*, March 1970, pp. 18–19.

Moorman, Travis. "Evidence That Hanged Chipita Circumstantial." *Corpus Christi Caller-Times*, 15 January 1959, p. 16.

———. "Date Recalls Woman's Hanging in Historical San Patricio Case." *Corpus Christi Caller-Times*, 13 November 1970, pp. 1, 20, Sec. A.

———. "Hanging Friday is San Pat Legend." *Corpus Christi Caller-Times*, 13 November 1959, p. 12.

———. "Houston Woman Won't Be the First Executed in Texas." *Corpus Christi Caller-Times*, 24 March 1963, p. 10.

Redding, Stan. (?) *Chronicle* reporter. "Chipita's Restless Ghost Slips Back Into Grave." n.d.

San Patricio County in 1976: A Bicentennial Perspective. Sinton, Tex.: Sinton Bicentennial Celebrations, Inc., 1976.

Smylie, Vernon. *A Noose for Chipita.* Corpus Christi: Texas News Syndicate Press, 1970.

LETTERS AND INTERVIEWS

Alaniz, Chon. Personal interview. San Patricio, Texas. September 23, 1978.
Conlan, Pat. Personal interview. San Patricio, Texas. September 23, 1978.
Farenthold, Frances T. (Sissy). Personal letter. April 29, 1978.
Havelka, Bill. Personal interview. San Patricio, Texas. September 23, 1978.
Hebert, Rachel B. Personal letter. June 23, 1978.
Klatt, Garrett. Personal interview. San Patricio, Texas. September 23, 1978.
McCown, Mrs. Eugene. Personal interview. San Patricio, Texas. September 23, 1978.
Moreman, Travis. Personal letter. May 3, 1978.
Norris, John L. Personal interview. Sandia, Texas. September 23, 1978.
———. Personal letter. April 15, 1978.

THE CAPITOL'S LADY

Audray Bateman

Texas Foundation for Women's Resources

The files of the Austin-Travis County Collection of the Austin Public Library are full of stories about the lady that stands atop the dome of the Texas State Capitol. Many will even dispute her origin—certain sources say she came from Spain, others say Belgium or Pennsylvania. One account tells us that the statue was made in France and lost at sea. A duplicate arrived in Austin in pieces a year later and was recast in a foundry on the Capitol grounds.

The legendary lady has many names. Some call her the Goddess of Wisdom, others say the Goddess of Victory or the Statue of Liberty. Most often she is known by the Goddess of Liberty.

The material used in the statue's construction is one point that would be easy for the researcher to check, but it may be a bit dangerous to climb the 300 or so feet to reach it. Some say the Goddess of Liberty is made of bronze; some say copper and even marble is suggested. One Austinite once claimed that his grandmother posed for the statue and that it was cast in a foundry set up on the Capitol grounds.

Documentation of the true facts is somewhat scarce, but recently we have discovered that the Goddess is made of zinc and that she was created by Friedley-Vorshardt Company of Chicago. The statue may have arrived in Austin in pieces and been assembled on the Capitol grounds before being lifted to its perch in 1888.

All sorts of stories are told about Austin's highest lady. Thomas T. Vorshardt, a nephew of the partners of Friedley-Vorshardt, was involved in one of the most delightful tales.

Vorshardt was a granite cutter and wanted desperately to work on the Texas Capitol. When asked by his co-workers why he wanted this particular job, Tom always replied that he had fallen in love with the Goddess of Liberty—the statue that had been made by his family's company. He insisted that he must at least make the pedestal on which she would stand. Disputes with the granite cutter's union made Tom's employment impossible. The state of Texas imported forty granite cutters from Scotland to supervise the building of the Capitol.

The story goes that when the Goddess arrived by train from Chicago the workmen brought her from the railroad station to the Capitol grounds on a specially built flat-bottom wagon. Soon she was ready and one of the Scotsman tied a rope around her neck to begin the job of getting her to the top of the Capitol dome. Suddenly Tom Vorshardt came galloping into the center of the workmen shouting at the top of his voice, "Get away from my lady! Get away from her!" The men backed away and Tom grabbed the rope that was around the statue's neck. He gave his horse a kick and started off with his treasure, only to be jerked from the saddle when the rope grew taut.

One of the Scotsmen helped Tom to his feet and asked him why in the world he was trying to carry off the Goddess. In response, Tom handed the man a picture of his wife. "The Goddess looks just like your wife," said the workman. "Yes," said Tom. "My wife posed for the statue."

"No offense," said the Scotsman, "but I think the Goddess is a mite prettier."

Tom replied, "The Goddess is not only prettier, but she is far less demanding and considerably more cordial."

The *American-Statesman* of February 25, 1925, dispelled another one of the myths: "Did you ever hear the legend that the giant cast iron lady in white on top of the Capitol dome was once blown off the foundation by a wind storm, hanging only by a twisted girder, and that a bunch of valiant men and boys including several University of Texas students, climbed to the top of the dome in the dark as the storm whirled and lightning flashed, and after heroic efforts, finally put her back in place again?

"'Impossible,' declared Capt. Hendrickerson (who was inspector of buildings of the Board of Control in the 1920s). 'For one thing the heroic maiden in white weighs several tons. It is firmly bolted in place, and the highest wind on record would not be sufficient pressure on it to move it. In the second place, if it were to topple over, it would go right through the dome and down to the basement. . . .'"

The best story of recent years is from an unknown source. "When the C. B. Moreland Paint Company was repainting the dome of the Capitol, the painters discovered bees using the nose of the Goddess of Liberty as entrance and exit. The resourceful painters plugged each nostril with a Budweiser beer bottle cork and proceeded to complete the job."

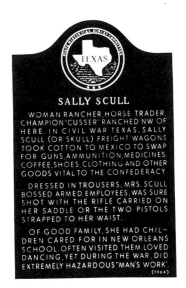

SALLY SCULL

WOMAN RANCHER, HORSE TRADER,
CHAMPION "CUSSER" RANCHED NW OF
HERE. IN CIVIL WAR TEXAS, SALLY
SCULL (OR SKULL) FREIGHT WAGONS
TOOK COTTON TO MEXICO TO SWAP
FOR GUNS, AMMUNITION, MEDICINES,
COFFEE, SHOES, CLOTHING AND OTHER
GOODS VITAL TO THE CONFEDERACY.

DRESSED IN TROUSERS, MRS. SCULL
BOSSED ARMED EMPLOYEES, WAS SURE
SHOT WITH THE RIFLE CARRIED ON
HER SADDLE OR THE TWO PISTOLS
STRAPPED TO HER WAIST.

OF GOOD FAMILY, SHE HAD CHIL-
DREN CARED FOR IN NEW ORLEANS
SCHOOL. OFTEN VISITED THEM. LOVED
DANCING, YET DURING THE WAR, DID
EXTREMELY HAZARDOUS "MAN'S WORK".
(1964)

TWO SIXSHOOTERS AND A SUNBONNET
The Story of Sally Skull

Dan Kilgore

The band of cowmen critically eyed the herd of horses approaching through the opening in the chaparral, scanning each rib and hip for a familiar mark among the intricate brands denoting the Mexican origin of the horses. High crowned sombreros with their wide flaring brims told the common heritage of the vaqueros trailing the herd. But a slatted sunbonnet shielded the hawk-like nose of the slight figure that spurred ahead to deal with the riders lined across the trail.

"Sally, we're missing some horses and we . . . ."

"Get around those horses; you don't cut my herds."

The piercing, steel-blue eyes under the bonnet's brim spoke with as much authority as her decided tone and the two cap-and-ball revolvers strapped at her waist. The horses continued along unmolested as the cowmen eased their mounts aside. They all knew Sally Skull by reputation and chose not to cross her.

Sally Skull made her own rules and defied convention in many ways other than riding astride when society dictated that ladies use only sidesaddles. A superb horsewoman, she roped and rode as well as any man. She could pick flowers with her blacksnake whip or with equal nonchalance leave the plaited imprint of its thong across the shoulders of an obstreperous man. Her language was strong and she was rated a champion cusser, her aim over the sight of either of the two sixshooters at her belt was true, and she delighted in either an evening of draw poker or of dancing at a fandango. In all, she took five husbands, and according to old legends, shot one of them and died at the hands of the last.

From the meager and scattered writings about Sally Skull, it would seem that she appeared in Texas fully armed during the 1850's to act out her violent role of cussing, fighting, and loving until she disappeared following the Civil War. In reality, she lived in the state throughout its most romantic and agonizing era, from the waning days of the Spanish empire in America to the time when the Union was sealed by the terrible war between brothers.

She came to Texas as a child with the first Anglo-Americans who settled Austin's colony, fled with her babe before Santa Anna's army while her husband fought to conquer the tyrant at San Jacinto, and worked to keep the Confederacy alive with her wagon trains. A restless soul, she ranged the trails all along the great arc of the Texas coast, and years before the first shot was fired at Fort Sumter, knew every meander in what became the lifeline of the Confederacy, the Cotton Road.

She has survived as a true folk character, through snatches of information recorded by some who knew her, in stories passed down among her many relatives and descendants, and by often embroidered tales of her escapades appearing in books and magazine articles. But beyond the tales that have come down orally, solid pieces of evidence about her activities show up in official records. She resided, worked and litigated in numerous areas of Texas from the Colorado River to the Rio Grande. Documentation of at least one incident in her life is buried in some recess of the courthouse of almost every county that existed in her day. And the roots of her wild and adventurous spirit come out in the chronicles of her pioneering forebears as they followed the long trail to Texas.

Sally's ancestors rode in the vanguard of pioneers who opened the American frontier. Her grandfather, William Rabb, learned the miller's trade from his uncle in western Pennsylvania, and as the line of settlement advanced, followed his trade west and then south into Spanish territory. He, his grown children, and his grandchildren arrived in Texas with the earliest settlers in Austin's colony. Perhaps his annual keel-boat trips as a youth from Pennsylvania down the Ohio and Mississippi Rivers to market his uncle's production of flour and rye whiskey at New Orleans kindled his desire to settle a new and farther country.

In 1801 Rabb moved his young family northwest from Pennsylvania into the Ohio Territory on the initial leg of a twenty-year journey ending in Texas. Five years later his family increased with the marriage in Warren County, Ohio, of his oldest child and only daughter, Rachel, to Joseph Newman of North Carolina.

Before 1810 William Rabb with his five children and grandchildren moved on to the Illinois Territory. He erected a four-story frame water mill with four grinding stones on a stream thirty or forty miles east of St. Louis, opened a store, and filled the office of judge of the court of common pleas. When Fort Russell was erected near the Rabb home during the War of 1812, Joseph Newman enlisted in a small cavalry company that waged a bloody campaign against the Indians. In 1817, the fifth of Joseph and Rachel Newman's ten children was born and christened Sarah Jane, but is remembered today as Sally Skull.

The financial panic of 1818 forced the Rabbs far southward out of the Illinois country to what was then Miller County, Arkansas Territory, but is now eastern Oklahoma. William may have built a mill in Miller County during his sojourn there but soon was forced to move again when his land was ceded to Choctaw Indians. He and his neighbors shifted their families only a short distance south across the Red River into the Spanish province of Texas in 1820.

During his stay in Illinois, Rabb probably knew or at least had heard of Moses Austin, who along with his other ventures operated a lead mine 60 miles south of St. Louis. As the leading stockholder in the Bank of St. Louis, Austin was wiped out when the bank collapsed in 1819. In a desperate attempt to recoup his fortune, Austin succeeded in obtaining a grant in December, 1820, from the Spanish governor of Texas to settle a colony along the Colorado and Brazos Rivers.

It appears that Rabb and his neighbors learned of the new colony as Austin journeyed home and spread the word on his route through Arkansas. His family, along with other residents of the Miller County area, was among the earliest colonists. Rabb received the largest grant in the colony, including the present site of La Grange in Fayette County, in exchange for his commitment to build a gristmill and sawmill on the Colorado River.

The Rabb sons made at least one preliminary trip to Texas to erect a house for the large family contingent, including six-year-old Sally, that arrived on the Colorado near present La Grange in December, 1823. Indians noted their arrival by stealing all the horses except one padlocked with a chain to the log house. During the early years of the colony, Indians remained a constant threat, prowling around the houses at night to steal what they hadn't begged during the day. When husbands were away at night, wives often blew out the candles and put the children to bed for fear the savages would shoot them through cracks between the logs of the cabin.

Some of the earliest tales of Sally and her family involve Indian episodes. Doors of the log houses often did not touch the floor and when one enterprising Indian thrust his feet in the opening to raise the door from its hinges, Rachel Newman removed his toes with one chop of an ax. On another occasion when the intruders decided to enter down the chimney, Rachel kindled the contents of a feather pillow in the fireplace to smoke them out.

A few years after she arrived in Texas, young Sally first assumed a man's place in the world when she observed two Indians creeping toward the house. She, her mother and a sister were alone with a male visitor, who was not one of the family. The frightened man removed the lock from his gun and pretended it was broken.

"I wish I was two men," he said, "then I would fight those Indians."

"If you were one man," cried Sally, "you would fight them. Give me that gun."

But Sally was only one young girl and could not stand off the savages forever. Rabb's mill grant was the northernmost grant in Austin's colony, and the continued theft of horses and corn by the Indians forced him out, forestalling the erection of his mill until the early 1830's. The entire family moved down the Colorado to a more settled area known as Egypt, upriver from present Wharton, where Joseph Newman and two of the Rabb sons obtained titles to their grants in the summer of 1824. Lean venison, bear meat, and honey constituted their diet until the men could burn off a canebrake and make a crop from corn planted with a sharpened stick. Sally spent her formative years here, without the benefit of any formal schooling. The death of her father in early 1831 may well have forced her into early maturity and marriage.

Sally's independent spirit is reflected in the first document of record involving her, entered in the Records of Marks and Brands of DeWitt's Colony at Gonzales on September 25, 1833, which reads:

> Sarah Newman wife of Jesse Robinson requests to have her stock mark and brand recorded which she says is as follows, Ear mark a swallowfork in the left and an underslope in the right and her brand the letters, J N which she declares to be her true mark and brand and that she hath no other.

> > her
> > Sarah X Newman
> > Mark[1]

The instrument makes clear that the brand is hers and appears on her livestock. Since her father died only two-and-a-half years before, it is obvious that the brand, her father's initials, as well as the cattle which bore it, was hers by inheritance. A modern Newman descendant said that her older brother, William, let things slide and the father's property wasn't divided for some time after his death. Sally finally told her brother, "William, I'm going down and cut out my part of the herd. If you want yours I will bring them." Although William told her to leave his, she proceeded to cut her share of the cattle from the herd.

Her mark in lieu of a signature attests to her lack of any formal education. Like her mother and many other young women on the frontier, Sally became the wife of Jesse Robinson at sixteen. The young couple resided on Jesse's grant in DeWitt's colony on the San Marcos River above the town of Gonzales. Their marriage was as yet unformalized, but they may have followed the common practice in colonial Texas of signing a marriage bond. In her later divorce petition, she declared they were married on October 13, 1833. Nine years later, in March, 1838, a wedding ceremony was performed and recorded in Colorado County, but this formality may have related to land titles Jesse was claiming for his military service.

It is abundantly evident that Jesse was a staunch fighting man. He migrated to Texas in 1822 and in the spring of 1823 joined a company of volunteers, predecessors of the Texas Rangers, organized to protect Austin's colonists from Indians. In March, 1824, he and several others rescued the Rabb and Newman families from 180 Waco and Tawakoni Indians who had surrounded their house, speared and ate their largest beef, and burned fires in the yard throughout the night. This may have been Jesse's introduction to Sally, although he was twenty-four and she was only a child of six or seven years.

He continued soldiering after their marriage and was a hero of the Texas Revolution. As one of Sam Houston's elite, he charged across the plains of San Jacinto and according to legend fired the shot that killed the cannoneer manning the center of Santa Anna's line. During the following summer of 1836, he served in Captain Lockhart's spy company of mounted volunteers, saw service again in August, 1841, under Captain January, and in September, 1842, participated in the Woll Campaign under Captain Zumwalt.

From the available evidence, both Jesse and Sally were contentious, and while he had an outlet through forays against Indians and Mexicans, he was the only available target for her wrath. Jesse sued for divorce in 1843, calling her a great scold and termagant. He charged Sally with adultery, particularly with one Brown, and of harboring and feeding Brown in an old wash house, to Jesse's great shame. He recited that she had abandoned him in December, 1841, and had taken one of their children.

Sally responded that she was compelled to separate from him because of his excessively cruel treatment. Her petition charged him with wasting her inheritance and asked that the twenty head of cattle and other property she brought into the marriage be restored to her. Both sought custody of the two children, nine-year-old Nancy and six-year-old Alfred. Following the trial, the jury rendered its verdict that all property be divided equally and did not rule on child custody.

Eleven days after the divorce, Sally married George H. Scull on March 17, 1843. While Scull's name remained attached to her despite her three later husbands, little is known of him. He was a gunsmith by trade and had served in a company of volunteers from Austin County in 1836. He and Sally took up residence on her strip of inherited land near the Egypt settlement in present Wharton County.

December 30, 1844, stands as a turning point in Sally's life. On that day she and Scull sold the last 400 acres of the land inherited from her father together with a yoke of steers, four cows, twenty hogs, a mule and a bay colt, and Scull's full set of gun maker's tools and farming implements. On the same day Jesse Robinson filed a petition in the District Court of Colorado County alleging that she and Scull had forcibly abducted young Nancy Robinson and refused to surrender her to Jesse. It appears that Sally had given up a permanent home to be with her daughter and may now have begun her life on the road.

Legend is that Sally placed Nancy and later her son Alfred in a convent in New Orleans to be educated, then Jesse located the daughter and moved her to another convent, with Sally later repeating the process. By tradition, the contending parents switched the children between convents several times. Sally was devoted to her children and always maintained contact with them.

While Sally's legend has largely survived through frontier mothers threatening their children with "You better be good or Sally Skull will get you," stories of her affection for all children are legion. When she called at a house for a coal to kindle her campfire, she would admire and pet the new baby. Other stories passed down through families tell of her taking young children to see a train, or to help her catch a wild hog, or to travel on short journeys with her.

Her attempts to educate her children may have occupied her time in the latter half of the 1840's, for few records of her activities during these years have been located. She reappeared in Wharton County in January, 1849, to acknowledge a deed to an earlier land sale and stated that she was then a single woman. Scull simply drops from the record without enough evidence to give him a personality. Although Sally declared in 1849 that he was deceased, he placed his mark on a legal instrument in northeast Texas in 1853.

By the fall of 1850 she was in DeWitt County, where the census taker found her living next to the family of Joe Tumlinson, husband of her sister Elizabeth. She recorded her brand "M" in DeWitt County in April, 1851, but in 1852 moved to Nueces County to set up a permanent base of operations at Banquete. She attended Henry Kinney's great fair at Corpus Christi that year and when John S. Ford wrote his memoirs years later, he recalled seeing her in action.

The last incident attracting the writer's attention occurred while he was at Kinney's Tank, wending his way homewards (from the fair). He heard the report of a pistol, raised his eyes, saw a man falling to the ground, and a woman not far from him in the act of lowering a six-shooter. She was a noted character, named Sally Scull. She was famed as a rough fighter, and prudent men did not willingly provoke her in a row. It was understood that she was justifiable in what she did on this occasion; having acted in self defense."[2]

This gunfight in the presence of numerous visitors at Kinney's Fair must account for the spread of her reputation of violence. While Ford did not record his memoirs until many years later, a European tourist reported the lobby talk of a hotel in Victoria in December, 1853, and published it in 1859 in his journal of the tour. He doesn't mention Sally by name but there can be no question of her identity and this seems to be the earliest contemporary description of her activities.

The conversation of these bravos drew my attention to a female character of the Texas frontier life, and, on inquiry, I heard the following particulars. They were speaking of a North American amazon, a perfect female desperado, who from inclination has chosen for her residence the wild border-country on the Rio Grande. She can handle a revolver and bowie-knife like the most reckless and skillful man; she appears at dances (fandangos) thus armed, and has even shot several men at merry-makings. She carries on the trade of a cattle-dealer, and common carrier. She drives wild horses from the prairie to market, and takes her oxen-waggon, alone, through the ill-reputed country between Corpus Christi and the Rio Grande.[3]

Sally was in full operation as a horse trader and freighter by the early 1850's. Banquete, where she headquartered, is today a sleepy village on State Highway 44 and the Tex-Mex Railroad about twenty miles west of Corpus Christi. In her day its dependable source of water from Banquete Creek made it an important stop on the first hug-the-coast Texas highway, the old Camino Real running northward from Matamoros to Goliad and beyond.

The growth of her business at Banquete is measured in the early Nueces County tax rolls, keeping in mind that horse traders and cow people are not noted for their accuracy in rendering all their livestock to the tax collector. The 1852 tax roll listed only four horses and four head of cattle in her name. In 1853 her assets appear on the rolls under the name of John Doyle, whom she married on October 17, 1852, as one horse, four cattle, two yoke of oxen and a wagon, indicating more emphasis on freighting. Her operation continued to expand in 1854 when she is listed as Sarah Doyle with thirty-three horses, fourteen cattle, four yoke of oxen and a wagon. The following year, in July, 1855, she purchased 150 acres of land on Banquete Creek.

She recorded her brand at the Nueces County courthouse in October, 1853. Today her brand probably would be called the Flying J, but properly it is the J Flor de Luz. A few years back an old rancher failed to identify it by oral description but seeing it traced in the dirt in the time honored fashion, remarked, "Aw hell, that's the J Fly Loose." And more than likely it was the J Fly Loose when Sally ran it along the Banquete Creek.

Together with her cousin, John Rabb, and his friend, W. W. Wright, Sally made Banquete an important horse trading and ranching center. She probably enticed the pair to come south from Karnes County to the greener pastures along Banquete Creek where in November, 1857, Rabb acquired the first of his numerous tracts of Nueces County land. He ran great herds of cattle bearing his Bow and Arrow brand and increased his holdings to the extent that after his death in 1872, his widow, Martha, enjoyed the title of Cattle Queen of Texas.

The Rabbs are long since gone from Banquete Creek but Wright, known as "W 6" from his brand, left numerous descendants who still live and run cattle on parts of his original holdings along the lower Nueces River north of Banquete. His great grandchildren today own what may be the world's largest longhorn herd. The ribs of these modern herds are burned with Rabb's Bow and Arrow rather than the family's original W 6 brand.

A few old timers still recall tales of how Sally and W 6 Wright dedicated themselves to outfoxing the other. She drew first blood by swapping him a horse with only one good eye. As the nag passed behind Wright's house and approached his underground cistern on its blind side, it stumbled and plummeted headlong into the ranch drinking water. The poor horse drowned and left Wright with the problem of removing the carcass and hauling in water until the next rain.

But W 6 found sweet revenge. Horse races formed a major diversion at Banquete and most cowmen kept a fast horse or two to match against anyone who thought he owned a faster one. Sally naturally always kept a good race horse and usually cleaned the boy's plows.

Somewhere Wright picked up a crowbait with the descriptive name of Lunanca, a good Spanish word meaning a horse that is "hipped" or with one hip knocked down. When Sally next returned to Banquete, he challenged her to a match race. She seized the chance to humiliate him again, and laid down $500, high stakes for that time, but W 6 covered. Lunanca's appearance fit his title, one hip drooped sadly below the other, but when he crossed the finish line, he was so far ahead that Sally could not distinguish the difference in elevation of his two rear joints.

Lunanca was one of Sally's few mistakes in judging horses. One old-timer recalled that she could out-trade anybody and her innate ability with and knowledge of horses gave her a distinct advantage. She acquired herds of up to 150 horses as far south as Mexico and traded them along the Gulf coast all the way to New Orleans. Except for the two six-shooters at her belt and a few Mexican vaqueros, she traveled the trading route alone. No one was permitted to inspect or cut her herds.

Many are the tales of her methods in acquiring her stock. She paid for purchased horses with gold carried in a nosebag draped over her saddle horn. Some hinted darkly that she didn't buy all her animals. One accusation was that after she visited the ranches in a neighborhood, raiding Lipan and Comanche Indians drove off the best horses which later turned up in her herds. Jealous wives spread the story that while she visited and made eyes at their men at the house, her vaqueros would be riding the pastures running off the horses.

Although her first three marriages occurred roughly at ten-year intervals, she acquired three of her five husbands within a span of eight years during the 1850's. Numerous legends survive that she killed one of her spouses, and if she did, the unfortunate one was either George Scull or John Doyle. Both simply disappear from the record.

Fertile minds have been devoted to the details of how she lost a husband. With her reputation as a marksman, one bullet should have accomplished the deed, but there are variations. One tale is that he intended to get her and laid in ambush, but made the fatal mistake of missing on his first try. They duelled for several minutes, before her superior aim prevailed, and he lost the contest.

Another improbable version has it that the couple spent the night at a Corpus Christi hotel after taking in a fandango. When he could not arouse her the next morning, he finally poured a pitcher of water on her head. Before she was fully awake she had grabbed her pistol, pulled the trigger, and lost a husband. She admitted she wouldn't have done it had she known it was him.

Rather than doing him in with her six-shooter following the Corpus Christi fandango, it is sometimes told that as he stopped for another drink at the whiskey barrel, she shoved his head into the potent liquid. Crying, "There, drink your fill," she held him under until he drowned. Which leads to the yarns of accidental drownings during river crossings.

As they approached a swollen river while on a freighting trip, the husband walked onto the ferry to stop the ox team and wagon. The oxen came down the steep bank with such force that he could not control them and all shot across the ferry and into the surging stream. Man and beast all drowned and Sally reportedly observed that she would rather lose her best yoke of oxen than her man. Others told it about that her husband chose to risk drowning rather than face Sally's ire after losing the team and wagon.

A possibly older tale goes that she ordered her vaqueros and her husband to cross the river on a big rise. The husband and his horse were swept away and he drowned. When one of her Mexicans asked if they should search for the body, she replied, "I don't give a damn about the body, but I sure would like to have the $40 in that money belt around it."

If she did kill one of her spouses, it wasn't the fourth one, Isaiah Wadkins. This marriage was short and anything but sweet. In her divorce petition filed in 1858, she stated that they married on December 20, 1855, but that she abandoned him on May 28, 1856, after he beat her and dragged her nearly two hundred yards. Her petition accused him of living openly in adultery with other women. Wadkins was served in Rio Grande City, and in granting Sally the divorce, the jury found that her charge of his living there openly in adultery with one Juanita was proven to be true. Her accusation was so well proven that the next Nueces County Grand Jury indicted Wadkins for adultery.

While the date of her fifth and final marriage to Christoph Horsdorff has not come to light, they were living as man and wife by December, 1860. It was a December and May affair, she was in her early 40's and he in mid 20's. Everyone called him "Horsetrough" for obvious reasons and as one old-timer remembered him, "He wasn't much good, mostly just stood around." Legends abound that he finally killed her.

The outbreak of the Civil War created an opportunity for which

Sally had spent years in training. The Union blockade of Southern ports virtually terminated ocean traffic between the South and Europe, but the mills of England demanded southern cotton while the Confederacy's survival depended on European manufactures. International law forbade the blockaders interfering with Mexican commerce and Texas cotton moved out freely in ships loaded on the Mexican side of the Rio Grande. Sale of the cotton provided funds for purchase of military supplies shipped into Mexico from Europe. The ancient Camino Real north from Matamoros became the Cotton Road, the lifeline of the Confederacy.

Alleyton, near present Columbus on the Colorado and only a few miles north of Sally's childhood home, anchored the northern end of the Cotton Road. The railroad from Houston terminated at Alleyton and thousands of bales of cotton arrived there by rail to be loaded on wagon trains for the dusty journey overland to Matamoros. On the backhaul, the lumbering wagons arrived at Alleyton loaded with government stores to be shipped throughout the South by rail.

Generally ten oxen or six mules pulled a wagon loaded with ten bales of cotton, although more animals were often required in the deep sands south of Banquete. The dense chaparral of mesquite and prickly pear bordering the road north of Brownsville turned snow white with bits of cotton snagged from the endless trains.

Long before the war, Sally knew every meander of the road like the back of her hand. Her headquarters at Banquete provided an ideal base of operations at midpoint of the road. She gave up horse trading for the more lucrative enterprise of hauling cotton and fitted out several wagons for a mule train. Her Mexican vaqueros became teamsters and she always accompanied her wagon train.

John Warren Hunter remembered meeting her in Lavaca County on the Cotton Road:

My visitor was a woman!—I met Sally at Rancho Las Animas *near Brownsville, the year before and subsequently had seen her several times in Matamoros, and strange to relate, she knew me.—Superbly mounted, wearing a black dress and sunbonnet, sitting as erect as a cavalry officer, with a six-shooter hanging at her belt, complexion once fair but now swarthy from exposure to the sun and weather, with steel-blue eyes that seemed to penetrate the innermost recesses of the soul—this in brief, is a hasty outline of my visitor—Sally Skull!*

Sally Skull spoke Spanish with the fluency of a native, and kept in her employ a number of desperate Mexicans whom she ruled with the iron grasp of a despot. With these she would make long journeys to the Rio Grande where, through questionable methods, she secured large droves of horses. These were driven to Louisiana and sold. This occupation was followed until the breaking out of the Civil War, after which Old Sally fitted out a mule train of several wagons, with Mexican teamsters, and engaged in hauling to the Rio Grande,—With all her faults, Sally was never known to betray a friend.[4]

Her slatted sunbonnet was ordinarily her only bow to femininity when on the road. She rode astride and men's clothes of no special kind made up her everyday working garb. At times however, her dress changed for practical or even esthetic reasons. Certainly she had raw-hide leggings for working in brush and one witness remembered her in a buckskin shirt and jacket. At other times she donned *chibarros*, apparently long bloomer-like garments tied at the ankles with draw strings, sometimes of rawhide or of coarse brown cloth in the summer but changed to bright red flannel for winter. Her grandchildren remembered playing with a fancy wrap around riding skirt and two French pistols which she could conceal in the skirt's folds. Her working costume was customarily accented by the two six-shooters holstered on a wide leather belt.

Even during her constant wartime travels, Sally maintained contact with her children. The Cotton Road passed near the home of her daughter, Nancy, at Blanconia in Bee County and many legends of Sally come from this area although there is no evidence that she ever lived there. Her son, Alfred, ranched about twenty miles northwest of San Patricio, where the road crossed the Nueces River. A moving reminder of the bitter days of the Civil War and of Sally survives in a letter from Alfred to his wife.

Alfred rode with a Texas cavalry company and wrote hurriedly from near Port Lavaca in December, 1863, when Union troops had captured Brownsville, occupied the island along the lower Texas coast, and threatened to overrun the southern tip of the state. He spoke of his arduous duties as his company ranged in the face of the Yankee peril, told his wife she was in great danger, and advised her to go east to Lavaca County with all the horses she could find. He wrote on, "Mother (could anyone refer to this two-gun terror as 'mother'?) promised me that she would assist you to get away. — — — I saw mother at King's Ranch but had not time to speak to her but a few minutes."[5]

But the war finally ended and the written record of Sally Skull ceases soon after. Sources that would have provided details on two intriguing events in her life shortly after the war went up in the smoke of two burned courthouses. One of the incidents shows up in the District Court minutes of Goliad County which record that on May 4, 1866, the Grand Jury of Goliad County indicted her for perjury. She certainly obtained her right to a speedy trial for on May 11, a jury rendered its verdict that she was not guilty of the charge. The specifics of the alleged perjury are unknown, for all records of the case other than the bare facts recited in the minutes were lost when fire destroyed the Goliad County Courthouse.

The brief notations of this trial are the last official records relating to Sally before she disappeared. Minutes of the San Patricio County District Court give a clue to the date of her disappearance, but again the pleadings in the case were lost when the San Patricio County Courthouse burned. In the October, 1859, session of the court, Jose Maria Garcia filed suit against Sarah Wadkins and her former husband, Isaiah, for reasons now unknown. The suit was not pursued and minutes of the court reflect that it was continued at each session all through the Civil War years. Finally in April, 1867, the case was again continued with the cryptic notation that "death of Defendant suggested."

Nueces County brand records lend another clue that she had disappeared in the late 1860's, for her son Alfred and the two sons of her deceased daughter Nancy recorded her brand in their names in June, 1868. But to confuse the issue, minutes of the San Patricio County District Court show that the case there was dismissed in October, 1868, on motion of the defendants, that is Sally and her former husband, Wadkins. Was the case dismissed by the lawyer representing her or did she resurface in the fall of 1868?

In any event she disappears from the record soon after the Civil War. Some say she rode away from Banquete with Horsdorff and that although he returned she never did. Others say he killed her. A man named McDowell claimed to have seen a boot sticking up from a shallow grave between the Nueces River and the Rio Grande. When he investigated he discovered her body; obviously she had been murdered. No one can prove that Horsdorff did it, but he certainly didn't live with her long after the war. He had moved north and remarried by July, 1868.

But was she really killed or did she just decide to abandon her old haunts and find a new life elsewhere? And when did she disappear? Some say she was seen around Goliad or Halletsville in the 1870's, which would rule out her death at the hands of Horsdorff. This writer has talked with two elderly citizens, both born in the 1870's and both in possession of their faculties, who claim they saw her as children.

One of these two, Mr. Charley Jones of Beeville, recalled that he and his brother would throw silver dollars in the air for her to shoot holes in them with her pistols. The boys would beg her for a perforated coin but she would say, "No, I will take it home, patch it up and use it."

If she wasn't murdered but disappeared on her own, the most likely theory is that she went west and lived out her days near El Paso, probably with a Newman relative. This story persists in one branch of the Newman family. J. Frank Dobie, writing of his early days as a school teacher at Alpine, lends additional credence to this story. He wrote that Alice Stilwell Henderson, who ranched in the El Paso area and possessed many of Sally's attributes in administering her own affairs and righting her own wrongs, sat up nights writing the life of Sally Skull. Mrs. Henderson as a child may have known Sally or could have written the story as Sally related it first hand in old age. Unfortunately her manuscript disappeared years before Dobie learned of it.

So let Mr. Dobie write Sally Skull's epitaph. He wrote "Sally Skull belonged to the days of the Texas Republic and afterward. She was notorious for her husbands, her horse trading, freighting, and roughness."[6] And her death remains as much a mystery as most of her life.

NOTES

1. Records of Marks and Brands in the District of Gonzales for 1829, DeWitt's Colony" (County Clerk's Office). Gonzales, Texas, p. 51.

2. John S. Ford, *Memoirs* (Austin: The University of Texas Archives) IV, p. 645.

3. Julius Froebel, *Seven Years Travel in Central America, Northern Mexico, and the Far West of the United States* (London: Richard Bentley, 1859), p. 446.

4. John Warren Hunter, *Heel-Fly Time in Texas: A Story of the Civil War Period* (Bandera: Frontier Times, 1936), pp. 57–58.

5. Dudley R. Dobie, "Lagarto Near Vanishing Point, Once Flourishing College Town," *San Antonio Express* (November 18, 1934).

6. J. Frank Dobie, "A School Teacher in Alpine," *Southwest Review*, XLVII (Autumn, 1962), pp. 273–274.

Sophia Porter at the graveside of her fourth husband,
Judge James Porter. An earlier husband, Holland Coffee,
was buried outside the fence.

SOPHIA PORTER
Texas' Own Scarlett O'Hara

Jack Maguire

Her name was Sophia Suttenfield Auginbaugh Coffee Butt Porter and her real life story reads like that of a fictional heroine in a historical novel "for mature audiences only."

She had four husbands, uncounted lovers, and a supposed affair with none other than Sam Houston. That dalliance led to the murder of one husband; a quarrel caused the death of another. Through it all, for more than half a century, she continued to preside over the grandest house in all of North Texas where she hosted some of the most memorable parties in the area. And it was there, at the gracious mansion she called "Glen Eden," that she also played the role of a "Scarlett O'Hara" to save a contingent of Confederate soldiers from capture.

Sophia was born in the frontier settlement of Fort Wayne, Indiana, on December 3, 1815, the second of William and Laura Suttenfield's seven children. Her father was the local saloon-keeper and had been a foot soldier in the U.S. Army. Her humble birth never concerned Sophia, however. As she did with so many biographical facts, later she "promoted" her father to colonel and always claimed that he commanded the fort.

Apparently life in Fort Wayne held little appeal for Sophia, although she had been popular with the soldiers there since she was thirteen. When she was seventeen, one Jesse Augustine Auginbaugh came through the town. When he left a few days later, Sophia accompanied him.

She always insisted that it was a case of love at first sight and that they eloped. However, no record of the marriage has ever turned up. Neither has any substantiation of her claim, in later years, that Auginbaugh had been a high-ranking officer in the German Imperial Army and that he was on his way to Texas to establish a business. His real profession appears to have been that of a sutler—a kind of male camp follower who peddled liquor and other provisions to the soldiers.

At any rate, the union with Auginbaugh was short-lived. Somewhere between Indiana and Texas, the couple separated and Sophia arrived in these parts about the time that Sam Houston and his army were settling matters with the Mexicans at San Jacinto. By her own account, she was the first woman to venture onto the battlefield after that skirmish and ended up nursing General Houston back to good health. Some historians, however, believe that the beautiful Sophia borrowed an idea from her ex-husband and became a sutler of her own. The product she sold, however, was her body and there is reason to suspect that Houston was one of her clients.

However the initial contact was made with the hero of San Jacinto, she and Houston apparently became good friends. He was in evidence in the capital because he was completing his two-year term as president of the Republic of Texas and enjoyed Sophia's company now and then. Also present at Washington was Holland Coffee, a dashing young colonel in the Texian Army and a member of the Third House of Representatives of the new nation. He was also reputed to be wealthy, and it wasn't long before Sophia decided that she was in love again.

The problem was that neither Sophia nor Auginbaugh had ever bothered to dissolve their marriage if, indeed, there had been one. Congressman Coffee, however, insisted that there should be some legal evidence that Sophia was free to marry him and insisted that she file suit for divorce. On July 25, 1838, she petitioned the Harris County District Court for a bill of divorcement. Since Auginbaugh's whereabouts were unknown, Judge James W. Robinson ordered that the decree would be granted only if the defendant was not heard from by "the fifth Monday after the fourth Monday in October."

When something went wrong with this proceeding and the divorce was not granted by the court, Sophia appealed to the Third Congress of the Republic to handle the matter. Although some of the members, preoccupied with debates over such weighty matters as the proposed Homestead Exemption Law, objected to taking the time to hear a divorce petition, Sophia's plea was referred to a "select" committee. On first reading, it squeaked through by only sixteen aye votes to fourteen nays.

After almost two months of debate, abetted by some adroit lobbying by both Coffee and Houston, the Senate and House finally passed a bill granting Sophia her divorce on January 15, 1839. She became Mrs. Holland Coffee the following February 20.

Coffee took his wife on a six-hundred-mile honeymoon trek by horseback. They rode up the Old San Antonio Road from Independence to Nacogdoches, then along the Trammel Trace to Clarksville, and finally along the Chihuahua Trail to Warren's Trading House on the Red River. At this stop they were honored at a grand ball by the settlers—the first of many such parties Sophia was to attend or host over the next half century.

Not far from Warren was the home to which Coffee had brought his bride and it was hardly her idea of a honeymoon cottage. It was more fort than home—a hundred-foot-square building of logs that served both as house and trading post. Located not far from the present town of Denison in Grayson County, it overlooked the Red River. The trading post had prospered because it was near a cut in the bluff that formed a natural chute for herding cattle into the river and Coffee's place was a popular rest stop for drovers going up the trail to the reservation and the northern markets.

There is no evidence in Sophia's own meager biographical notes that the lonely life on the trading post was not satisfying. There were frequent dances at Warren, and there was the company of cattlemen on their way north. She was pleased beyond measure, however, when Coffee decided to build her a home in which she could establish herself as a frontier hostess of some renown.

Exactly what Coffee built as Sophia's original "Glen Eden" has been lost to history. It probably was a single story, log cabin residence with a central hall and porches front and back. Later a second story was added to house a master bedroom and guest room. Much later, board siding covered the logs, and a brick kitchen and wine cellar became a part of the structure. Columns also were added, the house was painted white and it assumed the look of a Southern plantation mansion.

Sophia decorated the house herself, bringing in fine furniture by ox wagon from Jefferson, then a major port on the Sabine River. By now the Coffee's had acquired a retinue of slaves and she personally supervised the planting of gardens. When everything was ready to her satisfaction, she hosted a house-warming party that was to last for days and establish her reputation once and for all as the social arbiter of that part of the frontier.

Over the years, the guest list at Glen Eden would read like a "Who's Who" of early Texas times. A young officer named Robert E. Lee came often. So did a future president of the United States, Ulysses S. Grant. There seemed always to be handsome men in uniform from the army posts who dropped by, and anybody lucky enough to be invited to one of Sophia's parties gladly traveled days by horseback or wagon to get there.

It was a planned visit to Glen Eden by Sam Houston that brought the first tragedy into Sophia's life. Houston was coming to Sherman to dedicate the new county courthouse and planned to stay with the Coffees. However, Charles A. Galloway, husband of Coffee's niece, insulted Sophia by twitting her about her former relationship with Houston. She demanded that Coffee horsewhip his nephew by marriage for his remarks.

Coffee was reluctant to launder the family's dirty linen in public and this infuriated Sophia. She informed him that she would rather be the widow of a brave man than the wife of a coward and goaded him into a duel with Galloway. On October 1, 1846, Coffee instigated the fight and Galloway stabbed him to death with a Bowie knife. Later Galloway was tried by the Grayson County District Court but was acquitted "by public sentiment." The curious verdict probably resulted from the fact that both men were liked and respected by their neighbors and "public sentiment" was that each had been caught up in a conflict not of their own doing.

Now "the widow of a brave man," Sophia buried Coffee in a large mausoleum built at Glen Eden by slaves from bricks made on the property. Then she closed the trading post (the business never interested her) and devoted her efforts to her gardens and running the 3,900-acre plantation. She continued to host lavish parties and her guest list always included handsome officers from the forts. Social life at the Glen Eden was tame, however, compared with that of New Orleans, and the wealthy young widow took every opportunity to travel to the Crescent City, ostensibly to sell her lucrative cotton crops.

On one of these visits (Either 1848 or 1853—Sophia was always careless about recording dates.) she met another Army man, Major George N. Butt. He had left his native Norfolk, Virginia, en route to Texas to join the Peters Colony, but after a few coquettish glances from the curvaceous Sophia, he found himself accompanying her back to Glen Eden. She installed him as manager of the estate and began devoting more of her own time to the mangificent gardens she had developed and to the parties and dances she hosted on a continuing basis.

There is no record that the Butts went through a marriage ceremony in either New Orleans or Texas, but the union seems to have been her happiest one. Butt was the epitome of the Virginia gentleman: an authority on wines, a man who knew all the social graces and was handsome enough to turn female heads. He also was a genial host who enjoyed partying as much as Sophia did.

However, tragedy once again was about to intervene. In 1863, the Confederate guerrilla chieftain, William Clarke Quantrill (sometimes known as Charles W. Quantrell), moved into Sherman and began robbing and killing. Although both Sophia and Major Butt were Southern sympathizers, neither condoned Quantrill's actions. On one occasion, Butt and a member of the gang got into a violent argument over the tactics the guerrilla chief used.

Not long after, Butt went to Sherman to sell cotton. As he returned home that night, he was ambushed and killed. It developed that his murderer was one of Quantrill's men.

The murder of her third husband caused Sophia to mobilize the people of Sherman against Quantrill, and they succeeded in having him placed under arrest by General Henry M. McCulloch (brother of General Ben McColloch), who commanded a Confederate detachment at

Bonham. Quantrill and his men escaped, however, and crossed the Red River into Indian Territory.

After a short period of mourning her late husband, Sophia resumed her parties at Glen Eden. It was at one of these affairs that Sophia, like Scarlett O'Hara in Margaret Mitchell's novel, *Gone with the Wind*, was able to strike a blow for the Confederacy.

The incident began when Colonel James Bourland and a detachment of Confederates stopped by Glen Eden on their way to Fort Washita in the Indian Territory. Sophia, always the gracious hostess, gave a party for them. However, she had hardly sent them on their way when some Union scouts arrived in pursuit of Bourland.

Sophia not only welcomed the enemy soldiers, but turned on all of her considerable charms and opened her extensive wine cellar to them. Then she insisted that they stay for a sumptuous dinner. The delaying action worked exactly as she hoped it would. After her guests enjoyed the feast her slaves had prepared for them, Sophia invited them into the wine cellar for a night cap. Then she locked the drunken troops in the cellar and took her horse and forded the treacherous Red River. She rode straight to Fort Washita to warn Bourland that she had "captured" the enemy.

Confederate troops accompanied her back to Glen Eden, found the Union soldiers still enjoying the vintage wines and took them prisoner. Sophia had become a heroine.

She was to do even more valorous deeds. When Indians killed one of her neighbors and threatened to attack Glen Eden, Sophia threw up a barricade of cotton bales around the mansion and mobilized her slaves. They succeeded in holding off the attackers until the Indians finally gave up and quit the pitched battle in disgust.

Sophia never considered herself a fighter, however, and she decided to look for safer territory. One day she loaded a small fortune in gold coins into buckets, poured hot tar over them, strung the buckets under her wagon and headed south. When she reached Waco, two hundred miles south of her plantation, she stopped.

It was a fortunate decision because it was in Waco that she was to meet and marry the man who was to bring her long years of happiness. He also was a returning Confederate Army officer and a former judge. His name was James Porter and they were married in April, 1865. They returned to Glen Eden shortly after and lived there happily until his death in 1886.

By this time Sophia had been the mistress of Glen Eden for forty-three years. Her once great beauty had faded and she no longer could brag that men fought over her. The death of Judge Porter, admittedly the love of her life, left her desolate and disinterested in the social activities that had been her passion for so long. Like it or not, Sophia was growing old—and she didn't like it.

Mrs. Belle Evans, her long-time friend, became her companion at Glen Eden and the only bright spot in her existence. It was Mrs. Evans

who helped her haunt the shops in Denison and Sherman to search for new fashions that Sophia hoped against hope would help restore her youth. When that failed, she ordered new dresses by the dozen from New Orleans or else had Mrs. Evans, an excellent seamstress, make them for her. And it was Mrs. Evans, ever the thoughtful friend, who applied weekly applications of Ayer's Hair Dye to Sophia's locks in a vain attempt to restore the glossy black that once had made the hearts of dozens of suitors beat madly.

Aside from preserving or restoring her beauty, Sophia's other great concern in her later years was for her soul. Before Judge Porter's death, and at his behest, the couple had donated land for a Methodist Church at Preston Bend and had also given property to that denomination's Southwestern University at Georgetown. Until her husband died, however, Sophia had not been seen often at church and had not been baptized in the faith.

Not long after Judge Porter's death, Sophia attended a revival in Sherman. This time, the hell-fire-and-damnation sermon touched her and she got religion. She gave a convincing demonstration of her conversion to the congregation, crying and shouting as she ran up the aisle and confessing her sins so all could hear.

The preacher was unmoved. He was aware that Sophia had taken four husbands, perhaps three of them without a wedding ceremony. He had heard rumors of her affairs and of the soldiers she had entertained, often for days on end, at Glen Eden. He knew of the wine cellar there and the drinking. And from the pulpit he told her that "the sun, the moon and the stars are against your being a Christian." He admonished her that he would not take her into the church until she had served God "for at least twelve years."

The incident is probably apocryphal, as are so many others in the life of Sophia Porter. The fact is that she joined the Methodist Church in Sherman in 1869. The minister who received her was the Reverend J. M. Binkley. It was he who was with her on August 27, 1897, when she died quietly in the manor house over which she had presided for fifty-four years.

Now Glen Eden is gone, too. It was carefully pulled down in the 1940's because it lay in the path of Lake Texoma, the huge man-made lake created by the building of Denison Dam on the Red River. Each board of the old mansion was carefully numbered and the plan was to rebuild it on higher, safe ground and make it a showplace of an age that's past for the edification of generations that never experienced plantation life. One winter's night, however, an army contingent camping in the area found the pile of old lumber and used it as firewood. Thus the great old manor house died.

Not far away from where Glen Eden once stood, a social oasis on the Texas frontier, Sophia Suttenfield Auginbaugh Coffee Butt Porter is buried. Two of her husbands, Holland Coffee and James Porter, lie on either side. Above her grave is a simple stone that says: "I know that my Redeemer liveth."

ELISE WAERENSKJOLD
A Modern on the Prairie

Sherry A. Smith

Texas Foundation for Women's Resources

Known in local lore "as a walking newspaper," Elise Tvede Waerenskjold maintained a vital interest in writing, her Norwegian homeland, and her Texas immigrant community until her death at eighty. Out of her community interest and concern, she travelled frequently among Norwegian settlements in North Central Texas, where she was said to have been treated "like a bishop." She in turn offered hospitality to friends and strangers. Years after her death, she has been recalled as an unusually spirited woman of culture, books, and letters, a woman the entire community respected. Perhaps to the Norwegians she represented the most immediate link to the Old World as she carried news of people and events in Norway along with local tidings. And, doubtless, her unconventional past and her articulate convictions elevated her to a celebrity status in the eyes of both Norwegian and American neighbors.[1]

The most remarkable achievements in Elise's personal history occurred before she ever left Norway, but stories of them accompanied her to Texas. Born in 1815 into a family active in social and political affairs, she received a genteel education. At an early age she revealed a startlingly modern attitude as she breached Norwegian conventions with courage and intelligence. She opened a girls' handicraft school in Lillesand, Norway, when she was nineteen amidst hostile criticism; at that time it was not only unconventional but considered presumptuous for a woman to teach, let alone run a school. An early feminist, she is remembered in Norway as a woman leader (*foregangskvinne*) for espousing and pursuing a visible public life outside the narrowly drawn boundaries then prescribed for women. She was a pioneer before she ever set foot on the frontier of Texas.

In keeping with her puritanical, albeit sometimes unorthodox, religious beliefs, Elise was the first woman in Lillesand to join the local temperance society in the early 1840's. She was probably the first woman in Norway to have temperance literature published. In her fervent battle against drinking, she asserted no reform of any kind could be achieved without women's support. Years later in Texas, her husband organized a temperance society, surely under her rigorous influence.

Elise married Svend Foyn, who later became very wealthy and famous for his innovations in the whaling industry, in 1839. Creating something of a scandal, she daringly separated from him in 1842 and resumed her family name. Stories of their separation imply Foyn couldn't tolerate her untraditional independent activities, which took her away from home and "wifely duties." Though they separated and finally divorced due to "incompatibility," they remained friends and Foyn occasionally helped Elise financially. Foyn's later celebrated reputation no doubt heightened the scandal of their divorce.

Already the published author of articles and pamphlets, Elise Tvede assumed the editorship of John Reinert Reiersen's monthly periodical, *Norge og Amerika* (Norway and America), in 1846. Of course, journalism was an uncommon occupation for a woman. The publication promoted Norwegian emigration by singing praises of the United States, with particular reference to Texas. The next year *Norge og Amerika* folded, and Elise left for Texas with a vision of finding a freer environment for her talents and interests.

Later in 1847, Elise took up residence in Four Mile Prairie, a Norwegian settlement founded by Reiersen southeast of Dallas. Shortly after her arrival, Elise married Wilhelm Waerenskjold who had been in her emigration party. They acquired a square mile of farmland to begin raising stock, but encountered numerous economic and climatic troubles over the years. Elise's energy was directed toward surviving as a farmer and raising a family, a likely reason for her avoiding the intense social and political activity in Texas that she was famous for in Norway. And, in such a remote agricultural region, what opportunities for these kinds of activities would have been available to her? In her travels in and around Four Mile Prairie and other Norwegian settlements, however, she did actively engender and preserve the community spirit she so valued. She also continued to be thoughtfully sensitive to religious and social matters. She was particularly intent upon establishing a school and engaging a Norwegian Lutheran pastor for the community. Moreover, she continued to advocate emigration to Texas, defending the state against visiting Europeans' remarks that it was a dangerous, fierce land.

Elise's religious devotion didn't restrain her from objecting to certain religious doctrines, such as that of the Trinity. As for other religions, any which expressly subjugated women (i.e., Islamism, Mormonism) met her intolerance. Embedded in her religious beliefs was a strong, rational objection to slavery: "Slavery is absolutely contrary to the law of God. . . . Let us ask ourselves if we would be satisfied with being slaves, with being sold like animals, with being separated from our mates and children whenever it might suit our masters. . . . To all this we must without qualification answer 'No'!" Asked if she would accept having a black woman as a daughter-in-law, Elise answered that she wouldn't be pleased with the situation, but she "would rather have it thus than to have grandchildren who are slaves."

The democratic ideals she expressed before leaving Norway and which prompted her immigration to Texas received confident articulation in her plain words: "I believe to the fullest degree that human beings are born with equal rights." Recommending immigration, Elise wrote that Texas laws were definitely more democratic than those of Norway. She favored especially the homestead laws that protected property rights of women and children.

Elise and Wilhelm Waerenskjold had three sons, Otto, Niels, and Thorvald. In her letters to friends, Elise expresses more care and love for her children than for anything else. She was continually concerned about their education and their Christian training; she suffered great anxiety that without a Lutheran pastor her sons might die unconfirmed. Her youngest son, Thorvald, "the dearest thing [she] possessed on this earth," died suddenly in 1866. She remained extremely close to her other two sons up to her death, living with Niels and his family in her old house at Four Mile Prairie until the last year of her life when she moved in with Otto and his family in Hamilton, Texas.

Late in 1866, a neighbor Methodist preacher fatally stabbed Wilhelm Waerenskjold. In the ten years that elapsed before the murderer was apprehended and tried, legend grew that Wilhelm was assassinated in a dispute over slavery, he being opposed to slavery. The date of his death and the trial records indicate this story was incorrect. After the preacher received a ten year sentence in the state prison, Elise wrote that she thought the punishment mild for "such a cold-blooded and long-premeditated murder."

Elise assumed total responsibility for her two sons, the crops, and the farm animals, managing quite well. When money was scarce, she sold books, took orders for magazines and garden seeds, and taught school. Occasional poverty notwithstanding, Elise remained vigorous and thoughtful, a vital force in her community. In a letter she wrote, "If I don't have anything to do for myself, I help my relatives or visit the neighbors."

Throughout her life in Texas Elise remained devoted to literature and to writing. She began a reading club in her settlement as early as 1857, but it failed to catch on. Elise continued to admire feminist writers, although she disliked Ibsen. In 1888 she was still subscribing to Norwegian feminist magazines, and she continually sought new books on many subjects. As *The Lady with the Pen* (a collection of her letters) shows, she never ceased writing letters. They provided a forum for her opinions and observations as well as a means of keeping in touch with old friends.

Since before she left Norway, Elise held avid interest in immigrant history. She wrote magazine articles about Texas Norwegian settlements for both American and foreign publications. Editors of *Billed-magazin*, published in Wisconsin, commissioned her to write the history of Norwegian settlements in Texas in 1869. She freely gave information to and critically read the other writers she knew to be studying this subject. Rasmus B. Anderson in *Norwegian Immigration* stated that Elise Waerenskjold wrote to her dying day in 1895 and claimed: "No other Norwegian in Texas was better known than she."

NOTES

1. All biographical information and textual quotations for this article were gathered from: *The Lady with the Pen.* C. A. Clausen, ed. Clifton, Texas: Bosque Memorial Museum, 1976. This book is a collection of Elise Waerenskjold's letters written in Texas.

TEXAS GETS CULTURE

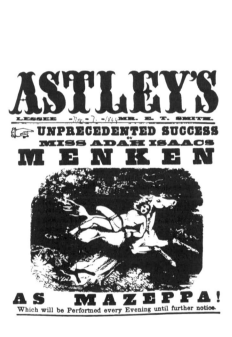

Adah in costume. The famous "Mazeppa" playbill attracted all London to see her sensational act.

ADAH ISAACS MENKEN
From Texas to Paris

Pamela Lynn Palmer

Through flashing lightning and rolling thunder, under falling snow, over painted mountains, fleeing the skulking shadows of wolves, came the wild horse bearing the noble Mazeppa. A murmur rippled through the darkened theatre. Women had played the part before, but always attired in bright Tartar costumes. Now clothed in flesh-toned silk tights and a hint of draped cloth, voluptuous curves accentuated in flashing light deliberately dimmed to create an optical illusion, the woman strapped to the side of the horse appeared to be, and many believed her to be, unequivocally nude. And so Adah Isaacs Menken, from one daring act on June 3, 1861, in the Green Street Theatre, Albany, New York, went on to take America and Europe by storm under an appellation which still survives: "The Naked Lady."

Adah's early career before her international celebrity in the 1860's is nebulous, in part because of her own journalistic sense of the sensational, and her instinct for the mysterious. Among her rumored birthplaces were Milneburg, Chartrain, and New Orleans, Louisiana; Nacogdoches, Texas; Memphis, Tennessee; and Spain. Her ethnic background was variously French, Spanish, Jewish, Creole, Scotch-Irish, and Negroid. Among the maiden names she confided were Rachel Adah Isaacs, Dolores Adios, Marie Rachel Adelaide de Vere Spenser, Adelaide McCord, and Adah Bertha Theodore, the latter two cropping up most frequently in Texas. She also revealed various names for her parents, brothers, and sisters to reporters and frequently spoke of a step-father, though she could not decide whether his name was Campbell, Josephs, or McCord.

Adah has been credited with as many as seven husbands, but only four are generally accepted: Alexander Isaac Menken, a Jewish musician and merchant; John C. Heenan, a New York boxer; Robert Newell, a journalist and satirist publishing under the pseudonym, Orpheus C. Kerr ("office seeker"); and James Barclay, a merchant and gambler. There may have been others for Adah was careless about her divorces and twice remarried before the divorce papers came through. The writer of a scathing obituary of her in *Blake's Semi-Weekly Galveston Bulletin* in 1868 speculated that she never married half the men she declared she divorced, announcing fake divorces to attract public notice.[1] Her public was willingly beguiled, and several journalist friends went along for the ride, including Thomas Peck Ochiltree, who was also a Texas Ranger, Confederate hero, and Congressman, and perhaps largely responsible for the Nacogdoches tales.

Shortly after Ochiltree's death in 1902, an article appeared in the *St. Louis Globe-Democrat* under the signature "Brazos," reminiscing about Tom's boyhood crush on Adah (then known as Adelaide McCord) in Nacogdoches in the early 1850's. In those days, the *Globe-Democrat* writer declared, Adah lived with her docile, illiterate, and unenterprising father and her hauntingly beautiful, educated mother in a log cabin. As a child she was strikingly pretty, and schoolboys vied with one another to carry her books, while old men were charmed into stuffing her pockets with gold coins. Adah's figure blossomed early and by her late teens she was already earning the reputation of a flirt.

Tom was not immune to her charms, though she was a couple of years older than he and had already collected a parcel of beaus. So smitten was he that he flattered himself she returned his affections, for upon arriving one Christmas Eve with a company of Texas Rangers from his first battle with the Indians, he watched her blush with pride as the others recounted the brave exploits of the sixteen-year-old carrot-top Tom.

That evening Tom and the rest of the men were entertained by the ladies of Nacogdoches with a banquet and dance at the cuartel (probably the original Stone Fort), a large building for sheltering troops, used as a refuge for the women and children in time of siege. About midnight the party was about to break up when someone announced that it was raining in torrents. The guests determined to spend the night in the cuartel. Adah urged Tom to hang up his socks for Santa Claus, hinting slyly, "There's no telling what kind of present you might get." Mrs. Rogers, the Captain's wife, seconded the suggestion, and there was much merriment as the women withdrew and the rangers strung a rope in front of the fireplace. As the others were hanging up their socks, Tom confided to the Captain that he was ashamed to display his for he had danced holes in them. Captain Rogers ordered him to hang up his boots instead. This done, Tom curled up in his blanket, with visions of sweet Adelaide dancing in his head.

The next morning, while the others were examining their presents from Santa, Tom woke with a presentiment of ill fortune. He remembered how Adah had teased him the night before, dancing most of her dances with Lieutenant Bailey. Soon Tom discovered to his dismay that not only had he received no presents but his boots were gone. He and his comrades searched, but his boots were not to be found. One fellow remarked, "If our belle of the ball is not a heartless coquette, I am no judge of women," while another suggested, "Some Mexican must have stolen them."

Supplied with a pair of borrowed slippers, Tom attempted to laugh the matter off, but he noticed at breakfast that Adah seemed to stay in the background, avoiding his eyes. When she finally drew near his table, Tom sprang to his feet, overturning chairs and knocking dishes to the floor, shouting, "Now I know what old Santa Claus has brought me. Look at her feet!" Adah had on Tom's boots.[2]

Adah soon left Tom far behind. From 1856 to 1860 she pursued an acting career in small theatres in Galveston, New Orleans, Shreveport, and Nashville. In this last city she ad-libbed her way through as Lady Macbeth, and in one memorable performance launched and squelched her career as a tragedienne. Thereafter the parts she landed were mostly melodramatic. She often played male roles since theatre managers were quick to note how the lines of male attire accentuated her natural allure. Until *Mazeppa* she met with little success, but in that part she sky-rocketed. The show toured across the United States in 1863 and hit London and Paris in 1864.

Adah was not one to allow fame to cause her to forget a friend. The following tale, occurring at the height of Adah's career between 1866 and 1868, has been set in Brussells, London, and Paris, places where Adah was a tremendous box office success and where Tom Ochiltree reportedly traveled as a banking associate and special correspondent of the *New York Tribune*, sent by Horace Greeley to cover the World's Fair. As the story goes, Ochiltree was sitting with a British nobleman in a sidewalk cafe when he saw Adah's carriage coming down the street and said, "I believe I'll ask Adah for a ride." His companion, not knowing of Ochiltree's previous acquaintance with the actress and aware of her tremendous popularity, bet Ochiltree a thousand dollars that Adah would refuse. When Ochiltree approached, Adah greeted him warmly and away they rode. Later he collected the bet.[3]

The Confederate general, George F. Alford, was another who claimed an early acquaintance with Adah in Nacogdoches, though he seemed careful not to mention any details of her life there. Instead he lauded her as a goddess of beauty, praised her voice (Most people said she was an indifferent singer.), and glossed her portrait with richness and glamour, citing among Adah's associates half the nobility of Europe and all the contemporary literary greats. He may be the one responsible for the rumor that she was the morganatic wife of the King of Würtemberg. He related a different version of the carriage incident:

"I met her . . . in one of my visits to Paris. Tom Ochiltree and I were sitting together in the court of the Grand Hotel. She was then the Queen of Wurtemburg, and at the zenith of her career. The King was with her when she drove in, but soon excused himself, begging her to continue her drive.

"A party of Frenchmen were admiring her and making extravagant wishes about having her acquaintance.

"Tom and I exchanged smiles. He arose and slowly walked toward her carriage.

"'Hello, Tom!' she cried, extending her hand, 'get in and take a drive.'

"Great was the surprise expressed by the Frenchmen, but greater still when the American with the ease of old acquaintanceship, stepped into the gorgeous vehicle, and was wheeled away to the Boulevard. The next day we both called on her and enjoyed a few hours in delightful reminiscences of our childish pleasures in old Nacogdoches." [4]

James V. Polk, an amateur Texas historian, also asserted that Adah spent her childhood in Nacogdoches. He told of her attending private schools and the old Nacogdoches University, where she joined a dramatic club. By age sixteen her beauty and talent had already attracted much local attention. Impressed with her ability, Polk's mother's cousin, Peyton F. Edwards, along with the other members of the club, urged Adah to go on stage.

Polk also credited Adah with the ability to read and write six languages. In her autobiographical notes Adah listed French, German, Spanish, Latin, Greek, and Hebrew among her linguistic accomplishments. But if she were schooled in Nacogdoches, could she have learned all these languages? Nacogdoches University offered all but Spanish and Hebrew. Still, Adah claimed New Orleans and Cuba as her places of education.

Polk listed among Adah's writer acquaintances Sir Walter Scott, James Fenimore Cooper, Lord Byron, and Thomas Moore. Byron was dead before Adah was born and the others were deceased well before she rose to public notice.

There is also a flaw in the Edwards story. Peyton was born in 1844, and although Adah's birthdate is unknown, by her own account she was born in 1835, and she would have needed to be twenty-one in 1856 to marry Alexander Menken without parental consent. So it is unlikely that Adah and Edwards went to school together.

Polk made one last family claim to fame by stating that as a child, Adah visited the home of his grandfather, I. D. Thomas, in San Augustine. Now if Adah were rich enough to attend those private schools and pay tuition to Nacogdoches University, she might have belonged to a social circle including that wealthy old plantation owner, whose dates were at least contemporary with hers. But her name, under any of various aliases, does not appear in any of the extant records of Nacogdoches University.[5]

Robert Bruce Blake, a court reporter of Nacogdoches and an East Texas historian, collected information on Adah, probably for his sketch of her in *The Handbook of Texas*. In an undated manuscript, most likely an early draft of his sketch, he glibly picked up the story of Adah's childhood in the "old Spanish pueblo" of Nacogdoches, and expanded the list of her girlhood companions to include such prominent local families as the Sternes, Taylors, Davenports, Millards, and Clevengers. Blake later decided Adah was born in Memphis, but still placed her childhood in Texas.[6]

Another story which persists is that either James McCord or Joseph Campbell, both of whom are referred to sometimes as Adah's father and sometimes as her stepfather, ran a mercantile or clothing store on the town square near the former site of the Old Stone Fort in the 1850's. There were no McCords listed in the 1850 Census for Nacogdoches County, but there was a family of Campbells with daughters in Adah's age range. Still, in the local lore she is always referred to as Adelaide McCord, and there were no Adelaides among the Campbells.[7]

In 1855 Adah appeared in Liberty, Texas, and if Adah's early personality were anything like her later one, it would not take more than six months' residence for her to have a lasting impact as she had on that town. As an aspiring poet, Adah was always fond of mixing with writers. She collected journalist friends throughout her career, aware of the effect of publicity on the acting profession. During her stay in Liberty from October 1855 to March 1856, she contributed poems and essays to *The Liberty Gazette* which she sometimes signed "Ada Bertha Theodore." She entertained the town with readings of Shakespeare as her first ambition was to be a great dramatic actress. Even off stage she retained the tragic mood, rarely smiling and sighing frequently in view of the other guests at the dining table of the City Hotel. Her morose expression attracted comment and people speculated on the cause of her mysterious sadness. She had no girl friends but was often seen in the company of young men, especially that of *Gazette* editor Henry Shea and Abner B. Trowel, a young lawyer. Her rather homely sister Josephine accompanied Adah as chaperone on these nightly strolls. One Liberty resident recalled seeing Ada Theodore and her sister Josephine perform in Galveston in 1850, where they danced, and Adah, in pink tights, walked the high wire.[8] Adah frequently claimed to have begun her career at the age of twelve, performing with a sister in New Orleans. She may have learned to ride while touring with a circus in the early 1850's.

Either before or after her stay in Liberty in 1855, Adah was captured by the Indians. In journalist Ed Kilman's version, she was engaged in hunting buffalo near Port Lavaca when taken. She was rescued by a band of Texas Rangers led by Frederick Harney, who adopted her at the age of twenty and procured a tutor to teach her sculpture and painting. When Adah and her tutor fell in love, Harney sent her away. A more flamboyant version has her adopted by Sam Houston, who already had a number of children. She soon grew restless in that domestic scene and joined a ballet troupe bound for Mexico. In Bob Bowman's biographical sketch, a young Apache brave renounced his tribe for her. The length of Adah's captivity ranged from three weeks to three years, sometimes featuring a Chief Eagle Eye who taught her to ride and toughened her up for her later perilous rides as Mazeppa.[9]

A month after her last known contribution to *The Liberty Gazette* in March 1856, Adah married the man traditionally believed to be her first of several husbands, and from whom she derived her stage name, Alexander Isaac Menken. It is uncertain where they met; however, they were both members of the company at Neitsch's Theatre in Galveston in 1856, she as a dancer and he as a musician. They eloped to Livingston, Texas, where they married on April 3, 1856, Adah using the maiden name of Ada B. Theodore. They might have chosen to tie the knot at the Polk County Courthouse while en route to or from Nacogdoches. From Livingston the newlyweds might have gone to Liberty, for a resident there recorded in her reminiscences dated sometime after 1869 that the couple stopped at the City Hotel in 1856, where Alexander Menken attempted to set up a folk dancing class. Or they might have stayed awhile in Galveston, where old timers used to point out the Menkens' bridal chamber in the old house which once stood on the southeast corner of Market and Center Streets. Others of Galveston recalled that Menken engaged in a successful cotton trade there during the Civil War.[10]

After a couple of years' attempt at domesticity, Adah yielded once more to the siren's call of fame and performed in Shreveport in 1858. But her husband no longer cared for show business and they soon quarreled and went separate ways. In 1859 in New York Adah met John C. Heenan and, assuming Menken had divorced her, she married the boxer. But Menken had not yet divorced her and a scandal ensued. Heenan deserted her, leaving her pregnant with a son who died a few weeks after birth. Destitute in a time of war when there was little demand for actresses, Adah poured her troubles into poems which she read in coffee houses and sometimes published in the *Israelite*, consoling herself in the Judaic religion she was either born into or adopted upon her marriage to Menken. Then along came *Mezeppa*—not enough amusement to stop a war but worth at least a couple of hours' respite. One story which Texans, as Southerners, are fond of repeating is that while in Baltimore during the Civil War, Adah flew Confederate flags from her window until she was arrested. She charmed a Union general into releasing her, though, and he allowed her to continue flying the flags. In a review of Paul Lewis' biography, *Queen of the Plaza*, John K. Hutchens related the story of nine Union generals attending the opening of Adah's *Mazeppa* in New York on June 14, 1861, speculating that her feminine charms effectually muddled the heads of the generals who planned and lost the First Battle of Bull Run fought a month later.[11]

A remarkable woman with spectacular career, Adah longed for a more solid claim to fame through her poetry. She attracted some of the literary giants—Mark Twain, Walt Whitman, and Charles Dickens, to whom she dedicated her one volume of poems. She and Alexander Dumas, *père*, scandalized France with their affair in 1866, and in 1867 she formed a liaison with young Algernon Swinburne, something he later denied in his prudish dotage. But like the boy who cried "wolf," even in her poems she was mistrusted. The writer in *Blake's Semi-Weekly Galveston Bulletin* accused her of hiring well-paid ghostwriters for her poetry.[12] But the poems in Adah's *Infelicia*, though sometimes honestly emotional with occasional fine passages, are mostly as confused as the accounts of her life. Consider these lines from "Myself":

> *Now I gloss my pale face with laughter, and sail my voice on with the tide.*
> *Decked in jewels and lace, I laugh beneath the gas-light's glare, and quaff the purple wine.*
> *But the minor-keyed soul is standing naked and hungry upon one of Heaven's high hills of light. . . .*
> *Shivering in the uprising of some soft wing under which it may creep, lizard-like, to warmth and rest.*[13]

Between her affairs with Dumas and Swinburne, Adah managed to squeeze in a marriage to James Barclay, whom she married only long enough to give her second son a name. George Sand was godmother to this child and it is unclear what happened to him. A recent visitor to the Sam Houston Regional Library and Research Center in Liberty claimed to be a descendant of William Henry Harrison Davenport, alleged to have married Adah during those last frantic years. Learning of her affair with Dumas, he left her and sailed for Australia.[14]

Adah's decline came quickly. Although she made a fortune off her performances, she spent her earnings lavishly on clothes and splendid party feasts. Remembering her own struggling years, she was generous to less fortunate actors and actresses, doled out money to charities, and paid gambling debts for ex-husbands Barclay and Heenan. In the winter of 1867–1868, she attempted another tour of *Mazeppa*, this time through England. But a rival tour of the show preceded her, and the novelty of the act was wearing thin. The following spring her health began to fail. A revival of her other standby, the swashbuckling *Les pirates de la Savanne*, was scheduled to go into rehearsal in July 1868. She never recovered enough to rehearse.

Even Adah's death in Paris was shrouded in tales. The writer in *Blake's Semi-Weekly Galveston Bulletin* half-believed the announcement of her death would prove to be another publicity stunt. He was soon proved wrong. Some said Adah died nearly penniless, abandoned by all her illustrious friends, with only a faithful maid attending when a cruel theatre manager came with gendarmes to force the ailing actress to go to rehearsal, only to discover her recently expired. Some said she remained true to the Jewish faith she was either born into or adopted, and died with a rabbi attending. But the quaintest picture comes from Elizabeth Brooks in *Prominent Women of Texas*: "She donned her own white bridal robes to meet her last ghostly bridegroom, and thus attired and veiled, was borne to beautiful, peaceful Père-la-Chaise [cemetery]."[15]

Later her remains were moved to the Jewish section of Montparnasse and placed under a monolith inscribed, "Adah Isaacs Menken. Born Louisiana, United States of America. Died in Paris, August 10, 1868." On the side of the stone crowned with an urn are these most appropriate words: "Thou knowest." He is the only one who knows, because all the unsolved mysteries of her origin and life lie buried now, and God alone can see the naked soul standing on the hill of light.

NOTES

1. "Death of Ada Menken," *Blake's Semi-Weekly Galveston Bulletin* (Aug. 19, 1868), R. B. Blake Collection, 59: 27–28.

2. "The Christmas Present Santa Brought to Tom Ochiltree," George Louis Crocket Collection, Folder 64, Special Collections, Steen Library, Stephen F. Austin State University, Nacogdoches.

3. Capt. J. Terrell, "Reminiscences of Ochiltree," [*Dallas Morning?*] *News* (Dec. 13, 1902), The Hardin Papers, Sam Houston Regional Library and Research Center, Liberty: Frank X. Tolbert, "The Glamorous Adah Was from 'doches," *Dallas Morning News* (Nov. 9, 1961).

4. Elizabeth Brooks, *Prominent Women of Texas* (Akron, Ohio, 1896), pp. 159–60. [Quotation marks edited to conform to modern usage.]

5. Information in the paragraphs referring to and refuting Polk's narration come from the following sources: James V. Polk, "A Brief History of Two Texas Celebrities," Beaumont (1936), R. B. Blake Collection 59: 48–50; Nacogdoches University Records, Special Collections, Steen Library, SFASU; Adah Isaacs Menken, "Notes on My Life," in Allen Lesser, *The Enchanting Rebel: The Secret of Adah Isaacs Menken* (New York, 1947), pp. 255–257; George Louis Crocket, *Two Centuries in East Texas* (1932; rpt. Dallas, 1962), pp. 218–19.

6. Robert Bruce Blake, "A Nacogdoches Queen," (n.d.), R. B. Blake Collection, 59: 59; R. B. Blake, "Menken, Adah Isaacs," *The Handbook of Texas*, Walter Prescott Webb, ed. (Austin, 1952), 2: 174.

7. Frank X. Tolbert, *op. cit.*; Ed Kilman, "Hunting Deadly Wild Boars in Texas; One Ring-Tailed Panther," *The Houston Post* (Dec. 11, 1955); Carolyn Reeves Ericson, *The People of Nacogdoches County in 1850* (Owensboro, Ky, 1980).

8. Camilla H. Davis, Dallas, to Ethel Calbuth Mayne, New York. T.L.S. (June 5, 1926), The Hardin Papers, SHRL&RC; Miriam Partlow, *Liberty, Liberty County, and the Atascocito District* (Austin, 1974), p. 264.

9. Ed Kilman, "When Adah Menken, Stage Queen of the 60s Worked on Texas Paper," [*The Houston Post?* n.d. Attached to Allen Lesser, *The Enchanting Rebel* in Special Collections, Steen Library, SFASU.] Lesser, p. 242; Bob Bowman, "The Nacogdoches Strip Teaser," *They Left No Monuments* (Lufkin, 1975), p. 9; Joseph Galleghy, *Footlights on the Border: The Galveston and Houston Stage Before 1900* (The Hague, 1962), p. 58.

10. "A Menken Myth," Typescript excerpt from Ben C. Stuart, "Texas Play Actors and Matrimony," *Galveston News* (May 30, 1909), Rosenberg Library, Galveston; Miriam Partlow, *op. cit.*, p. 264; "Death of Ada Menken," *op. cit.*, p. 27.

11. Garland Roark, "The Naughty Queen from East Texas," *The Houston Chroni-*

cle (July 22, 1952); John K. Hutchens, "That's Why the Lady Was a Terror," *Saturday Review* (Oct. 24, 1964) 47:43:73.

12. "Death of Ada Menken," *op. cit.*, p. 28.

13. Adah Isaacs Menken, *Infelicia* (1868; rpt. Freeport, NY, 1971), pp. 47–48.

14. Joyce Calhoon, Director, SHRL&RC, Liberty, to Pamela L. Palmer, Nacogdoches, T. L. S. (May 29, 1980).

15. "Death of Ada Menken," *op. cit.*, p. 27; John S. Kendall, "'The World's Delight': The Story of Adah Isaacs Menken," *Louisiana Historical Quarterly* (July, 1938) 21:3: 867–68; Leo Shpall, "Adah Isaacs Menken," *Louisiana Historical Quarterly* (Jan., 1943) 26:1:168; Elizabeth Brooks, *op. cit.*, p. 160.

Elisabet Ney in her studio. Liendo plantation near Hempstead.

ELISABET NEY
Texas' First Lady of Sculpture

Mary Elizabeth Nye

"This is where I shall live and die," said Elisabet Ney, viewing the cleared park from the upstairs veranda of Liendo Plantation house near Hempstead, Texas, in 1873. She was buried there, in 1907. Events between those two dates are well documented, yet the folk who observed her had their own interpretation of her personality.

Elisabet Ney, born in 1833 of Alsatian-Polish parents in Münster, Westphalia, was the red-headed daughter of a stone cutter who was inordinately impressed with his uncle, Michel Ney, Marshall of Napoleon's armies. As a small child Elisabet set her goal, "to know great persons" as did her spectacular kinsman. Sharing Marshall Ney's foolhardiness as well as his bravado, she defied her parents in order to invade the man's world of sculpture.

With remarkable diligence she matched her father's carving skill. Growing up with and working alongside her father in his studio she soon was able to "secure the ground" at age eighteen in an all-male art school in Munich. Described by one biographer "as a beauty of bold courage, high enthusiasm and superb strength," she mastered the artistic as well as the physical requirements of a sculptor.[1] Older men were eager to assist the unconventional beauty toward her goal, although unwanted physical contact from men was put down with one of her "hard" looks. No man had captured her heart until, at age twenty, on a holiday in Heidelburg she met Edmund Montgomery, a young medical student.

Edmund, a story in himself,[2] was the shy son of a Scottish noble-man who never married. Edmund's mother, amply supported by the Edinburgh jurist, reared her son in Paris and then in Frankfurt. It was in Frankfurt that Edmund as a student became interested in the works of the philosopher Schopenhauer, who would later play a role in the career of Elisabet Ney.

At twenty she was attracted by Edmund's tall slender body and his walk of easy grace, and thought that he would make a beautiful model. She also found in him an ally in rebellion, a believer in freedom and self-fulfillment for both men and women. They were ardent idealists together.

Her circle of friends increased when, accepted as a pupil by the renowned sculptor Christian Rauch, she was adopted by his liberal friends such as Varnhagen von Ense, Alexander von Humboldt the naturalist, and Franz Liszt's daughter, Cosima von Bülow. From these stimulating personalities her philosophy, resembling the feminist stand of today, took shape.

Declaring herself a professional sculptress, she sought a person of fame as her first sitter, and at Dr. Montgomery's suggestion, selected the venerable Schopenhauer. The old man consented grudgingly, but as the sittings progressed, he was charmed by her. In his published letters are glowing descriptions: "Perhaps you know the sculptress Ney. If not, you have lost a great deal. . . . She is very beautiful and indescribably *liebenswürdig*. We walk; we are wholly sympathetic."[3]

Sixty years later an observer was to recall, "She was wearing a black velvet gown trimmed with a silver lace collar. Her head was a mass of short curls—I thought her to be a young man in skirts."[4] A portrait by Christian Kaulbach shows her as being tall, harmoniously propor-tioned, with auburn hair pushed back from a slightly domed forehead, with eyes a deep hazel and charmingly animated.

The Schopenhauer bust was an artistic success and was followed by commissions from such famous personalities as Jacob Grimm and Richard Wagner, which attracted the attention of Hanover's King George V. For this celebrity existence she was to pay a high price. Eventually Garibaldi posed for her; from him she acquired a taste for political intrigue. Not long after she finished a portrait of Bismarck, she was approached by Prussian agents who had plans for her in the court of Ludwig II in Bavaria.

In the meanwhile, Elisabet and Edmund, keeping in touch as their careers were developing and their respect for one another deepening into love, were faced with a decision. She had rebuffed marriage as a form of bondage until Edmund, having recovered from a bout with tuberculosis, took a firm stand. On the island of Madeira she agreed to a civil ceremony, with the proviso that it should remain a secret forever and that she should always be addressed as Miss Ney.

Ludwig II, new to the throne of Bavaria, was resisting Bismarck's plan to add his country to the alliance of German states since he feared the dominance of militant Prussia. To build a palace for the arts was

Ludwig's obsession, and Elisabet, as one of the artists, was summoned by the King's secretary. Their first encounter was a memorable one. Ludwig, then a youth of eighteen, was not noted for his patience, especially with women. When he arrived for his first sitting, Elisabet spent some time studying him in silence, only to have her royal subject bark out, "Begin!" The grand niece of Marshall Ney merely stated, "I shall begin, Your Majesty, when I am ready," and picking up a ruler proceeded to measure the nose, forehead, and other pertinent parts of Ludwig's anatomy as impersonally as if she were handling carpet.

In subsequent sittings the impersonal treatment continued, but it was the King who kept aloof, preferring to listen to a reader. Noting that the book in question was about Iphigenia, Elisabet had a Grecian gown constructed, memorized some lines, and at the next sitting was able to act the part and to quote some of Goethe's lines in the bargain. Ludwig responded to her cleverness and thenceforth conversation flowed more easily between them.[5]

Once his confidence was gained, theorizes one biographer,[6] Elisabet was able to coax Ludwig into Bismarck's trap. Her reward was an estate and studio-home of her own in a suburb of Munich. The unsuspecting young monarch, eager to please her, helped plan a handsome villa. Elisabet's version of the villa's financing was that Edmund had amassed a fortune in his medical practice and had provided the money for the construction. Be that as it may, after the villa was built, Edmund lived there, his laboratory next to her studio. They lived in ducal splendor. An intelligent German housekeeper named Cencie commanded a retinue of servants. In this stimulating capital of arts and sciences the talented pair might well have reached their full potential.

In spite of that, they abandoned the estate suddenly and accompanied by Cencie went quietly to America. Some biographers[7] say the appearance of open sin was too much for local Munich society to bear and that finally the pair was ostracized by the court. More likely, however, Elisabet was called to account by the agents of Bismarck and fled because she could not deliver Ludwig to the Prussian alliance.[8]

Why America? In general, they chose America as the land of the Enlightened Thomas Paine.[9] Specifically, an invitation to join a Utopian community in Georgia from a German nobleman seeking a climate suitable for consumptives appealed to Edmund, himself a fellow sufferer. The opportunities on the frontier for enlightened people to demonstrate humanitarianism in an atmosphere of tolerance appealed to Elisabet. It may be noted also that at this time she was pregnant.

In Georgia Elisabet did much to enlighten but little to charm the natives. She and the doctor, living with the von Stralendorffs at Mecklenburg Farm near Thomasville until their purchased farm could be the site for a house, were objects of curiosity for their innovations. On projects for the commune she ". . . don't like being left out of any business consultation though she has not the first idea of business. Then, she wears bloomers and other outer costumes that she calls practical."[10] When it was obvious that she and Edmund occupied the same house and that the baby was theirs, they became objects of scorn. Arthur, named for Schopenhauer, was referred to in town as "that poor little bastard out at Ney Castle," the habitation was a "den of iniquity," and its inhabitants "an indecent, sinful lot."[11]

The commune dissolved when the Baron went back to Germany to die. Elisabet and Edmund did not sell out for another year. They traveled through the East and Mid-west, during which time a second son, Lorne, was born. When they returned to find their farm a malarial swamp, Elisabet looked toward Texas, the newest frontier.

In 1873 they settled finally at Hempstead in Southeast Texas, a hamlet then nicknamed "Six Shooter Junction." This was a town filled with carpetbaggers and violence,[12] an unlikely home for such a pair. They soon occupied a nearby plantation named "Liendo" with which Elisabet had fallen in love. The glamour of previous owners, the family of a Col. Leonard Groce, and the ducal existence it seemed to suggest, made her disregard a friendly planter's warning of the high cost of maintenance.[13]

The mansion at Liendo, still standing today, is a colonial-style clapboard house of eleven immense rooms. It stands in a great grove of live oak trees heavily hung with Spanish moss, and as Miss Ney phrased it, "The place is something in a dream." By mid-summer, the dream had turned into a nightmare. Disregarding her neighbors' sensitivity to her unorthodox behavior, Elisabet alienated friendly callers to achieve the privacy she desired, and when tragedy struck she had to manage by herself.

In late summer the first-born, Arthur, died of diphtheria a few weeks after a romp in those beautiful woods. She made a plaster death mask and then cremated the little body in the fireplace of the east parlor. There are many versions of what happened that night, one in a popularly circulated children's rhyme:

> *"She took it out, rolled it in the yard*
> *To coat it with clay, put it in the chimney. . ."*

Another variant contained the line, "Elisabet Ney baked it wif' clay."

This chant shows the cruel glee with which the plantation Negroes punished their eccentric mistress. Biographer Vernon Loggins quotes an old Negro, Aunt Laura, "who will sing for two-bits or a swig of rum" the following song:

> *"Dey burn little Artie by the big house do',*
> *Dey burn up de ten little toes,*
> *Dey burn up de legs and de yaller hair,*
> *Dey burn up de pink little nose.*
> *But dat little boy ain't afeelin' no burn,*
> *He's up dere in de sky,*
> *He's got on his wings, go flippity-flop,*
> *How dat little boy do fly."*

The view held by his kinfolks in Hempstead, says septuagenarian Otis Dozier, was that "the cremation didn't go well at all; the fire wasn't hot enough."

This fits with another ending. As no casket was ordered, nor a hearse seen going to or away from the plantation "THEY" must have buried the remains down by Ponds Creek. Undertakers are presumed by family friends to have circulated this story.

How did the death mask story get out if no one outside Cencie and the parents was there? In one story even the father was not present. Dr. Montgomery was away on a trip and she, when the baby died, incased it in plaster to make a statue. She put this statue, which "was a little bit bigger," in the hall. When the father came back she pointed to the statue and said to him, "Behold, my friend, all that remains of your first born."

The family version, probably through Cencie, is that Dr. Montgomery was present all the time and that he diagnosed the case and fearing the spread of the highly contagious diphtheria, sent the house servants into town and ordered Cencie to make a big fire in the southeast parlor. Miss Ney did make a death mask (a custom in high favor in Europe in the 19th century). She then laid little Artie on the flaming logs and went out in the back yard to watch the sun come up. Afterward Cencie prayed at a bush in the yard where she had a religious emblem hung in the branches. Then she returned to the house and shoveled the ashes into a leather pouch. Elisabet hung the pouch on a nail to one side of the fireplace where it remained. When Dr. Montgomery died the pouch was put in his coffin. Years later Lorne is said to have pried open a small trunk that was always locked, thinking it had valuables because it went with Miss Ney everywhere. In it he found the plaster cast of a small boy's body.

The Texas Fine Arts Association, which keeps Miss Ney's letters, has a recent missal from a lady whose grandmother was told this story by a Dr. Nutt, who was requested by a Mr. Lafevre to go to the plantation to attend the sick child: "When the child was pronounced dead by Dr. Nutt, Miss Ney could not restrain herself." She grabbed the body in her arms, rushed to her boudoir, and locked herself in for the night. It is said she made a death mask but the whereabouts of it are unknown. Dr. Nutt persuaded Elisabet Ney to have the child cremated to prevent the spread of diphtheria. This she did and Dr. Nutt quarantined the place from the local people.

Meanwhile, there were the other son Lorne whose daily and hourly needs claimed attention, the stock to care for, and the field hands to supervise. They all looked to Miss Ney; the Mister was in his laboratory, reading and writing. Following the example of the Georgia planters, someone from the Big House had to ride the rounds. Miss Ney learned to be a good horsewoman, riding astride like a man. She patrolled the fields swathed in veils over a wide straw hat. As a planter, she was said to be a smart go-getter, "a match for any two white men in getting work out of a nigger." But as was the case with other plantations burdened with former slaves and a mortgage, all too often a deficit at the end of the year proved to be the only harvest.[14]

As her son grew up, Elisabet had in mind his filling a role as a young laird worthy of the Liendo image, the equivalent of his Gaelic cousins in Argyllshire. For him she designed a court suit of satin and lace, a kilt, and a tunic. The first time Lorne wore his tunic into town, he was subjected to jeers of "Shirt-tail out!" from the street urchins of Hempstead. This was the last time he willingly obeyed his mother. As the years went by, alienated by his mother's eccentricities and aloofness from what she snobbishly described as "the common herd,"[15] Lorne joined them and became for a time one of Hempstead's rakehells.

That Lorne was called "little bastard," his mother a "queer woman, a witch," his parents "atheists, imps of the Devil, unlike other people," was probably told to him by his forbidden dusky playmates. Jim Wyatt,[16] who had been from boyhood her body servant, said that one of the chores he dreaded doing for Elisabet (He called her "Miz 'Lisabeth.") was driving the mules that pulled the sled on which she sometimes rode into town. Wyatt said she dressed "like an *Ayrab*" or "folks in the Bible stories" (her Grecian robes), and apparently he too was confounded by her uninhibited behavior while shopping in Hempstead.

Jim said that Dr. Montgomery was "a mighty fine gentleman, always ready to doctor a person or a mule," and had only kind words to say of him. In contrast, he said that "Miz 'Lisabeth was meaner than bat manure, mighty haughty and careless with other people." When he heard horses running at night, after Elisabet's death, he said he was afraid that Elisabet had "come back as a booger" and referred to her habit of riding bareback around the plantation near the hour of midnight. Jim testified further that his mistress "lived on cat meat," and that she was hunting for cats on her rides, "although," he added, "I never saw her skin a cat." Jim was witness to many of Elisabet's tantrums, stating that at such times Dr. Montgomery would take refuge by sleeping in a tent in the yard.

Her tantrums increased until two events occurred. First, Edmund took charge of Lorne, who was sent East to college. Then, Governor Oran M. Roberts invited Elisabet to Austin to do some sculpturing. Though the legislators she was asked to address failed to be impressed by her, she succeeded with a ladies' commission seeking likenesses of Texas heroes for the Chicago Centennial of 1893. This opened the way to re-establishing Elisabet, now in her fifties, as a sculptress.

Dr. Montgomery raised money by another mortgage[17] on the plantation and helped Elisabet build a studio in Austin. The place, named Formosa, was a miniature medieval castle north of the University, at the corner of Avenue H and 44th Street. At age fifty-eight, in 1891, Elisabet no longer had the beauty which had opened doors for her in Europe, but she retained her wit and charm and was full of schemes to obtain commissions. Still, her eccentricities and the costume and actions required of a working sculptress remained little understood, and she soon became the most talked about woman in the capital. Many of the stories were cruel and vindictive, but others were merely good-natured raillery.

Some of the blacks dubbed her "The Witch Woman," and whispered that she made clay models of her enemies and hung them in the closet, that she could cast spells, and that she had the hide of her horse for a "coverlid." No wonder, it was said, her folks built her place near the insane asylum. It would be handy, just in case.

Certainly, some of her conduct was fey enough. At a friend's housewarming she strewed goldenrod in every nook and cranny of the new dwelling, sprinkled wine on every hearth and declared that she must appease the Lares and Penates, acting the part so well that some of the guests thought she was actually reviving old Roman rites. The rigidly righteous wanted her disqualified from a competitive commission, recounting all the gossip which had traveled from Hempstead to prove that she had not been properly churched, and pleading that State money should go only to a Christian sculptor.

As late as 1906, when she was seventy-three, stories circulated about her alleged sexual appetites. It was said that she had picked up a lover in Italy, and that the scoundrel had followed her to America to get more money out of her. When she added on to Formosa, she fired a number of workmen for their sloppy work, and they in revenge told stories about her. A fragment of one of these tales was collected recently by the author from an informant who blurted out, "Ney—she was the one who had three guys—" and then abruptly guarded his tongue.

Her costumes, it was agreed, always covered her but most often stopped short at a different length from the current fashion, the gap between hem and floor being filled by boots or gaiters. Recently, an eighty-two-year-old woman[18] recalled that as a child she was taken to see the famous artist, but stated, "I was terrified of her; she wore draperies, bloomers, and boots up to her knees." She favored a toque tight enough to stay on her head while driving her gig, informing her milliner that the headpiece would be tested overnight; if it were still on in the morning, she'd pay for it.

A favorite story of the Pease-Graham clan concerns the time Elisabet was discovered crawling over a fence on the grounds of Woodlawn, the home of Governor Pease's widow. The shocked gardener, seeing the aged sculptress in breeches and later driving off in her gig with gray cape flying behind her, thought he'd been talking to a witch. On another occasion, upon being invited to the Pease home for dinner, she accepted with the proviso that no one else at the table eat meat, since she herself was a vegetarian. Again, at a time when commissions were slow in coming, she would help herself to the back porch ice-box of her friends the Albert Burlesons, leaving a witty note in recompense for the food. Invited to spend the night, so the tale ran, she would often as not request that instead of a bed to sleep in, a hammock be slung for her in a corner.

In addition to all this, she was given to haranguing the Texas legislators in her heavy German accent for having an insufficient appreciation for the fine arts. She displayed the same fervor when she scolded the burghers of Münster for failing to place her sculptures in favorable light. She had confronted the burghers while on a trip to Europe in 1895, where a new generation effusively welcomed the sculptress whom they thought to be the victim of an Indian raid. In Munich she saw her statue of Ludwig placed in the Linderhof Castle garden, gathered her other works that she had abandoned twenty-five years earlier, sold[19] the villa, and returned to Austin.

Back in Texas, the legislators finally relented under pressure from the ladies who rallied around Elisabet, especially after she succeeded in getting William Jennings Bryan to sit for her. A sum of $32,000 was appropriated so that Elisabet could finish the statues of Sam Houston and of Stephen F. Austin for the Capitol building in Austin and the National Capitol at Washington. Once again, a large sum of money was in her hands.[20]

With the reward for her labors, Elisabet bought marble in Italy and brought an expert stone finisher to Austin to complete her last show-piece, a statue of Lady Macbeth, now in the National Gallery of Art in Washington. In addition, there was a gift to Edmund of a trip to Europe, productive of tender love letters between them. In the same spirit, she had one of the Doctor's manuscripts published elegantly, a work which elicited the sour comment from son Lorne, now overseer of the deteriorating plantation, that "not forty people will read it."[21] Also, additions were made to Formosa, and Elisabet began to enjoy visitors. One Austinite who had objected to the shocking creature who ran about in trousers, attended a lawn party which was memorable for the sound of an orchestra playing from the tower, and upon being shown the studio, remarked, "One look at the scaffolding and one could see why skirts would be a hindrance."[22]

As the years passed, the stories continued to multiply. Jan Fortune and Jean Burton in their breezily written *Elisabet Ney* relate how Miss Ney, then almost seventy and prosperous at the turn of the century, hired an Indian servant named Horace and purchased a canoe for the little lake on her property near the studio. Once when instructing Horace in the proper use of the paddle, Elisabet stood up in the canoe to belabor the unfortunate redman. Onlookers were treated to the sight of a capsized canoe and of a dripping goddess-like figure wading ashore amid a welter of floating cushions.

On another occasion, Miss Ney was entertaining a group of young ladies on the studio grounds when a male friend, Morton M. Shipe the real estate developer of Hyde Park where Formosa was situated, drove up on his maiden voyage in his new steamer automobile. Elisabet accepted his offer of a ride, but in getting the car out of the grounds the driver struck the picnic table, sending glassware and china in all directions. Undismayed, Miss Ney and Shipe drove on, until something went wrong with the car's plumbing and clouds of steam began to arise from beneath the seats. "Jump for your life!" yelled Shipe, and jump they did. A variant of the story insists that after striking the table, the steamer with its passengers plunged into the creek.[23]

So, it would seem that at last Elisabet gained acceptance in Texas. Biographer Bride Neill Taylor writes: "Those who had helped over the years in the struggle for culture were rewarded with invitations to *al fresco* suppers at Formosa, definitely the center of culture in Austin!" This center frequently consisted of a rude table with a ruder bench under a fine old oak on the banks of the lake. To the accompaniment of a bass chorus from immense bullfrogs, conversation played back and forth between the artist and her guests. "Elisabet was so indifferent to bodily comforts that it never occurred to her to doubt the adequacy of her menus. She dispensed ascetic suppers, sometimes of clabber only, sometimes of dry bread, cheese and tea, seasoning the plain fare with generous outpourings of high thinking."[24]

The tenor Caruso, pianist Paderewski, and ballerina Pavlova called on her (Paderewski was said to have been partial to the clabber.), and one of the famous, Mme. Schumann-Heink, became a fast friend with whom Elisabet corresponded over the years. Another visitor was Lorado Taft, sculptor and art historian, author of a history of American sculpture, who dwelt at length upon the sculptress at Austin at a time when she had just finished her memorial for Albert Sidney Johnston and had begun her statue of Lady Macbeth.

Taft dubbed the Johnston Memorial "a work of high order," and in his book lists her as one of the best equipped of women sculptors. He lauded her good taste, "in that the picturesque, the literary motif, the anecdotal . . . make no appeal to her," but added that her work was sometimes uneven, stating that "Her isolated life has not resulted in that growth which accompanies generous rivalry."

Edmund was often at Formosa, commuting to Austin by train. Elisabet in her turn went frequently to Liendo, oftentimes driving in her gig, staying the night at hospitable farmsteads where she would sling her hammock between two trees in the yard. Her "dearest friend" Edmund was at Formosa the night she died after experiencing a year of difficult breathing. This was the night of June 29, 1907, and she was taken to Liendo to be buried in the grove of trees she and the doctor had planted in their first year, about a hundred feet west of the house. At Austin a large crowd gathered to pay its last respects, but at the railroad station in Hempstead, there was only Lorne with a team and a wagon. Into the casket, later, with the body of Elisabet was placed the death mask of little Arthur.

Someone, perhaps the garrulous Jim Wyatt, launched the legend that $10,000 in gold was buried with Elisabet in her grave. At any rate, Jim was quoted as saying that he doubted his former mistress was resting easy, that "She couldn't buy her way into Heaven with $10,000." When a six-by-two foot slab of granite was placed over the grave, some of the tenants expressed relief, saying, "the ole witch is finally pinned down."

Elisabet had wished her collection to be part of the University of Texas which she had adopted as her own. She attended every event held in the main auditorium, always occupying the same box. Edmund made certain that Formosa would continue to house the collection, and it is now a museum, kept open by the Texas Fine Arts Association.

Nowadays, Liendo may be visited by appointment with Mr. and Mrs. Carl Detering of Houston. Although the mansion cannot be seen from Wyatt Chapel Road, an offshoot of State Farm Road 1488 three miles east of Hempstead, it may be viewed in a T.V. serial called *Texas*, an NBC soap opera which was released in 1980. One can imagine that Elisabet, with her questing, independent spirit would have been de-lighted with the new art form and its limitless possibilities.

NOTES

1. Vernon Loggins, *Two Romantics* (New York: The Odyssey Press, 1946), pp. 32–33.

2. I. K. Stephens, *The Hermit Philosopher of Liendo* (Dallas: Southern Methodist University Press, 1951), pp. 11–12.

3. Loggins, p. 82, got the quote from Eugene Müllers, Schopenhauer's letters.

4. Loggins, p. 96. The description was given sixty years after the boy, now an old man, had seen her step out of a shop.

5. Wilfred Blunt, *The Dream King, Ludwig II of Bavaria* (Baltimore: Penguin Books, 1973), p. 157.

6. Loggins, pp. 120–21, 126–28.

7. Bride Neill Taylor, *Elisabet Ney, Sculptor* (Austin: Thomas F. Taylor, 1938), p. 46. Elisabet's version: "She was disgusted with court intrigue." (Taylor gave a sympa-thetic ear to the aged Ney in recounting her life and motives. Loggins and Stephens had access to copious notes, diaries and files of Ludwig's court.) M.E.N.

8. Loggins, p. 149. Elisabet was ashamed to face Ludwig after delivering him into other agents' hands after he began to trust her.

9. Paine was read in Europe, the R. Hachette edition, 1856.

10. Mrs. J. W. (Willie B.) Rutland, ed., *Sursum! Elisabet Ney in Texas* (Austin: Hart Graphics and Office Centers, Inc., 1977), p. 3.

11. Jean Burton and Jan Isbel Fortune, *Elisabet Ney* (New York: A. A. Knopf, 1943), p. 192.

12. Stephens, pp. 177–78. A Texas joke concerns a Houston drunk who, once settled in the chair car, was awakened by the conductor who demanded his ticket. "Ain't got no ticket." "Where do you think you are going without a ticket?" "Goin' to Hell." "Very well. Give me a dollar and get off at Hempstead."

13. Bracken and Redway, *Early Texas Homes* (Dallas: Southern Methodist University Press, 1956), p. 144. Before the war Groce's cotton receipts had been $80,000 but afterward Liendo became an economic liability, bankrupting the owner. Elisabet, enrap-tured, promised to pay Groce Jr. one-fourth of $10,000 down in gold and two additional payments at the end of the next two years.

14. Loggins, pp. 39–40.

15. Samuel W. Geiser, in *Dictionary of American Biographies*, Vol. VII (New York: Charles Scribner's Sons, 1957), 478–79. "Elisabet Ney was marked by an independence of spirit that broke everything to her will. . . . She possessed a haughtiness and an uncalculating ambition that surmounted all personal and material obstacles."

16. Frank X. Tolbert, columnist of the *Dallas Morning News* and author of many books on Texas History, accompanied I. K. Stephens and Allan Maxwell to "Liendo" and wrote about it April 15, 1951, and after hearing the plantation was in new hands, on

June 18, 1962. In 1951 the aged Negro, Jim Wyatt was able to talk to a journalist with a good ear for folklore. The descriptions of "Liendo" plantation house are Tolbert's also.

    17. Stephens, p. 294, had the letters and library of Dr. Montgomery which were given to and are available in the DeGolyer Library at Southern Methodist University from which he deduced the incomes of the couple. Dr. Montgomery's "only sources of revenue" were an annuity of $1,000 and farming, dairying and goat-raising which barely equaled the outlay." Poured into the plantation were Edmund's legacy from his father's estate of nearly $75,000, and savings from his practice from which he made $1,000 annually. Elisabet had a legacy and money from her commissions. Her response to each year's deficit was to purchase more acreage, disregarding the mounting debt. In the end the original amount of acreage was doubled as had the mortgage.

    18. Mrs. Clifton L. Moss, Jr., Dallas, 1980. Her grandfather was Miss Ney's attorney from Hempstead days, Judge Thomas Sidney Reese, who looked after her investments in Austin. "Grandfather was fond of her and we would go on Sunday afternoons to call at the studio. . . . Her hair was grey and stringy down to her shoulders. Just terrified me."

    19. Loggins, p. 129. The villa was an estate in the Schwabing Valley on the North side of Munich. It resembled a Tuscan villa. This "abode was a gift of (the) King to a woman of Prussia (Elisabet). With Prussian cleverness she secured unqualified title to the property."

    20. Taylor, p. 98. "Money leaked out of her hands like water . . . not spent on herself . . . she had few personal needs but wasted with ill-considered generosity . . . to a tale of need. . . ." (An ingredient of a legendary character in the making—selfless generosity.) M.E.N.

    21. Loggins, pp. 331–32. On the occasion of Dr. Montgomery's seventy-third birthday, copies of his book arrived. Lorne, remembering crates of unsold pamphlets from a previous publishing venture, must have gasped at the expense of this one. Its title was *Philosophical Problems in the Light of Vital Organization*, an edition of 500 being published by Putnam. Advertising was also to be at Montgomery's expense. As none was arranged, no books were sold, a few copies being distributed to friends.

    22. Memoirs of Emma Shapard Stedman of Austin, unpublished letters.

    23. Anecdote related in 1980 by Joseph Jones of Austin.

    24. Taylor, p. 97.

Mollie Bailey with her favorite horse and buggy.

Show time at Lockney, Texas, July 4, 1906, near the end of more than 25 years on the road.

MOLLIE BAILEY
Circus Entrepreneur

Martha Hartzog

Texas Foundation for Women's Resources

Mollie Bailey was born in 1844 on an Alabama plantation, her conventional destiny that of southern lady, wife and helpmeet to some aristocratic scion. Instead, she ran away from home at the age of fourteen to marry the son of a circus owner. During the course of a long and eventful career, which ended only with her death in 1918, Mollie Bailey was show boat entertainer, Civil War nurse, Civil War spy, mother of nine children, benefactor of charitable causes, and one of the few female entrepreneurs in circus history.

The bare facts of Mollie Bailey's life would qualify her to be an extraordinary woman, but she attained an even higher status. She became an institution among Texas people, respected and beloved. "Aunt Mollie Bailey" brought the magic of the circus, one of the oldest of folk events, to rural Texans whose lives were dominated by crops, livestock and the seasons. She helped Texans celebrate one of the most important occasions of the time—Old Soldier's Day. And by purchasing town lots and donating money to charitable causes, she became a part of every community where her circus stopped. Many stories were told of her exploits, some factual, some apochryphal. During her lifetime, Mollie Bailey achieved the stature of female folk hero.

Mollie Arline Kirkland was born in the autumn of 1844, on a plantation in Sumpter County, Alabama, near Mobile. Her father, William Kirkland, and her mother, Mary Arline, doubtless assumed that Mollie would live up to the rigid ideal of perfection expected of Southern women of genteel birth and extolled in story and song. But Mollie failed to fit into the mold.

Family stories of her childhood paint a picture of an active, strong-willed, inquisitive, adventuresome child. Mollie early exhibited her theatrical abilities, leading the other children—sister Sally and half-sister Fanny—in thinking up new role-playing games, for which Mollie was the director and major actor. And Mollie mimicked the walk and manner of speech of everyone, from servants to visitors, behind their backs. She was always asking questions, and she followed her father around like a boy, listening and watching as he managed the plantation. Later on she would show that she knew how to manage a large operation.

William Kirkland quite typically predicted that Mollie would outgrow the tomboy stage, meaning that she would turn to more traditional, ladylike pursuits. And while by the time she was twelve years old she had grown into a beautiful young girl, her father's prediction did not quite turn out to be accurate. At twelve, Mollie was described as being "gypsy-like in appearance, dark hair, flashing black eyes, and a vivacious manner . . . a graceful, charming young lady, a belle of the day."[1] Her family sent her to be educated at the ladies academy at Tuscaloosa, near Mobile. Boarding schools of the time emphasized correct female deportment over intellectual growth. The school principal wrote to Mr. Kirkland commending Mollie's excellence in "Dramatics and the Tableaux" and praising the sampler she made which consisted of a quote from Milton's Lycidas: "Fame is no Plant that Grows on Mortal soil."

When she was around fourteen years old, Mollie returned to the plantation on vacation. It is at this tender age that she makes her fateful decision! Though accounts differ as to when she met her future husband, how long she had known him before they married, and her age when married, it is agreed that in the early spring of 1858 Mollie declared her love for Gus Bailey, the son of a circus owner, and himself the circus band leader. Her father refused her request to be married, so Mollie ran away one night and married Gus on March 21, 1858.[2] Mollie and Gus spent their honeymoon on the road with Gus's father's circus. She returned home twice to ask her father's forgiveness, but was turned away each time. Her father subsequently disinherited her.

The strong outlines of Mollie's character begin to show up now: ambitious, quick-witted, and determined. The story goes that one night, by candlelight, using a trunk lid as a table, Mollie persuaded Gus that they should have their own show. They were hindered of course by lack of money and equipment. Though Mollie was later to rail against dishonesty, she stole home to the Sumpter County plantation and "borrowed" some horses and a couple of wagons from her father.[3]

Mollie and Gus's first show, vaudeville rather than circus, lasted only a few years. The Bailey Family Troup went from town to town playing in schoolhouses or opera houses in Alabama, Mississippi, the Carolinas, and later Arkansas. Gus was fiddler, leading man, orchestra leader and comedian. His brother Alfred Bailey was contortionist and musician. Mollie was leading lady, soloist, and organist. Mollie's half-sister Fannie joined the show to dance and act—undoubtedly causing William Kirkland additional grief and raising a serious question as to the idyllic nature of life on a southern plantation, at least under the rule of this particular patriarch. Fannie and Alfred were to continue with Gus and Mollie's shows for many years afterward.

On May 20, 1861, Gus enlisted in the 44th Alabama Infantry at Selma, Alabama. The winter of 1862–63 he transferred to Company 13 of the Arkansas Infantry, a regiment in Hood's Texas Brigade. Gus became leader of the Third Arkansas Band and performed with the Hood's Minstrels, a group of actors, musicians and singers who were Brigade members. Mollie volunteered to serve as nurse and left her first child, an infant daughter, with friends in Richmond, Virginia. During the winter months, while the Brigade was in semi-permanent quarters, Mollie and her sister Fannie joined the Hood's Minstrels, entertaining the troops with their song and dance acts. Though she did not talk about it later, leaving the task of recounting her exploits to Confederate veterans, Mollie also served as spy for the Brigade.

Female spies are said to have been fairly common during the Civil War. When caught they did not receive the same treatment as men, who were often hanged. Instead, the women were either threatened or sent to prison, the double standard working in their favor for once. Several incidents are recounted of Mollie's spy exploits. Two of them illustrate her resourcefulness and thespian skills.

Hearing that the Third Arkansas soldiers were in need of quinine, Mollie volunteered to take it to them. Her idea was to have the powdered quinine wrapped in small packets, then hide the packets in her hair which was combed in a large pompadour, according to the fashion of the day. Upon hearing the plan, it is said that the officer in charge remarked, "Depend on a woman to think up a good scheme."[4] The plan worked and Mollie returned safely. Another time, by making up like an old woman—complete with downturned mouth and stooped stance, she infiltrated the enemy camp in order to obtain vital information. Hobbling about dispensing cookies, she went unnoticed by the troops and got her information.

It was also during the War that Gus Bailey, with the assistance of one of the musicians in the band, wrote the song, "The Old Grey Mare, She Ain't What She Used to Be," which became popular during the War and was used as the official song of the 1928 Democratic Convention held in Houston, Texas.[5]

When the War ended, the Baileys found themselves broke in Arkansas with three daughters to feed and Gus weakened by chilly bivouac nights. Though it is never overtly mentioned, Gus evidently contracted consumption during the War. The Baileys took employment with a dramatic company which played on a "boat show"—the term Mollie preferred. After a few years and more children, including sons, Gus and Mollie quit the boat show to form the Bailey Concert Company. It played in schoolhouses in the rural sections and small towns of the South. Mollie played the organ, Gus the fiddle, the older boys sang, and they had a few dancing acts.

In 1876, the Baileys purchased a home in Prescott, Arkansas. The concert company had grown until it was a tent show which travelled by wagon. There was a trapeze act, singing and dancing acts, a contortionist, blackface comedy, a stringed orchestra, and a band. Mollie's acrobatic sons and singing daughters formed the nucleus of the performers, together with Alfred and Fannie. It was a show that "nice people" felt good about attending—no con games, no cheating—a show run by a family for families. Because of Gus's increasingly poor health, Mollie was the show's actual head. And really it is clear that she had been the driving force behind the steady growth of the operation from the very beginning. In 1876 Mollie was thirty-two years old. She is described at that time as a short, rounded figure of a woman, with a small waist and a positive walk. Well dressed in dark, rich materials, her skirts billowed as she walked, her eyes sparkled, and her lip gave "mother wit."[6]

Since before the War, the Baileys had felt a strong attraction for Texas and had been trying to move the show there. The attraction is said to have begun one day in 1860 when Mollie and Gus had visited a small Arkansas town. On the main street was a crowd staring at a swaybacked covered wagon. A whiskered man who sat beside a bonneted woman described a land he had seen: "'Grass enough for the whole kit and billin' of you and some left over!'"[7] The many pioneers moving to Texas at that time saw it as a land of opportunity and plenty. Gus and Mollie too caught the Texas fever and vowed to go, but before they had a chance the War broke out. Serving in Hood's Texas Brigade proved another tie to Texas and one that would contribute to the later success of the circus.

After several unsuccessful attempts to move to Texas, in 1885 they were able to purchase a winter home in Dallas, at South Preston and Young Streets. From then on, for over thirty years, Texas was their home. After having used tents off and on since 1875, by the spring of 1887 they had become a tent show once and for all, and exhibited the three basic elements of a circus: the ring acts, clowns, and the ring itself.

The Bailey's Circus was called "A Texas Show for Texas People." Three flags flew over the three-pole tent: the Republic of Texas, the Confederate States of America, and the United States of America. The circus played to small Texas towns rather than to the larger ones—an economic decision made early by Mollie and Gus since playing in small towns meant not competing with circuses already established and didn't require much advertising. The usual route was to leave Dallas in early spring for the sawmill section of East Texas, thence to South Texas, then back through Dallas and the cotton section to the Panhandle and West Texas. Finally, the circus returned in December to its winter quarters in Dallas.[8]

Imagine how dangerous it was to take a small playing company out on the road to rural Texas during the latter part of the nineteenth century, especially with your own young children. Here is a favorite story about Mollie which displays her courage and ingenuity. One night, in camp between two Texas towns, whose identity is not given, the Baileys had arranged their wagons in a circle as usual. The evening meal was being prepared when Mollie saw shadows moving between her and the sun. These became a group of Indians circling the wagons. Mollie fired several shots in the air with an old pistol she had carried through the War, but this had no effect. She then was inspired to beat on the big bass circus drum. It worked! The Indians rode off in terror, evidently thinking the drum was a cannon like the one the soldiers had at the fort. Years later, when the circus was in Quanah, Texas, Mollie told the story to Quanah Parker, famous Indian chief. He enjoyed it immensely and each year when the show came to town he would ask Mollie to tell it again, doubling up in laughter.[9]

The arrival of the circus in the small towns was a big event. Nineteenth century Texas was far removed from older, more settled portions of the nation. According to circus historian G. G. Sturtevant, the circus was probably the first form of professional entertainment to visit Texas, and its appeal was instant and very strong.[10] Over and over again accounts by the people who lived in the small Texas towns where Mollie played speak of the excitement her circus brought. Picture this scene, a typical one throughout the history of the Mollie Bailey Show.

The circus arrives in town, very early in the morning, its brightly painted wagons drawn by mules. As always, Mollie rides in the lead wagon, her star garnet pin at her throat, her diamonds flashing, bowing right and left to the crowds that are gathering. The brass band that follows has red uniforms. Daughter Birda is on a big black horse, riding skirt almost sweeping the ground. The wagon for her trained birds is "a hack pulled by one mule and filled with the cages and perches housing and holding birds of all kinds. Macaws, cockatoos, myna birds, and canaries kept up a raucus chatter as the circus caravan moved along the country roads and through the town streets."[11]

Son Allie's "trained canines" follow, then the "educated ponies" of son Brad's. Finally the clowns! One rides a bucking mule. Another clown—with red circles painted on top of his head—follows on foot, periodically trying to hang onto the mule's tail and shouting funny verses. Or dancing up to the sidelines to let loose a jack-in-the-box to the excited children. The menagerie includes zebras, anteaters, bears, deer, antelope, coyotes, a trained pig, a leopard cat, and a camel. There is even an elephant named "Bolivar." The larger animals walk. The others are in cages.

"'When are you going to bring us a lion, Aunt Mollie?' a small town groceryman once teased her. 'When I start charging a dollar for my show,' she retorted."[12]

In 1890 Gus retired to Blum outside Houston because of ill health and the show officially became "The Mollie A. Bailey Show," what country people had been calling it for years.[13] It was the Golden Age of the show: country fairs waited for it, Confederate veterans dated their reunions with its appearance, schools let out for half-a-day when the circus came to town. The eminent men and women of the period—war heroes, politicians, civic leaders—came to see Mollie's circus. Governor James Stephen Hogg, Governor of Texas from 1890 to 1894, presented her with a wild boar's tooth mounted in gold and with her name inscribed in the center.

At its peak the show had thirty-one wagons, 170 head of stock, twenty-one trained ponies, and a collection of walking animals. Here is how the show has been described at its Golden Age: Mollie always stood at the entrance, in her later years, a stout, dark-skinned, confident woman. Inside the big top were tiered seats on the three sides. On the fourth side was a stage with a leafy proscenium and a curtain on which was painted a river. With a blast of trumpet, the show began. In tumbled the clowns. There were at least six and one of them was dressed up like a woman, and with a more innocent motive than possible today, flirted with whatever public dignitary was in the crowd.

After the clowns was the "stupendous panoply of color." In rode daughter Birda on her black horse, Shetland ponies in tandem pulling a phaeton full of trained canaries. Next was a float of "college canines"— white as statues against the black floor of the tent, their protruding tongues as red as lollipops. A shepherd dog drew a doll buggy in which rode a pig in a lace cap. Another clown ran in, fleeing for his life from a tomahawk-wielding Indian.

The acrobats began the ring show. Son Allie was dressed in white flannel trousers and a bright silk shirt for his slack wire act. Son Brad had a tight wire act that scared everyone when he pretended to fall. Daughter Birda performed with her birds: they climbed miniature swings and swung on little trapezes. Allie showed his trained dogs, Brad his educated ponies. The vaudeville show followed, with singing and dancing and dramatics on the curtained stage. Birda did a serpentine dance wearing a dress made of yards of tulle on which colored lights flashed.

Mollie was an excellent manager. Anyone who has ever seen a circus unload knows how many details there are to manage: animals, people, equipment—all must be happily maintained. To the last Mollie attended to every detail herself. She paid in cash out of a big dark purse as she went along. In 1917 Mollie returned to Houston to nurse sick Birda and still managed the circus by post, telephone, and telegram. Birda died in September 1917. A year later Mollie fell and broke her hip. Unexpectedly, she never recovered and herself died in October 1918. It is said that her heart did not stop beating for two hours after her death.[14] Her four boys—Eugene, W. K., Allie, and Brad—carried on the show for awhile, but moved on to other pursuits after a few years. Mollie had done what many other strong and determined people have done before her and will continue to do, she failed to train anyone to take over when she was gone. When she died her circus essentially died with her.

There are many tributes that have been made to Mollie Bailey, but here is one that illustrates why she became a folk hero to thousands of Texans. In 1952, Mrs. J. C. Byers of Coolidge, Texas, wrote a letter to the editor of *Texas Parade* describing with fondness the devotion her husband and son had given to Mollie Bailey many years before. When she asked her husband why he persisted in seeing the same old show over and over, he replied, "'Why it's just like turning down your own folks to turn her down. She is every thing a show should be—clean, wholesome, no skin games. She's . . . well, she's Mollie Bailey, and I'm going to her show as long as she comes over the road.'"[15]

Finally, let these stanzas from Frank W. Ford stand as an epitaph for this woman who is still "coming over the road" in the memories of Texans:

It was cotton-picking time down in Texas
And the leaves of all the trees a golden brown.
The children and the old folk all were happy
For the Mollie Bailey show had come to town.

A line of gay and fancy-colored wagons,
Loaded down and painted with her name;
A sight that made the little kids all happy.
Those golden days will never come again.

The Mollie Bailey Circus now is over;
And time has rung the golden curtain down,
And very few of us are left who then
Performed our act or painted as a clown.

When that day breaks we'll meet you,
We'll talk of your great fame.
In Southern hearts you'll always live
Your life, your love, your name.[16]

NOTES

1. Olga Bailey, *Mollie Bailey: The Circus Queen of the Southwest*, p. 26. This is a highly anecdotal account of Mollie's life, told by her daughter-in-law, and is the source of much of the information about Mollie.

2. Most accounts agree that Mollie married at fourteen. However, if she were born in the fall of 1844, she would only be thirteen and not fourteen when she married. It is interesting to note that Olga Bailey extends Gus and Mollie's courtship longer than anyone else. One account, by Marshall Monroe which appeared in the *Houston Chronicle* (October 27, 1929), gives sixteen as her age, perhaps in deference to more modern marriage customs.

3. This enterprising deed is not mentioned in Olga Bailey's biography, but appears in several articles, notably Vivian Richardson's *Dallas News* feature (June 1, 1930). Richardson's article, based on firsthand accounts, is also a rich source of information about Mollie.

4. Bailey, pp. 35–36.

5. In 1964 Texas erected a granite monument to Gus Bailey as a memorial to him and other Confederate soldiers and the songs they sang (*Dallas News*, September 12, 1970).

6. J. Marvin Hunter, Sr., "Mollie Bailey, The Great Showwoman," *Frontier Times*, V, 27, No. 7 (April 1950), p. 188.

7. Vivian Richardson, "The Life Story of Mollie Bailey, Pioneer Southern Show Queen: Courage and Canvas," *Dallas News*, June 1, 1930.

8. When the circus' winter quarters were moved to the Houston area in 1890, the itinerary remained essentially the same. And though when it became a railroad show in 1905, the route had to be altered somewhat, it still played to small Texas towns.

9. Bailey, pp. 54–55.

10. G. G. Sturtevant, "Old Circus Days in Texas," *Frontier Times*, V, 9, No. 11 (August 1932), p. 481.

11. Virginia Browder, "Molly Bailey & Her Circus," *The Giles Chronicle*, 1956. Virginia Browder's description is one of three firsthand accounts of Mollie's circus that the author has received while writing this article. Browder, of Memphis, Texas, made a typescript of her article which appeared in 1956. Hilde Faulkner of Coldspring, Texas, sent reminiscences of two Coldspring citizens who remember the circus, and a copy of an article by Cecil B. James which appeared in the Centennial edition of the *Hamilton Herald-News*, in 1958, was sent by Phillip Campbell. All these responses came as a result of an item placed in the *County Chairman's Bulletin* of the Texas Historical Commission.

12. Hunter, p. 191.

13. Gus died in 1896 and Mollie continued without him. It might be mentioned at this point that the claim often made by writers that Gus was distantly related to the James A. Bailey of Barnum & Bailey Circus appears to be unfounded. James A. Bailey assumed that name in honor of his adoptive father, Fred H. Bailey.

14. Hunter, p. 193.

15. *Texas Parade*, V, 12, No. 11 (1952), p. 4.

16. Bailey, pp. 18–19.

MARTHA WHITE McWHIRTER
And the Belton Sanctificationists

Frieda Werden

Texas Foundation for Women's Resources

Martha White was born in Jackson County, Tennessee, in 1827. At age sixteen, she joined the Methodist Church there. Her early Methodism was probably pentecostal in practice, but was a mainstream religion of the day, unlike the Shaker colonies which existed nearby her area and practiced celibacy and ostensible equality of the sexes, as well as a form of collectivism. She married George McWhirter in 1845, and ten years later, after having a number of children, the couple moved to Bell County, Texas. After the war, when George came home a major, they moved to town, settling in Belton. There George went into the mercantile business, they built a large stone house, and Martha had several more pregnancies. They had twelve children in all.[1]

George and Martha McWhirter founded and ran a Union Sunday School in Belton for all the Protestant denominations, and were religiously active. However, Martha McWhirter found she was not satisfied with her religion. One hot day in August, 1866, after sitting through a long end-of-summer revival which did nothing to comfort her for the recent loss of a brother and two of her children, Martha heard a voice, audible, but inside her head, saying "Ask yourself if this is not the devil's work." The next morning while doing her dishes she had a pentecostal baptism—a spontaneous experience of speaking in tongues (not uncommon in those days)—which convinced her that the voice she'd heard the day before was the voice of God. From this time forth, she believed in a theology that held with the sanctity of the individual's own dreams and revelations as a source of spiritual guidance. She taught this doctrine, which she called Sanctification, in her Sunday School classes, and met to discuss it with a group of other women at regular meetings.

When the Methodists built themselves a church and broke away from the Union Sunday School, the McWhirters opposed the move on the grounds it was sectarian. Her women's discussion group, while largely Methodists, also consisted of five Baptists, two Presbyterians, and a Christian Cambellite. They met at the new Methodist church for a time, but after being locked out once and having to climb in a window to hold their meeting, they went back to meeting where the Union Sunday School met. The Union Church building was eventually abandoned by all the other denominations, and the sanctified women were the only ones who continued to meet there.

Gradually, the group evolved a working methodology and a set of tenets. One of the main tenets was that religion should be a spiritual rather than a physical practice, and they opposed the eating and drinking of the sacrament and baptism in water. This led to the five Baptist women being formally ejected from their church, and other members being elbowed out of their denominations. All the members of the group sought what they called the "second blessing" or pentecostal baptism such as Martha McWhirter had experienced, and they also evolved a method of discussing their dreams and revelations together so as to have a sense of the group will to guide them.

Perhaps it was the group will of women who had had more children than they wanted that led them to develop the doctrine that it was not good for an unsanctified person and a sanctified person to sleep together. At one of the divorce trials that arose, McWhirter testified that the justification for this decision came from First Corinthians 7:12–15. A wife had a duty to try to keep peace with her husband, because her sanctification would keep him sanctified; but if he once left her, or threw her out, she was under no obligation to take him back.

In 1877, Martha McWhirter accused her husband of flirting with a hired girl. Offended, he withdrew from her room, and she never took him back. Years later, she related a sad scene in which neither of them could sleep, and he asked her, "Do you *have* to believe this way? Couldn't you take some other religion?" But her revelations were all pointing to one conclusion. Unlike many other husbands, George McWhirter never filed for divorce, and he continued to live with his wife in a celibate relationship for a number of years until the children were grown. Nevertheless, he never really understood her religion, believing only that she was honest and fully sincere.

In addition to withdrawing from sexual relations with their husbands, the sanctified women also withdrew from economic relations. Sensing the tacit connection between money and sex in marriage, and wishing to get out from under the dependency that the laws of the day enforced on the wife, they began to save money in a common fund, and to plan for the possibility of all living together. One was a teacher, others sold milk and butter, and wove rag carpets on a loom purchased out of the common money. Late in 1879, one of the sanctified sisters was hired by Mr. McWhirter at $8 a month, mainly so that she and Mrs. McWhirter could be together. The $8 was paid into the common fund. Then the $8 was used to rent a room from Mr. McWhirter for another of the sisters. When he began turning the rents over to his wife, she stopped collecting them. Gradually, the McWhirter house became Sanctificationist headquarters. All the women gave whatever they had to each other as it was needed; and by 1879, none of them was any longer accepting money from a husband, except as wages for housework.

There was never any rule in the Sanctificationist code that excluded men from membership in their group; and in 1879, two young men from Scotland came to Belton with the express intention of joining the sect. They had belonged to a similarly named group in Scotland; and, indeed, Mrs. McWhirter herself claimed that her doctrine was precisely the same as that of John Wesley. While the men of Belton had fumed, they had not felt justified in physically attacking a group of religious women, no matter how infuriating. This taboo did not apply to men, however—the threat was more than some angry husbands could bear. In February, 1880, on the very day the Dow brothers' elderly parents had arrived from Scotland to live with them, a group of angry husbands took the two male Sancties from their house at midnight and whipped them severely. The boys refused to leave town after being threatened with their lives, so on February 17 an insanity hearing was held in District Court. The boys were found insane and sent to the asylum in Austin. There they were released, but only after promising never to return to Belton. (One of them did later return, but did not try to join the sanctified group again.) The records of the insanity hearing provide insight into the workings of the sanctified group. For instance, one woman testified that she had left her husband in obedience to a revelation, not to any generalized principle of their religion. Another trial was held that same year, the divorce proceeding of E. J. Rancier vs. Josephine Rancier. Perhaps the publicity did the group good, as it was at its largest—fifty members—at this time. More violence took place when a posse of angry husbands fired at the McWhirter house. A bullet hole can still be seen in its door frame. Another husband lured his young son away from the Sancties' premises and kidnapped him from his mother.

It is significant that the population of Bell County and Belton had been growing at a phenomenal rate since the war and continued to do so. In 1881, the first railroad line reached Belton, bringing more business expansion and population growth. This population growth was almost entirely among whites, a statistic that assumes significance when one considers the laundry. Since the early days of Texas settlement, doing the laundry had been an economic niche occupied by black women. Now, white women in Belton complained that they couldn't get anybody to do a decent job of washing for them. Having realized as early as 1878 that they were no longer accepted into polite society, the Sanctificationists had little to lose socially by accepting "nigger-work." They began to take in washing to earn money for their common fund, doing the wash at each woman's house in turn. They were to accumulate quite a nest egg in this way, enough that they invested some of the money in an interest-bearing note secured by a mortgage. Ignorance of the homestead act nearly lost them their money, since a homestead cannot be foreclosed upon under Texas law; but the honesty of the recipient of the loan saved them in this instance. Soon they would be quite savvy in the use of capital, and Mrs. McWhirter developed excellent accounting skills. Their ability to think things out together and work out any uneasiness through both practical and dream work stood them in good stead as investors and entrepreneurs.

But in 1882, they still had a long way to go. One day they took the laundry to the J. C. Henry home—a posh place—and Mr. Henry caught them setting up the washpots. He was probably drunk (Prohibition had passed the Belton electorate in 1877, only to be voted out again in 1878.), and he was definitely abusive. He ordered the women off the place, but they refused to leave. Then he started throwing things, and gashed his wife severely in the head. The women left, but gathered at the house again in the evening, determined to carry through their plans. Mr. Henry had them arrested. They were convicted of assault, and five of them were fined $20 apiece—which was paid out of the common fund. With the same common fund, the sisters built Mrs. Henry a home on a lot belonging to Mr. McWhirter. They hired a professional carpenter for one day, doing the rest of the work themselves and with the help of their sons. When Mr. McWhirter found out that the house was being built, he complained mightily, but Mrs. McWhirter pointed out that she had brought property into the marriage, and she had the moral if not the legal right to use it. The house exhausted the common fund, but it was soon restored.

In 1883, Sister Johnson's husband died, leaving her an insurance policy worth $2,000. She refused the money, saying she had not accepted money from her husband when he was alive, and she wouldn't take it now he was dead. Her brother then had her convicted of lunacy and himself appointed receiver of her estate so that he could get the $2,000. After praying for a way to get Sister Johnson back, a member of the group dreamed that Martha McWhirter wrote the governor and obtained her release. Mrs. McWhirter did so, Sister Johnson was released, and returned to Belton bringing $90 she had earned working as a seamstress at the asylum in Austin, which was added to the common fund.

That spring of 1883, the sisters began to get requests to hire out as servants. They were cautious about what sort of work they would take, but by summer accepted applications for a cook and a house-girl. They eventually took many such jobs—sometimes weeping when the orders came in, but agreeing that it was right for them to humble themselves; and of course it was right to make the $1 or $1.25 a day. They did good work but would not talk with their employers about anything except the job. As former members of the Belton elite, their comedown excited much comment. Two of the women had a horse each, and they bought a wagon and harness. Then they purchased standing wood at 25¢ a cord, cut and hauled it, and sold it for $3 a cord. Mrs. Henry—she of the haughty husband—had charge of this operation. One Belton woman reminisced years later that seeing those fine ladies do hard manual labor like that upset her more than anything she could remember. But the women were making money fast: milk and butter made them $5 or $6 a day, wood $8–10 a day, and laundry up to $200 a month.

In November 1883, Mr. Henry died. Sister Henry as the widow took over their large house, and since it was in a good location near the railroad depot she turned it into a boarding-house and it prospered. Then in 1884, a woman hotel-keeper in the nearby town of Temple sent for two sisters to help her. In 1886, she asked for three more, paying them $1 a day. This was to be both a major source of revenue and an excellent training ground. Meanwhile, the sisters built three more houses on lots belonging to Mr. McWhirter. He complained again, but suffered his wife to collect the rents. In 1885, she fixed him a room in one of his houses on the square, and he moved out of the McWhirter home, leaving it entirely to the sanctified women. His daughter and her children had moved into the house, and it must have been getting rather crowded.

In 1886, the sisters stepped up their investment program again. One of the Dow brothers had brought a steam laundry to Belton and tried to make a go of it in the old Methodist church building, but failed. The sisters bought it for $5,000 and ran it, doing almost all the work themselves. They also took over the Henry boarding house and began enlarging it to make a hotel. The Central Hotel, as they called it, was across the street from the laundry and the livery stable, near the Wells Fargo Express depot, and beside the tracks of the railroad spur. When the sisters took over and raised the rent, almost all the old boarders left, and for a year it was boycotted by everyone in town; but in 1887, after George McWhirter's death, it suddenly filled up and became popular. Townspeople went there to board, and the best people found quarters there. The sisters no longer hired out as servants, but all pitched in to run their own hotel and their laundry. Soon the laundry was used only for hotel laundry and the sisters' own washing.

The death of Mr. McWhirter is one of the more uncertain moments in the life of his wife. The Sanctificationists had a general rule that they did not visit the unsanctified, though any member of their families might come to visit them. Mrs. McWhirter was torn over whether to go visit her husband in his illness, and she decided that she would go if she had a revelation to do so, or if he sent for her. She never had the revelation, and he never sent for her (Later she confessed that it hurt her that he would lie there and never ask her to come.). Nevertheless, he made no attempt to cut her out of her share of his estate, and made her executor of the children's share, saying he knew her to be honest and fair. He had held an important position in the town; some reports mention that he was a prominent jurist, and he was an important leader of the Masons and the Methodists. Perhaps his trust in Mrs. McWhirter inspired the confidence of other townspeople. Perhaps the change of heart among the citizens was more due to her support of civic efforts— donating $500 to bring the railroad spur, supporting a building fund for an opera house, and so forth. She eventually became the first woman elected to the Belton Board of Trade—a precursor of the Chamber of Commerce. Clearly, widowhood was considered a more becoming state than that of a woman separated from her husband.

Another major divorce case was filed in 1887, by the husband of Mrs. McWhirter's daughter. The husband won the first round of Haymond vs. Haymond in the courts, but the Sanctificationists could afford good lawyers, and they appealed to the state supreme court. There it was ruled that evidence of the defendant's religious conviction should not have been admitted, and further that the husband was a resident of British Columbia not Belton at the time the suit was filed. Ada Haymond turned around and filed for divorce on her own behalf, winning back custody of her children.

The same year, 1891, the Sanctificationists incorporated as the Central Hotel Company. This was not an adequate legal vehicle for their entire holdings, however, but only for those enterprises which directly supported the hotel. They held a lot of improved real estate in Belton and three farms managed as adjuncts to the hotel. Half of one of the farms they worked themselves, with some hired help, to supply the hotel and feed their livestock. Their net income was now about $800 a month. The hotel, completed at last, had thirty-five bedrooms. The work was shared by all members of the group equally, and each had to work only four hours a day at an assigned task. That summer, a history professor from the University of Texas visited and wrote an article about the group, describing it as a successful commune. He found thirty-two members: two married men, two unmarried men, three boys, nine widowed or divorced women, eight unmarried women and girls over age sixteen, and eight girls under sixteen. Two of the girls were unrelated to adults in the group, but had been consigned to the sisters to raise. One of the women was a dentist—self-taught—who worked on townspeople for just the cost of materials since she didn't have a license. One of the men was living in New York trying to set up a business selling pianos. In 1890, all the members of the group had traveled to New York for vacations in three shifts, living in a house near Central Park rented for the occasion by Mrs. McWhirter. In the next few years, search parties would travel as far as Mexico City, San Francisco, and other places, looking for a place to which the group would eventually move. Meanwhile, the group lived comfortably but not too elaborately, hired tutors for their children, subscribed to many magazines and newspapers, stopped having prayer-meetings, but still held sessions to talk over their dreams and discover the group will. Mrs. McWhirter was the acknowledged leader of the group, but it operated very much on the basis of feeling and consensus. The delicate group sense could determine when something was wrong, and dreams would point out what was to be done about it—whether the solution was to sell one of the farms, fire a German piano teacher, or encourage a disloyal group member to go ahead and get married.

In the late 1890s, the group leased and operated two hotels in Waco. It is significant that though they kept to themselves in many ways they were very open to the public, sometimes even doubling up in their quarters to make more rooms available to guests. When testimony came out in a divorce case that Mrs. McWhirter had permitted prostitutes to board at the hotel, she admitted that this was so, but said that they had behaved themselves and caused no problems. In 1898, the Women's Wednesday Club of Belton met at the Central Hotel and voted to found the city's first public library, starting it the next year with more than 350 volumes in one of the smaller rooms of the hotel.

In later years, Mrs. McWhirter would confess that she could have made a great deal more money if she had wanted to work harder on her investments. However, in 1899, the group decided to shut up shop and get shut of Belton. A search party had found the right location for them—Washington, D.C.—and they were anxious for the older members to enter semi-retirement and the younger members to have a more stimulating environment. They sold all their Texas property and bought a large house at 1437 Kennesaw Avenue for $23,000 cash, spending ten thousand more for renovation. This was all paid in cash, as Mrs. Mc-Whirter was dedicated to cash transactions as one of the bases of her success. It was rumored that sales of the Texas property had netted the group about a quarter of a million dollars. No men followed the group from Belton, though they did bring one black hired man with them, as he had been in their employ for a great many years. They told an interviewer that men simply did not enjoy their harmonious lifestyle, and that no man had ever stayed longer than nine months because "they want to boss," but "they find they can't." An article in a 1901 Washington newspaper was headlined "A Happy Home Without Husbands," and described them as selling little messes of food to the neighbors, keeping a few cows, and waiting for it to be revealed to them what their next big project would be. Members of the group frequently appeared in the galleries of Congress, and they permitted themselves various amusements. One of the members was now said to be a physician; the dentist was still there; another made and repaired shoes; others were milliners and dressmakers—though all still dressed in simple attire. They taught their own children, including two grandchildren and one great-grandchild of Mrs. McWhirter. The youngest, a boy of three, was reported to be able to "gravely lisp the signs of the zodiac." They called themselves the Woman's Commonwealth.

On April 21, 1904, Martha McWhirter died on the communal farm in Maryland. Though it had been predicted that the group would die with her, it held together until the death of all the original members. In 1908, a daughter of one of the members ran off to Philadelphia to marry a young man and was written up in the newspapers. In 1918, some members were reported to be still living on the Maryland farm.

The values of this group, their apparent contentment, and their success, give the lie to many of the myths and rumors that spread about them both while they were alive and in later years. Magazines are still reprinting an obvious falsehood by a Belton townsman who claimed to have witnessed an attempt by Mrs. McWhirter to fly from the roof of her house with a feather-duster in each hand. Other distortions include attempts to claim the Sanctificationists as Marxists (They were clearly capitalists.), feminist separatists (They were feminist, perhaps, but not in the modern sense, and they did admit men.), and so forth. I expect them to be written up soon as foremothers of the New Age Aquarian Conspiracy, and their way of thinking together justifies this idea, too, though their life-style was rather strait-laced. It has been pointed out by Dr. Harriet Andreadis that they were an "historically reasonable phenomenon"—a coalescence of the movement toward women's benevolent societies, Wesleyan Methodism, experimental communities, and let us add capitalist expansion and the availability to white women of new economic niches. They are unique in the annals of women's history, and the most amazing thing about the Sanctificationist legend is that it is true.

NOTES

1. The major bibliographic sources for this article were George P. Garrison, "A Woman's Community in Texas," in *Charities Review*, v. 3, no. 1, Nov., 1893; Eleanor James, "Martha White McWhirter (1827–1904)," in *Women in Early Texas*, ed. Evelyn Carrington, Austin, Pemberton Press, 1975; Margarita Spalding Gerry, "The Woman's Commonwealth of Washington," *Ainslee's (Magazine)*, Sept., 1902; and Frieda Werden, "A Sanctificationist Time Line," unpublished document, Texas Foundation for Women's Resources, Austin, 1980.

AUNT DICY
Legendary Black Lady

James W. Byrd

Legends touch upon the whole spectrum of folk culture, and folklorists have long been aware of the difficulty of describing the legend, a "capricious genre."[1] An appealing definition is one by Friedrick Ranke: "The folk legend is a popular narrative with an objectively untrue imaginary content. It is printed in the form of a simple account as if it would have really happened."[2]

Legends, it has been said, are based on some bit of factual or of historical truth. That applies to the legends of Aunt Dicy, as does another old saying, "Legends are the bearers of the early tradition of a people." There is, it seems, only a shadowy line between legendary figures who have come down to us as part of a people's folklore and the imaginary creations of a group of writers whose characters have acquired a legendary quality (from Rip Van Winkle to Paul Bunyan, from Uncle Remus to Aunt Dicy).

Legendary figures, famed by Anglo-Saxons in song or story, are "historical or semi-historical figures distinguished from everyday people by either their physical prowess, exceptional skill, or ethical superiority." So begins the discussion of most folklore dictionaries, and they follow with a list of "heroes," not heroines. A study of the works of J. Mason Brewer, the greatest black collector of black folklore, shows that these dictionary definitions (and examples) may be too limited.

Once upon a time in Texas, all Negroes knew who Booker T. Washington was, and all snuff dippers knew who Levi Garrett was. Garrett's product, "the best snuff in the world," was more widely distributed than Washington's product, education. Thereby hangs a tale worthy of introducing an unlikely legendary black woman from the unlikely place of Dime Box, Texas, in Brewer's second folklore book, *Aunt Dicy Tales* (1956).[3]

> *One Sunday . . . Aunt Dicy read an article in an Austin newspaper announcing the fact that the great Negro leader, Booker T. Washington, principal and founder of Tuskegee Institute, Tuskegee, Alabama, was scheduled to speak at Woolridge Park, in Austin, on the next Friday night.*
>
> *Aunt Dicy and Uncle June had heard about Booker T. Washington and his great work, so they decided to go to Austin and hear him speak. When they reached the park where Mr. Washington was scheduled to speak, the crowd was already seated and nearly all of the seats were occupied. But Uncle June finally found two seats vacant near the back of the audience and he and Aunt Dicy sat down. Shortly after they had taken their seats, Booker T. Washington, his secretary, Emmett J. Scott, the mayor of Austin, the members of the City Council and a few Negro preachers mounted the platform that had been built for Mr. Washington to speak from. After the singing of the Star Spangled Banner by the audience and the offering of prayer by one of the Negro ministers, the mayor rose and introduced Booker T. Washington.*
>
> *The subject of Mr. Washington's address was "Great Americans and Their Contributions." He mentioned George Washington, and his contributions to the country; Abraham Lincoln, and his contributions to the country; Benjamin Franklin, and his contributions to the country; Jefferson Davis, and his contributions to the country; Sam Houston, and his contributions to the country; Thomas Edison, and his contributions to the country, John D. Rockefeller, and his contributions to the country; Frederick Douglass, and his contributions to the country; and many others.*
>
> *After Mr. Washington had finished his speech, the crowd, Uncle June among them, applauded so much that the great Booker T. Washington had to take several bows. But Aunt Dicy did not join in the hand clapping. So Uncle June turned to her and said, "Dicy, how come you are not clapping for Mr. Washington like everybody else? Didn't you enjoy his speech?"*
>
> *"Humph! No, I didn't," replied Aunt Dicy. "He ain't said nothing about Levi Garrett—he wasn't nobody's fool" (p. 54).*

That (in a shortened tale) is Aunt Dicy Johnson, heroine of *Aunt Dicy Tales*, the second book by J. Mason Brewer, a black Texan who gained world attention with *The Word on the Brazos: Negro Preacher Tales* (1953). She was praised and promoted in reviews by J. Frank Dobie and Roy Bedichek, but it was a female Austin reporter who saw Aunt Dicy for what she was—"an authentic Negro Folk heroine." Ms. Lorraine Barnes wrote in *The American-Statesman*:

> Aunt Dicy Tales . . . *may fill a void in American literature by giving it an authentic Negro folk heroine. Oddly enough, while the folklore of the country has produced such popular heroes as genial Uncle Remus and powerful John*

Henry, the Negro matriarch—so much a fixture in the rural life of the South— has never been typified effectively.[4]

Oddly enough, Brewer's sister, Dr. Stella Brewer Brooks, wrote *Joel Chandler Harris: Folklorist* (Athens: University of Georgia Press, 1950), a volume which made Uncle Remus an acceptable folk hero for Blacks in America (Harris wrote for white readers.). Ms. Barnes, in her column "Reporter at Large," correctly prophesied the arrival of a female in the same heroic mold. She wrote:

Brewer hopes, and believes, that Aunt Dicy of Dime Box, Texas, is going to catch on people's thinking. She is the compelling Reconstruction Era person- ality around whom his work centers, various episodes in her life being Brewer's device for interpreting folk way, tales and beliefs connected with the snuff- dipping habit. Other characters—her family, her pastor, and her neighbors, black and white, who dwell in the vicinity of Dime Box and in Giddings—come to life in the magic of Aunt Dicy's storytelling.[5]

How did Aunt Dicy Johnson happen to become Brewer's greatest character creation? How was she born? Or had she, like Topsy, "jes' growed"? Brewer never said in the years that I knew him (1963–1974) while we watched *Aunt Dicy Tales* become his most sought after and expensive rare book (Only four hundred signed copies were sold.).

Aunt Dicy probably came into being while Brewer was collecting tales for *The Word on the Brazos*. One tale tells of the Sunday that "El- duh" Walker preached a sermon entitled "Who Can Go to Heaven" and encountered some opposition in the congregation. The concluding di- alogue, as Brewer records it, is an amusing comment on human nature. The preacher is in the midst of his strong sermon:

He say, "None of you liahs, you cain't git in." "Tell de truf!" shout Sistuh Flora. "None of you gamblers, you cain't git in," say de Elduh. "Speak outen yo' soul!" squall Sistuh Flora. "None of you whiskey drinkers, you cain't git in," say Elduh Waller, "Tell de truf!" shout Sistuh Flora. "None of you snuff dippers," say Elduh Waller, "you cain't git in," an' when he say dis heah, Sistuh Flora what got her mouf full of snuff rat den, jump up an' p'int her finguh in Elduh Waller's face an' say, "Wait a minnit, Bub; you bettuh say, not ez you knows of."[6]

This anecdote caused Brewer to mine a rich lode of folklore. Three years later, he published *Aunt Dicy Tales*; it contained fourteen "snuff-dipping tales of the Texas Negro." A tale similar to the above anecdote illustrates the difference, as well as the similarity, of the two characters. Aunt Dicy is the protagonist here, as the title suggests; and she becomes annoyed with her pastor. As Brewer concludes the tale,

. . . when Reverend Jackson got up to preach he started out as usual listing the kind of people who were going to Hell. "All you drunkards," he said,

"You're going to lift your eyes in Hell one of these mornings; all of you liars, you're going to lift your eyes in Hell one of these mornings; all of you gamblers, you're going to lift your eyes in Hell one of these mornings; and all of you snuff-dippers, too," he continued, "you're going to lift your eyes in Hell one of these mornings." And when Reverend Jackson said this Aunt Dicy jumped straight up from the bench she was sitting on and yelled, "Look ahere, Reverend, you've done stopped preaching and gone to meddling now." [7]

J. Frank Dobie, Brewer's patron in folklore (after Brewer abandoned an abortive avocation as a poet), reviewed *Aunt Dicy Tales* in the Austin, Dallas, and Houston papers, predicting accurately that "it will become a rare, rare item." He added, "Each of the fourteen tales is, in effect, an episode in which Aunt Dicy pops the whip at the end with a dip, a splatter, a pinch, or a bottle of snuff." More seriously he concluded that the book "is social history as well as folklore." [8]

Dobie's favorite tale was the last one in the book, "Aunt Dicy at the Heavenly Gates." Although Aunt Dicy's pastor, Rev. Jackson, suspected her tragic flaw, snuff dipping, when she was "funeralized" he preached her right into heaven "with the choicest angels" and predicted that the heavenly band would be very happy to have a good old soul like Aunt Dicy join them.

But when Aunt Dicy reached the heavenly gates and asked for admittance, St. Peter asked her who she was, and what she wanted. "I'm Aunt Dicy Johnson, a true and tried pillar of the Mount Zion Baptist Church of Dime Box, Texas," replied Aunt Dicy, "and I want to come in; you just look over the roll book and I'm sure you'll find my name there some place." So St. Peter got the roll book and began to turn its pages and look for Aunt Dicy's name. He turned, page after page, but was unable to find Aunt Dicy's name, so he finally turned to her and said, "I can't find your name anywhere in the roll book, so I'll have to ask you to leave."

"Now, hold on there a minute, St. Peter!", replied Aunt Dicy, "I tell you what you do; give me that roll book and let me see if I can't find my name listed there somewhere!"

"All right," said St. Peter, "Come on over here to the desk and look in the book, and see if you can find it!"

So Aunt Dicy got up out of the chair in which she was seated, walked over to the desk and started to turn the pages of the roll book. She turned, page after page, just as St. Peter had done for a long time, without finding any trace of her name, but finally, when she got to page seven hundred and seventy-seven she saw a name blotted out with dried snuff-juice all over it, so she turned to St. Peter and said, showing him the name that the snuff-juice had blotted out, "See here! This is me right here in this spot where this dried snuff-juice is" (pp. 75–76).

Roy Bedichek, a kinder and more generous man than his friend Dobie, wrote the foreword and, Brewer said, "offered valuable suggestions as to the best approach to the subject." In the foreword Bedichek characterizes Aunt Dicy as a strong and admirable woman, a heroic folk figure:

Although Aunt Dicy is a personality built around the vice of snuff-dipping, she has qualities which endear her to us. There is nothing negative, mealy-mouthed, or wishy-washy about her. She takes a stand and stands by it. She dominates each situation as it arises, while her one vice seems to throw her virtues into sharper relief.

For illustration, when her pastor, the Reverend Jackson, suspects her of snuff-dipping, judging from certain evidences he sees on the ground within spitting range of where she is standing, she laughs him out of countenance. She had been chewing up Hershey's chocolate bars, she explains between bursts of laughter, on doctor's prescription and had had to spit the vile stuff out on account of its evil flavor. But when the same "reverend" chose to preach a sermon against snuff-dipping and was consigning all snuff dippers to the nether regions, it was no laughing matter. Aunt Dicy jumped to her feet from the front row and shouted, "Look here, Reverend, you done quit preaching and gone to meddling now."[9]

Bedichek thinks it significant that she publicly criticizes the great Booker T. Washington "whose word was the generally accepted gospel. . . ."

Thus to take a stand for good and sufficient reasons and to maintain it against the mass—or herd-opinion, indicates that quality of character we call the "courage of non-conformity," itself a sign of spiritual strength. The "courage of one's convictions" is the basis, also, of the virtue of loyalty, so highly prized in its purer forms—i.e., unadulterated with self-interest—because it is so exceedingly rare.

Brewer could develop Aunt Dicy's character and be highly amusing at the same time. "Aunt Dicy in the Courtroom" and "Aunt Dicy's Train Trip" best illustrate this. Her visit to the courtroom came about when her son Pomp was arrested for shooting dice:

When the day came for the trial Aunt Dicy went to the Court House in order to pay Pomp's fine. As a general rule, when Aunt Dicy went to public places she always carried a paper bag with her to spit snuff-juice in after she had dipped it, but she was so worried about Pomp that particular morning that she forgot to bring a paper bag with her to the Court Room. So after taking a big dip of snuff and enjoying it she spit on the Court Room floor. One of Aunt Dicy's neighbors, named Bill Wilson, saw her spit snuff-juice on the floor, so he went over to where she was seated and said, "Aunt Dicy, don't you know it's a five dollar fine to spit snuff-juice on the Court House floor?"

"No! I didn't, Son," replied Aunt Dicy taking three "five dollar" bills out of an old handkerchief in which she carried her money, "so I tell you what you

do; take this fifteen dollars and give it to the Judge for me right now, 'cause I'm going to spit two more times before I leave the Court House" (pp. 41–42).

After Pomp got out of trouble about gambling, he ran off to Houston and got a job "as an engine wiper at the Southern Pacific round-house." He received a pass to ride the train free and sent it to his mother to come for a visit. Aunt Dicy had never been on a train but undaunted she packed a shoe box with chocolate layer cake and fried chicken and a straw suitcase with an outing flannel gown, two percale dresses, and her black satin Sunday dress. Thus prepared, she went to the station.

Aunt Dicy boarded the train, and shortly after it left the station she took out a can of "Levi Garrett" snuff and took a dip. They had spittoons on the train coaches at that time, since so many people chewed tobacco and dipped snuff. But Aunt Dicy had never seen a spittoon before. She didn't know what it was. Consequently when she got ready to spit her snuff-juice out, she spat on the other side of the spittoon to keep from spitting in it. Every time Aunt Dicy would spit snuff-juice on the floor the Negro porter would pick the spittoon up and put it in the spot where Aunt Dicy had spit last.

This kept up for a long time until finally Aunt Dicy called the porter over to where she was seated and said, "Look a here Bub; let me tell you something— you better take that thing and put it out of the way, 'cause if you keep on putting it over here close to me, I'm going to spit in it afterwhile" (p. 60).

In "Aunt Dicy and the Mailman," the one story that combines history and folklore (but firmly believed by Brewer, Dobie, and Bedichek, among others) proved to be controversial.[11] It also proves a point about legendary characters.

The first tale in the book tells of Aunt Dicy's independence after emancipation. She and her family moved from the old plantation (which had a store or commissary) to work a small farm way out in the country. The major hardship was having no place to get any snuff, and Aunt Dicy was making life miserable for herself, her husband, and her three kids.

This kept up for almost a month until one Saturday when Aunt Dicy was out in her front yard she looked down the lane and saw the mailman from Lexington loping his horse towards Mr. Schultze's mail box so she ran as fast as she could towards the mail box and reached it just in time to catch the mailman before he got back into his buggy and drove off.

"Mister, mister," said Aunt Dicy handing him a dime, panting and almost out of breath from running so fast, "Would you mind bringing me a dime box of snuff from Lexington the next time you come to bring the mail?"

"I'd be glad to, Aunty," replied the mailman. So the next Monday morning when he came by the Schultze farm Aunt Dicy met him at the mail box and he gave her the box of snuff she had sent for.

Every Saturday, from that time on, as long as Aunt Dicy lived on the

Schultze farm she would meet the mailman and give him a dime to bring her a dime box of snuff. Everybody in the little community knew about Aunt Dicy's practice of sending for snuff by the mailman, so they called a meeting one night and decided to call the little community "DIME BOX OF SNUFF" in honor of Aunt Dicy. They shortened it later to just "Dime Box" and to this day, this little community still goes by the name of DIME BOX (pp. 17–18).

John Biggers' painting of Aunt Dicy meeting the mailman was published with several reviews; in Austin, it met with "scholarly" refutation. An unnamed Austin woman told the *American-Statesman* that she doubted the story of Aunt Dicy and her dime box of snuff "being the legendary practice that inspired the naming of the community in the eastern part of Lee County." She quoted the following paragraph from *Texas Towns*, a "complete compilation of nomenclature" published by Fred Massengill in 1836.

Before there was a post office in this section early settlers erected a community mail box on the road to San Antonio and the freighters would pick up mail for a service charge of a dime for each round trip, which was from one to four times per month. When petition for the post office was sent in, Dr. R. H. Womack requested it be named Dime Box, that the old community mail box be not forgotten.[12]

Lorraine Barnes refutes Massengill's story by quoting another "legend" (with other names) from the then current *Handbook of Texas*. If Dobie had been asked, he would have told them that the Aunt Dicy tales are as true as most folk tales. "Facts" have a way of becoming elaborated and obscured in oral tradition. By the time Brewer heard it, a legend attributed to earlier figures had been associated with Aunt Dicy. The tale added a historical and geographical dimension to an already legendary figure.

Tales about Aunt Dicy fit Brewer's belief that folk legends must have historical longevity and geographical spread. Brewer's volume illustrates historical longevity, while geographical spread can be illustrated with an out-of-state example from Tennessee, one of the parent states of Texas. John T. Scopes, the central figure in the famous "monkey trials" of 1925 (on the teaching of the theory of evolution in Tennessee schools), tells of visitors during the trial in Dayton, Tennessee, seeking entertainment at a black church.

Each person testified as the spirit moved him. One heavy-set woman suddenly and spiritedly erupted with a homily on "those old snuff-dipping womens." She went on for several minutes, verbally flaying her targets.

The testifying amazed the sophisticated urban newspapermen. The worshippers were getting worked up. Shouts rang out: "Glory be to God! Glory be to the Lamb!" Some became incoherent.

Suddenly the testifying woman stopped short in her denunciation of the fast, snuff-dipping women, as though she had run out of breath. As visitors

gaped through the window the kerosene lanterns flickered, casting grotesque shadows inside as the circle of Holy Rollers swayed and moaned. The big woman turned abruptly toward the nearest window and aimed a monumental spit of snuff juice. Bystanders scattered frantically, some of them jumping too late to miss being splattered by amber spittle.[13]

Though unnamed, there stood Aunt Dicy, practicing her only vice, all virtue else.

Many readers who were not black admired this legendary character. Brewer received letters like this one from U. T. Professor of History Carlos E. Castañeda, dated November 19, 1956;

Aunt Dicey, with her inseparable snuff dipping, is the seer, the wise counselor and the caustic commentator of her day, who distills with her tobacco juice the essence of common folk philosophy, exalting common virtues and condemning petty failings.

J. Frank Dobie wrote to Brewer's sister after she published *Joel Chandler Harris: Folklorist*: "Uncle Remus is by far the richest and most outstanding folk character that America has given the world. People interested in American folklore, particularly Negro folklore, will be grateful [to this creator]."[14] One could not use such hyperbole with Aunt Dicy, but she is the one black old lady in folklore who can be compared to Uncle Remus.

Brewer went to great personal expense to publish the tales because he felt that a legendary character was being recorded who represented the flesh and spirit of rural Texas Negroes, a folk heroine of all the common black old ladies. Aunt Dicy unburdens herself with the robust wit and common sense typical of an alert woman of the people. As Langston Hughes wrote, "The snuff-dipping stories are repositories of both Negro soul and wit." Aunt Dicy's vivid reality on paper achieved the dimensions that have earned her comparisons to Joel Chandler Harris' Uncle Remus in folklore and Langston Hughes' Jess' Simple in black literature. Negro *soul* is steadily revealed by this folk character who is the womanly equivalent of Hughes' Negro "Everyman."

Aunt Dicy Johnson is indeed a legendary figure in American folklore. For every Afro-American there is much in her to love; for every American there is much in her to learn.

NOTES

1. Dan Ben-Amos, ed., *Folklore Genres* (Austin: University of Texas Press, 1976), p. 93.

2. Friedrich Ranke, "Grundfragen der Volkssagenforschung," *Niederdeutsche Zeitschrift fur Volkskunde* 3 (1925): 14.

3. J. Mason Brewer, *Aunt Dicy Tales* (Austin: privately printed, 1956). Four hundred copies, numbered and signed, were printed and bound in leather. Elaborate art work by John T. Biggers would make the book too expensive to republish. Some

copies sell for over $100.00 today. Page numbers from this volume will be given after each quote in the text of the article.

4. Lorraine Barnes, "Reporter at Large," *The American-Statesman*, September 27, 1956, p. 4.

5. *Ibid.* Brewer makes a legend of the naming of Dime Box. Ms. Barnes admits that it may be controversial. She writes.

Dimes and a box had something to do with the naming of Dime Box, that's for sure. According to the Handbook of Texas, *the Lee County settlement was known as Brown's Mill and the postman, one John Ratcliff, used to shop for the settlers for a fee of 10 cents per errand. The money was deposited in a box in the neighborhood store.*

Later on, when the town got a post office, Brownsville objected to the name Brown's Mill as obviously too similar in sound if not in spelling, and so, the Handbook *relates, the people chose Dime Box. The present community on the Texas and New Orleans Railroad is really New Dime Box, about two miles away from the original site. Biggest recent doings in Dime Box (pop: 350) occurred in 1944 when the National March of Dimes was kicked off right there.*

6. J. Mason Brewer, *The Word on the Brazos* (Austin: University of Texas Press, 1953), p. 85.

7. *Ibid.*, p. 46.

8. J. Frank Dobie, undated clippings.

9. Roy Bedichek, "Foreword" to *Aunt Dicy Tales*, pp. ix–x.

10. *Ibid.*, p. x.

11. See f.n. 5.

12. Undated clipping.

13. John T. Scopes and James Presley, *Center of the Storm: Memoirs of John T. Scopes*, (New York: Holt, Rinehart and Winston, 1967), p. 96.

14. Book jacket, Stella Brewer Brooks, *Joel Chandler Harris: Folklorist* (Athens: University of Georgia Press, 1950).

First Chance   Last Chance

Miss Tille Howard
307 South Utah

Gems   Fine Cuts

REMEMBER- The Alamo-
The Maine-
ME-
PEARLE
HARBOUR!

Main-41   El Paso

Calling cards circa 1900 & 1943. Madame Etta Clark.
"Lovers All": Chippa, Edna, Kate, & Rosie, Alice Abbott's employees.

Oval: Madame Alice Abbott, recipient of the "Public Arch" award/1886.

EL PASO MADAMS

H. Gordon Frost

On assuming office, one of newly elected President Franklin Delano Roosevelt's first actions to stem the country's rampant financial woes was to recall all gold coinage. The citizens were given a deadline by which they were to exchange their gold for silver-backed currency, and lines of treasure-holding Americans became a common 1933 sight in banks throughout the nation. In El Paso, a bored teller at one of the city's largest financial institutions looked up from his neatly stacked columns of the sun-god's tears and recognized his next customer, one of the town's leading madams. In an attempt to alleviate the monotony of his job, the teller jokingly referred to the two bulging leather pouches being carried by the madam. "Well, Faye," he quipped, "it looks like you've been doing a little hoarding."

Lifting the heavy sacks to the teller's cage, the madam replied matter-of-factly: "Yep, I whored this bunch and my sister whored the other."[1]

While the above-related anecdote might bring a smile to the reader's face, it does serve to illustrate two undeniable facts: first, as long as men live, they will always be interested in womanly charms, purchased at whatever price is required. The second fact illustrated by the "hoarding" anecdote is that, as in all other western cities, prostitution was a major industry in early-day El Paso. "Sin was a business, like shoes and real estate," writes historian C. L. Sonnichsen. "The city government for many years made ends meet by demanding payoffs from prostitutes and license fees from gamblers, money which paid the salaries of the policemen who kept the girls and gamblers in line."[2]

It is highly probable that without the prostitute the west would never have been "won," for there was a dearth of so-called respectable women who had the fortitude to accompany their men in the early stages of the western movement. Many of those wives who chose to dare destiny with their husbands did so out of a sense of marital duty rather than one of adventure. Without available women, most hard-living frontiersmen would have battled the elements and fought savage Indians in an attempt to gain the silver and gold treasures of the mountains, then return to New Orleans, St. Louis, and Chicago where, for a price, they could prove their masculinity. On the other hand, though, the availability of prostitutes in western communities took care of the sensual needs of the adventurers, leading many of them to eventually settle down and form the nucleus of many of today's major cities.

Once referred to as the "greatest whore in the west," Sarah Burgett was the first prostitute/madam-of-record to appear on the El Paso scene. Attaining fame for outstanding bravery under fire during the Mexican War, this massive camp follower gained the sobriquet of "The Great Western." Standing over six feet tall, she caught the lustful eye and erotic imagination of many a gringo soldier during the conflict. "You can imagine how tall she was," wrote George Washington Trahern, "she could stand flatfooted and drop these little sugar plums right into my mouth."[3]

While in Mexico, Sarah opened and operated the American House, a Saltillo-based brothel for Yankee soldiers in the area. On more than one occasion, Sarah was seen to have risked the fatal kiss of angrily humming enemy bullets to rescue wounded soldiers and carry them to her "house," which was used as a hospital by the Americans during nearby battles. Too, there exist eyewitness accounts of the Great Western's picking up rifles of fallen soldiers and firing them at the enemy, further endearing herself to the memories of the campaign's veterans.

Once, while applying for a job as a camp laundress, Sarah was told that military regulations prevented single women from accompanying soldiers on expeditions in the Mexican hinterlands. She would have to marry one of the troopers in order to accomplish whatever goals—patriotic or professionally passionate—she had in mind. "I'll marry the whole squadron and you thrown in but what I go along," she was reported to have responded to the startled officer who informed her of the rule. She didn't have to take this drastic measure, however, as one of the soldiers took her up on her offer to be the husband of the woman with the biggest "thigh" in the whole American army.

Leaving military life at the end of the Mexican War, Sarah arrived in El Paso in April, 1849. Merging assets with Benjamin Franklin Coons, she erected a restaurant-hotel-brothel in the Pass City. Combining concupiscence, cuisine, and cordiality, the Great Western achieved a measure of amatory fame, as reflected in letters of the period. Her partner stayed in the dusty village long enough to give the community a temporary name, Franklin, then went to California. Sarah left the area in 1850, then opened brothels in Yuma and Patagonia, Arizona. She died in

Yuma on December 23, 1866, and was buried with full military honors, reflecting the country's gratitude for services rendered *hors de combat*, and possibly, *combat des whores*.[4]

There is little documented information on prostitution in El Paso from the Great Western's departure until 1873. At times, though, the researcher is able to find whoredom referred to in nearby Fort Bliss records, such as the "release of female prisoner Lottie, sentenced to one week for venereous persuasions," in 1863, but mostly, this victimless crime goes unnoticed in southwestern annals for the period.[5]

The fact that prostitution was an established trade in early El Paso is evidenced in the city charter of 1873, when it decreed that the council had the power to "suppress and restrain disorderly houses, houses of prostitution or assignation. . . ." And, "to restrain and punish vagrants, mendicants, street beggars and prostitutes. . . ." Also, "to prevent and punish the keeping of houses of prostitution within the city or within such limits therein as may be defined by ordinance. . . ."

It is interesting to note that this latter section of the city charter provides for the establishment of an officially tolerated Red Light District in El Paso. Sanctioned or not, though, the girls began to come to the Pass City, and sex raised its ugly head along the north bank of the Rio Grande.

Pioneer El Pasoan George Look reminisced that around 1878 he was living in Johnny Doyles' saloon on Utah Street when a prostitute known only as "Slim Jim" died. Lumber was scarce, so Look donated wood from an old Organ Box for her coffin. He had purchased the box to make a door for his room in the rear of the saloon, but thought so much of the girl that he made the great sacrifice.[6]

The world came to El Paso in 1881, for it was in that year the railroads first entered the community. Along with those farmers, cowboys, merchants, and professional men who came looking for a better life were the denizens of the *demi-monde*: the gamblers, gunfighters, con-men, madams and whores, all anxious to make it easy for John Q. Citizen to indulge in his basest desires, no matter what they might be. El Paso soon became known as a place where "everything goes and nobody gives a damn," as one letter writer informed his brother in Philadelphia.[7]

The resulting influx of what Owen White referred to as "durable sinners" gave El Paso a reputation of tolerated lawlessness which would last well into the Twentieth Century. "It was said," writes C. L. Sonnichsen, "that New York, New Orleans, El Paso and the Barbary Coast were the four hottest spots in the United States."[8]

While the first prostitutes who arrived at the Pass laid the groundwork for future sisters of sin, it wasn't until Madame Alice Abbott came to El Paso that the classic bordello made its appearance in the southwest. Called either "Big Alice" or "Fat Alice" behind her ample back, she was the first of what has been referred to as the "Big Five": El Paso's most noteworthy madams.[9]

By the time Madame Alice arrived in El Paso in the early fall of

1881, the so-called Sporting Set had established South Utah Street—now called South Mesa—as that area where Sodom could meet Gomorrah and was able to raise Cain; where girls, guzzling, and gambling were the order of the day and night.

Alighting from the train, Big Alice looked around at the dusty village and decided that both men and money could be made in El Paso, then sent for her girls in St. Louis.

First establishing her brothel at 19 Utah Street, Alice settled for a two-story, wooden frame building that had a parlor and six bedrooms. Her house became well known as "Number Nineteen," and the madam prospered in the location for nearly five years when she moved to a more opulent, larger bordello at 202 Utah.

Alice kept a photo album which not only affords us with Victorian visages of vice, but allows the peruser to learn of her feelings about several prominent early El Pasoans. For instance, next to the picture of saloonkeeper George Roller, she penned in red ink: "King of the Texas Longhorns." John Selman, killer of the notorious outlaw, John Wesley Hardin, had a red "X" drawn across his groin, and the photo of rival Madame Etta Clark was captioned with what at that time was the ultimate of trade insults: "Hore to Niggars."[10]

Etta Clark, the second of the "Big Five," arrived in El Paso close on Alice's well-rounded heels. According to her photo, Etta was a good-looking, diminutive-sized madam. But what she lacked in height, Etta more than made up for in spirit. At first establishing her sex emporium in a one-story, four-bedroom, wooden-framed house at 27 Utah Street, Etta became Alice's chief competitor. Rivalry between the two women blossomed into extreme jealousy, and dirty tricks—including stealing each other's top performers—became commonplace.

On the evening of April 18, 1886, Alice stormed across the street to Etta's parlor house to retrieve busty Bessie Colvin, a former employee. Refused admission to the house, the six-foot meretrix hurled her 200-pound body against Madame Clark's door, smashing it open. Startled, Etta struck Alice with a flimsy gas lighter, but this only served to further enrage the seething cyprian, and she hit Etta, knocking the tiny madam against the wall.

Contemptuously sneering at her prone opponent, Big Alice then grabbed terrified Bessie by the wrist and began descending the stairs to the street. Screaming, Bessie vainly tried to resist her captor.

Meanwhile, Etta rushed to her bedroom, where she snatched her .44 revolver from the bureau drawer and followed the struggling strumpets to the stairs and fired. The shot missed Alice, but caused her to turn and face her assailant. Etta pulled the trigger once more and Alice fell to the dusty street, blood gushing from a bullet hole in the left side of her pubic arch. She was quickly carried to her bedroom for treatment of the serious wound, while Etta was arrested and charged with assault with intent to murder.

The *El Paso Times* reported the incident the next day, but a typographical error stated that Big Alice had been perforated in the "public arch"![11]

Alice survived the shooting, and after a lengthy trial, Etta was acquitted on grounds of self-defence.[12] The incident had almost been forgotten, when three years later, Alice, aided by several paid colored accomplices, burned Etta's place to the ground. Alice and her conflagratory conspirators were arrested and charged with the crime, but the case against them was eventually dropped due to the lack of incriminating evidence.

Etta rebuilt her brothel, locating it at 401 Utah Street. It was an impressive place: a three-story, 32-room brick pleasure palace. Photographs of the exterior and interior of Etta's bagnio, along with some of Madame Tillie Howard's sex emporium, were included in El Paso's 1901 Mid-Winter Carnival's souvenir booklets. Descriptions accompanying the pictures portrayed the houses as being opulently elegant, with the very latest innovations in furnishings, plumbing, and decor. The only known photo of Etta Clark's parlor bears this out, as it shows the large room to be equipped with both an elaborately decorated piano and organ, deep-pile Turkish rugs, flocked wallpaper, and gold-leafed, hand-carved furniture.

The third member of the Big Five, Gypsie Davenport, opened her large place in 1883. Apparently, Gypsie and Alice Abbott became fast friends, as they cosigned many complaints against rival madams for petty violations of the law. In most instances, the complaints were ignored, as the local police knew that, if any of El Paso's madams should be accused of peccadillos, La Belle Davenport would head the list, for the lady was full of tricks—in more ways than one.

Traditionally, most madams refuse to engage in commercial copulation with their "house callers," as they are too busy keeping things running smoothly. But Gypsie Davenport was one of the few exceptions to the norm, and was well known for her wanton willingness. Of course, the customer had to pay a premium for the madam's undivided attention, but according to those who chose to "buck the tigress," the extra investment was well worth it.[13] There were some of Gypsie's personal customers, however, who regretted their choice, as they became victims of the madam's infamous "morning after" scheme.

The "morning after" artifice consisted of Gypsie's getting a customer passout drunk in her bedroom, then removing most of her good furniture and replacing it with some that had been broken up. The madam would then add many empty champagne bottles to the scene, and when the hungover customer woke the next morning, she would present him with a greatly inflated bill for the "drinking and damage" he'd done the night before.[14]

May Palmer was another famous El Paso madam. In business from 1894 until 1910, May appears to have been one of the city's quieter madams, as there are few police complaints which mention her name. Like many of El Paso's brothel-keepers, May advertised her place, issuing crimson-colored calling cards to those who might be interested. Her cards bore the legend: "Madame Palmer's Gentlemen's Club, 309 S. Utah, Bell 142, El Paso, Texas."[15] No more than a dozen of the cards are known to still exist, hence are highly prized pasteboards of a passionate past.

In an effort to help control the redlight district's potentially explosive customers, El Paso's police department issued each madam a two-tone whistle which they were to blow if a man got too unruly. The police knew the madams liked to handle their own difficulties, hence when the bobby-type sound pierced the air, they responded immediately.

The most famous El Paso madam was the elegant Tillie Howard. Opening her first bordello in 1892, Tillie quickly established a community reputation of being a "respectable, sensitive, compassionate madam," who went quietly about the business of operating an orderly house. There are many stories connected with Tillie's many cats and kittens in the madam's carriage house in the rear of her San Antonio Street residence. Naturally, the neighborhood children referred to the happy place as "Tillie's cat house."[16]

Another pet-related story deals with a Mexican parrot that escaped from its cage. Tillie and her girls searched throughout the brothel but were unable to find the missing bird. They were forced to abandon the chase when the evening's business began arriving, and during the ensuing "action," the bird was forgotten. But the brightly colored cageling would not allow this to pass for too long. Selina Winston, Tillie's most popular girl-of-the-moment was vigorously entertaining an important customer when the man emitted a blood-curdling shriek and jumped to his feet. Holding his bloody derriere, the lacerated lothario looked about for his assailant but could find none. Selina hurried downstairs and told Tillie of the mysterious attack. The madam sent for a physician to tend the customer.

A bit later, Tillie and her girl nervously attempted to assuage the enraged customer while the doctor stitched the wound. As they were conversing, the parrot made his presence known when he waddled from Selina's bureau and squawked the only English phrase he knew: "Hey, Joe, wanna have some fun?"[17]

Tillie left El Paso in 1897 for Johannesburg, South Africa, where she ran a brothel for nearly two years. Returning to Texas' westernmost town with a fortune in diamonds, she had a copper-roofed bordello erected across the street from her first place. Possibly influenced by her European venture, the well-traveled madam named the new brothel the Marlborough Club, and ran it until her death in 1915.[18]

Tillie's death caused sorrow throughout the community. Those who patronized her place realized an era had ended: the city's newly found morality would no longer allow the refined casualness of bordello sex. Instead, the hoariest of professions was to be outlawed, its participants forced into dark alleys and hotsheet hotels.

Many of El Paso's more respectable citizens also missed the madam. The merchants could no longer count on Tillie's monthly purchases of hundreds of dollars' worth of beautiful gowns, perfumes and other items needed to maintain her brothel's reputation as the finest between St. Louis and San Francisco. Various church leaders would notice the lack of Tillie's generous monetary donations to their fund-raising drives, for she was always among the first to contribute to a worthy charity. And the children, of course, would lose the fun of playing in her "cat house."

Many El Pasoans dropped by the funeral parlor to pay their last respects to the madam. Among these were Bob Neil and Maury Kemp, prominent community leaders. Tillie lay in state in a six-thousand-dollar coffin which was much too large for her remains. Pillows were packed around her head, reminding Neil "of a man with a size 6½ head hid in a 7¾ size hat."[19] Kemp, an extremely successful lawyer, discovered the coffin had originally been ordered for a Mexican general, but it was rejected by the soldier's family as being too expensive. The undertaker tried to pawn the coffin off on Tillie's estate, and would have succeeded, except for Kemp's alertness. The lawyer quickly recognized this was a clear-cut case of the mortician's attempting to do to the madam in death that which she had made a profession of while living, so Kemp convinced the opportunistic businessman to bury Tillie in a smaller, less expensive casket.[20]

In addition to the lavishly appointed bordellos, Utah Street was graced with many small, one-story, two-room sin dens which were called "cribs." These were occupied by the lower-class whores, referred to as "crib girls." While the attractive prostitutes that worked in the brothels were able to charge from three dollars upward for a "trick," the crib girls received only fifty cents to a dollar for their amatory efforts. Strangely, though, the crib girls made more money in their humble surroundings than their fancier competitors. The reasons behind this fact were twofold: first, the customers were always of the "quicky" variety, not being allowed to undress or even take their shoes off. As a matter of fact, most of the crib girls had a piece of oilcloth placed across the bottom of their beds so the men's shoes wouldn't get the bedspreads dirty. By limiting their customers to the "quickies," the girls could service many men in a night's work. One ex-crib girl told this writer that, on some pay days, she had as many as fifty soldiers, and the other girls were just as productive.[21]

The second reason for the crib girls' financial success was low overhead, as their only expense was the weekly fifty dollar rent. They didn't have to buy fancy, expensive dresses, nor did they have to give a madam half of their proceeds. But the crib girl didn't have the prestige accorded the bordello beauties, and they missed the occasional big tip sometimes left by a satisfied "house player."

As long as prostitution was confined to a well-regulated area in South El Paso, the venereal disease rate was low. The girls were required to be checked by a doctor every week, who initialed their health cards which they had to display above their beds. The girls were "fined" from five to ten dollars per month by the city, and a policeman was assigned the job of going to every brothel and crib to make the collection. Those who balked at paying were hauled off to jail, given a brief trial, then fined the monthly amount plus rather stiff court costs, which at least doubled the initial fine. It didn't take a newcomer too long to learn a good lesson in economics, and she soon joined her sisters in voluntarily adding to the city coffers.[22]

The heyday of prostitution in El Paso covered a twenty-year period, from 1885 until 1905. After 1905, a series of moral reforms swept the city and the tolerance of vice began to diminish. The redlight district boundaries were decreased during various city administrations, then, by 1938, totally eliminated. But the closings hardly inconvenienced the girls; they would either go across the Rio Grande to Juarez, Mexico, or spread out to various apartments in the city where they practiced their trade unchecked. Predictably, when the district was eliminated, the mandatory weekly venereal disease checkups were eliminated, and the rates of syphilis and gonorrhea soared.

With El Paso being the site of a major military training area, the two World Wars brought a flood of whores to the city. Attempts by civil and military authorities to eliminate prostitution were, at best, marginally successful. If the young soldiers couldn't find commercial sex in El Paso, there were the Juarez prostitutes who were always available. Many El Pasoans still remember Juarez-bound streetcars overloaded with our nation's finest patriots, bound for "Boy's Town," laughing, whistling and shouting in anticipation of the events to come in El Paso's sister city.

During the Second World War, the venereal disease rate at nearby Fort Bliss became so high that the base commander made it mandatory for all military personnel returning from Juarez to get the sometimes painful and always embarrassing prophylactic treatment at one of the international bridges. One evening in 1944, the commanding general, his staff and their wives were returning from an elegant banquet in the Mexican city when they were stopped by a military police corporal who absolutely refused to allow the party to reenter the United States until the officers had received the ordered treatment. Reminding the general that, according to the order, there would be no exceptions, the corporal was adamant in following his orders. After arguing in vain, the commander and his staff finally agreed to have the required treatment. It is reported that their wives were convulsed in laughter all the way back to the base. The sheepish men could only grin sickly like the gentlemen and officers that congress had declared them to be.[23]

Like their predecessors, the prostitutes of World War Two often advertised. One rare calling card from the period has the Statue of Liberty emblazoned on it, with the phrase: "Remember the Alamo/ Remember the Maine/ Remember me: Pearle Harbour/ Main 41/ El Paso, Texas," printed therein.[24] The phone number was that of the Mansion House, a brothel located at 306 West Overland Street. The building, currently being used as a low-income apartment house, is El Paso's only former whorehouse still standing, the others being razed over the years to make room for such community improvements as gas stations, banking facilities, and vacant lots.

Professional passion at the Pass of the North still exists, of course, but pay-for-play sex has changed greatly since the days of the "Big Five" madams. El Paso's elegant parlor houses, seamy cribs, and Redlight District are but faded memories for a few old-timers, and these, too, shall soon be gone. The cheerful call of "company in the parlor, girls," has been replaced by the sounds of a decaying slum area. Those streets where ostrich-plumed madams once proudly drove their fancy horses and buggies now teem during the daytime with rattletrap cars and trucks adding their cancerous breath to the polluted atmosphere. At night, the scene shifts to the fearful cries of gang violence and *sotto voce* drug transactions. But more than this, society's attitudes of tolerance and understanding of innate human nature have been forgotten, being replaced with stone-casting hypocrisy and cynicism. Man often uses the cliche, "the good old days," but ignores its true meaning: a time in which people were genuine, their needs simple, and there was no obsessively destructive passion for so-called "progress."

NOTES

1. R. E. McNellis, interview, August 20, 1979.

2. C. L. Sonnichsen, *Pass of the North* (El Paso, 1968), 277.

3. El Paso Journal, December 31, 1974, 4. Sarah Borginnis was also known as Sarah Bourgett.

4. Ibid.: S. M. Buchanan (ed.), "George Washington Trahern," SWHQ, LVIII (July, 1954), 84.

5. El Paso County Deed Records, Book B, August 27, 1863, 234–382.

6. George Look, *Reminisces*, June 13, 1909, MS.

7. Jim White to H. B. White, July 13, 1885. Original letter in possession of HGF.

8. Sonnichsen, *Pass of the North*, 277.

9. Ibid., 287.

10. Alice Abbott's photo album in possession of HGF.

11. Sonnichsen, *Pass of the North*, 289.

12. "The State of Texas versus Etta Clark," April 27, 1886. Original holographic trial transcript in possession of HGF.

13. O. C. Dowe, interview, December 22, 1970.

14. Sonnichsen, *Pass of the North*, 291.

15. Calling card in possession of HGF.

16. Sonnichsen, *Pass of the North*, 301.

17. R. R. Deason, interview, April 20, 1957.

18. Ibid.

19. Robert Neil, *Reminisces*, MS.

20. Ibid.

21. "Ruby," interview, April 10, 1978.

22. Ibid.: Pete Leyva, interview, March 14, 1978.

23. Ibid.

24. Calling card in possession of HGF.

EARLY 20TH CENTURY

The famous rolltop desk/1926. Inaugural gown.
Jim and Ma in Austin. Home.

PARDON ME, GOVERNOR FERGUSON

Maisie Paulissen

Miriam Amanda Ferguson's inauguration as Governor of Texas on January 20, 1925, suited her to a "T." The whole scene was Texas-elegant. The platform upon which she sat was decorated with bunting, the band was playing her campaign song "Put On Your Old Gray Bonnet," and the words of the song were being sung by an operatic soprano in a very high-brow way. Down below, the people that were on her side were milling around their parked Fords and farm wagons in anticipation of the swearing-in ceremony. As Miriam Ferguson's secretary, Miss Gladys Little, said about her, "Mrs. Ferguson was always perfectly groomed,"[1] and today, on her inauguration, she was decked out in a black satin suit trimmed with chinchilla fur, and, like gilding a lily, a fluffy ivory feather boa hung around her neck. Above her face, which she kept stony so as not to smile, and above her curly brown hair that she had controlled with pomade, she had set a large-brimmed black hat covered with bird feathers.

Miriam Ferguson was the first woman governor of Texas, but to her disappointment, she was the second lady governor of the United States. Wyoming had jumped the gun on Texas by inaugurating Mrs. Nellie Tayloe Ross as that state's governor only fifteen days before Mrs. Ferguson's ceremony.

Now in her forty-ninth year, "Ma" Ferguson stepped forward. Her nickname had been invented by Frank Gibler of the *Houston Press*, who, writing her campaign stories, shortened the name "Miriam Amanda" to "M.A." But she never did like the name, saying that it "didn't suit her dignity."[2] She looked down, still not smiling, at the crowd of cotton farmers, working men, and business friends who shouted up pleasantly the campaign slogan, "Me for Ma, and I ain't got a dern thing against Pa!" "Pa," that is, James Edward Ferguson, had been elected governor of Texas in 1914 and again in 1916 but had been impeached from office in 1917 and legally barred from holding office in the state; he sat beside her on the platform within touching distance, occasionally leaning over to whisper something in her ear, something for her to do or not to do.

She spoke loudly enough to be heard and simply enough to be understood by even the least educated of the "common people" who made up her audience. She said that she freely admitted her inexperience in governmental affairs and, while in office, would ask the advice and counsel of "others." Most people in the crowd understood that by "others" she meant her husband, Jim. But testimony to the contrary by those who knew her, insists that Miriam Ferguson was not merely her husband's shadow, his stand-in, but an individual person in her own right, a quiet woman who only pretended to be pretending that she was Governor of Texas. In reality, she really was the chief executive of the state, some said.

During the campaign Miriam Ferguson had not been offended by her husband's heavy-handed treatment of her, because she had been in on the joke. The two of them were putting something over on their political enemies. When her husband had been asked in Fredericksburg, Texas, what he thought about women's suffrage, Jim had answered, "If those women want to suffer, I say, let them suffer!"[3] And Miriam had set her face so the little lines around her eyes did not crinkle into a smile, because she knew as well as he that these German men wanted their women to stay in their places in the kitchen. As a matter of fact, each of the Texas voters felt as though he personally was in on a happy deception in electing the disenfranchised Jim by voting for Miriam.

When Miriam and Jim had appeared before a group in San Marcos, Texas, Jim had winked at his wife as he assured the crowd, "Don't worry, you'll get two governors for the price of one. I'll be carrying in the wood and water. I'll tell her what to sign and what not to sign."[4]

Moving back toward Austin from San Marcos, the Fergusons had sat through a commencement before she had risen from her place, stepped to the podium, and announced, "My husband will make the speech." Then she had sat down, and that seemed to tickle the crowd. They had applauded and called out words of encouragement.[5]

Usually the pattern for these public appearances was that she spoke first, asking the mothers, sisters and wives of Texas to help her clear her family's name, which had been sullied by their enemies. She said that she was just an ordinary home-loving wife and mother and grandmother, and she ended her speech with this plea:

"A vote for me is a vote for my husband, who cannot be a candidate." When Jim got up to talk, he told the voters it was all right with him if it was his wife who was getting elected and not him: "If God's in his heaven and a Ferguson is in the Governor's Mansion, all's bound to be right with Texas," he said, and Miriam had nodded approval.[6] By using this method, a homespun housewife defending her husband's honor, the Fergusons managed to get both the newly franchised women of Texas and the men of Texas, still cleaving to the frontier ethics of the free-wheeling hero and jokester, on their side.

Midway through the campaign Miriam began to realize that she had a chance to be elected, and she enthusiastically posed for pictures of herself wearing a sunbonnet as a symbol of her days growing up on a farm. Then she went into her kitchen where all the materials for making strawberry jam were set before her, so she could represent a Texas housewife. She was even photographed stepping out the back door to sweep down the steps and then to feed her chickens. Throughout Texas other women who identified with "Ma" Ferguson put on sunbonnets as a sign that they were on her side. And Jim saw to it that the band played "Put on Your Old Gray Bonnet." Somebody else picked up the saying that the political contest between "Ma" Ferguson and the Ku Klux Klan's Felix Robertson was "the sunbonnet pitted against the hood"—or, "a petticoat against a bedsheet." The Fergusons represented the everyday Texan and his wife to the voters rather than the shadowy, hate-filled Klan member who was out to get somebody, who might happen to be the voter himself.

"Ma" defeated Robertson in the primary and went on to defeat the Republican, University of Texas Professor George C. Butte, in the general election, although William Hobby's *Houston Post* pointed out that "Many will vote for Ma Feguson, but no one, not even the editor of the *Chronicle*, will vote for her because he thinks she is more capable than Dr. Butte."

In some respects Miriam Ferguson had been dominant over her husband from the moment the two had met back in Bell County; while he had been very poor, she had been something of an heiress in a down-to-earth Texas fashion. Her father, Joseph Lapsey Wallace had died, leaving his family a legacy of cash, bank stock, land, and cotton gins. At the time of her father's death, Miriam's mother had called in a lawyer to help her settle the estate. And who should this lawyer be but young James E. Ferguson, who was a nephew of her father's first wife? Jim Ferguson always told his wife afterwards that he fell head over heels in love with "the little curly headed girl four years his junior." The two saw each other frequently, "always properly." Miriam, who knew the difference between right and wrong, had seen to that, she had explained later.

The man whose chair had been placed on the platform within touching distance of hers listened as she delivered her brief inaugural address. She had moved into the Governor's Mansion with him in 1914 and stayed on with his re-election in 1916; she had accepted the honors with humility, not changing anything she found in the mansion, with the exception of the greenhouse which she had built on the south side to house the flowers she loved to grow and to decorate with when she had parties. When he had been impeached by the legislature on September 25, 1917, she had said nothing at all but moved back home and kept house as she always had.[7] When he bent over to whisper to her, she could see his wide black suspenders over a diamond embossed white shirt underneath his black alpaca suit; he wore a black string tie at his neck and in his lap lay a wide-brimmed black "city-man's" hat. One of Jim's friends describes him as "slow moving and deliberate except when his temper got him."[8] On the other hand, the Ferguson's daughter, Dorrace Ferguson Watt, when comparing her mother and her father explains, "Daddy was the soft-hearted one. Mother wouldn't forgive so easily. She wanted things done right, and if you didn't do things right, then she was against you."[9]

It was Jim who had pursued Miriam during their courtship. She had a pleasant life in the Wallace home in Belton. Her father had indulged his children with everything his money could buy in a pioneer community, heaping upon them the Central Texas luxuries of a tutor when they were small and a log cabin education in a school in Salado. He had even sent his daughter Miriam to college, the Baylor Female College in Belton in 1898.

On the other side of the tracks, Jim had struggled through his young years. When his enemies wanted to say unkind things about him, they said he was an unworthy son of a worthy father: Jim's father had been a circuit-riding Methodist preacher before his death when Jim was five years old. The hard times that befell the Ferguson family at the father's death brought out two sides of Jim: his hard work on a cotton farm gave him understanding for underdogs, and yet, he learned to use his cunning to bolster his career in a rugged world. Ferguson told his daughter Dorrace how his mother used to give him a gun and three shells and "he'd better bring back a squirrel." His mother did not want him to be just hunting around in the woods for pleasure. She wanted him to kill a squirrel and bring it home for the family to have a meal.

By the time Jim Ferguson had returned home to Belton from working in odd jobs across the country and after he had managed to pass the bar exam from studying in borrowed notebooks, Miriam Ferguson was comfortably settled in the Wallace home. She had grown up, as she put it, "in an atmosphere of culture" and indulgence. When Jim Ferguson asked her to marry him, she quickly turned him down. But he pursued her, and after several months of his persistence, she consented, marrying him on December 31, 1899. He never forgot that he took her from the comfort of her home. He never got over the awe of the prize he had won in this intelligent girl from a rich family and always conceded to her that she was superior to him both in education and in breeding.

And in Miriam's breeding, her family background, can be found the clue to her character which gave her the courage to be the first woman in Texas to serve as Governor, the endurance to survive the humiliations that arose from scandals attached to the Ferguson family, the self-confidence to ride out the folklore which described her as the ignorant wife of a trickster governor engaged in nefarious activity. In *Texan Who's Who*, under Miriam Ferguson's name, is the entry: Member of the United Daughters of the Confederacy and Daughters of the Republic of Texas. Membership was earned for her when her grandmother and grandfather settled on the banks of the Little River in Bell County during the last days of the Republic of Texas, and when their son, her father, at the outbreak of the Civil War, served in the Confederate Army, returning only after Lee's surrender. Miriam described her father as a "steady, God-fearing person, the type that is the backbone of a nation," a phrase which can be applied to her character. She believed that when duty beckoned her, when her husband needed her, she must, without tears or complaint, answer the call. As her daughter Dorrace comments, "When Daddy asked Mama to run for governor, I suppose she just thought she had to."

In his *Texas: The Lone Star State*, Rupert Richardson writes, "During the second Ferguson era (1925–27) reform took a holiday."[10] Everybody in Texas, even the Fergusons' friends, passed on stories about the bribes that Governor Miriam was accepting in exchange for pardons that she granted state prisoners, and everybody told stories about how the governor had loaded all the state agencies with "friends of the family." "Ma," whom her enemies accused of being "dominated from the bedroom," appointed her husband to the Highway Commission, and he made the most of his position. Governor Miriam later named the accomplishments of this administration as taxing gasoline for highway improvements and taxing tobacco for school financing, but more importantly, because of her temperance beliefs, in putting through a more strenuous bootlegging law. She even tangled with the prestigious Amon C. Carter of the *Fort Worth Star Telegram*, demanding that he resign as chairman of the Board of Directors of Texas Tech College in Lubbock because he had been seen imbibing liquor, in fact "as drunk as a biled owl," at a Texas-Texas A&M football game. Carter answered the lady governor's order with his refusal to resign.

"Ma" ran for governor because she thought she had to, and she stood by her husband, because that was what she thought a wife was supposed to do. When she became governor herself, she remained steadfast against serving alcoholic beverages, no matter on how many state occasions she entertained. Neither did she allow swearing or card playing; she did put up with her husband's smoking a large cigar. In contrast to the talk spreading across the state that Miriam Ferguson was growing fabulously wealthy off the graft she was collecting from her position as governor, the Ferguson home was a quiet, straight-laced place, where the evening meal was put on the table at exactly six o'clock sharp, where the lady governor and her husband spent the evening, very often, with work they had brought home from the office, papers to be signed and decisions to be made. Dorrace remembers:

Everybody said my father was so fiery, that he must be terrible at home. But he was actually gentle and quiet. He said he didn't dare push his weight around with three women to buck him. But he did like things kind of routine. We did the same thing night after night. He'd come home from the Capitol at five— Mama had come home at three—and he liked to read and be quiet, maybe just sit out on the front porch and be still for a minute. We would eat dinner, and he'd sit around and figure. Do you know what I mean? Play with figures. He'd find out if he bought hogs at a certain price and then sold them at a certain price, how much the profit would be.

On the topic of her father's "figuring," Dorrace ponders that he might be "figuring" because he was wondering why he could never again make money as he had in Temple, Texas: "He used to tell us over and over, 'There was a period there—about ten years—when everything I touched turned to gold. I just couldn't keep the money from pouring in.'" And then Dorrace remembers her mother's point of view on the subject:

My mother was always saying that if my father had taken all that money people said he had, she wished she could see some of it, because my father never did have the money later on that he made in banking in Temple.

The Ferguson daughters—Ouida Ferguson Nalle and Dorrace Ferguson Watt—remember strict discipline at home, mostly from their mother. Miriam's rigid morals contrast with the more broad-minded Jim in the recounting of this incident that happened when the girls were growing up:

We really had all we wanted—more than was good for us, I guess—and we went to the Temple High School. That town had several good schools, and Ouida always could stir things up and she got this friend called Mattie Ann Locke, and all we heard was that girl. My mother finally said, "Well, who is this girl? Where are her people?" and Ouida answered, "They travel with a carnival," and that was the end of her with mother. Pretty soon we began to miss pencils and money and we suspected Mattie Ann Locke. Then one day Ouida had a particularly nice white sweater and she made the mistake of leaving it at school when she came home for lunch, and when she got back the sweater was gone. Well, Ouida knew she was in for some punishment when she got home, so she ran in and said, "I know Mattie Ann Locke did it. I know." Well, the next day she ran in again and said, "Now I really know. She dyed it black and wore it to school today." She was going to school and tell the teacher, but my father said, "No, don't. That girl probably needs that sweater." And my mother said, "Why, you're crazy. Do you want to condone dishonesty?"

"Well," he answered, "I don't think it's condoning if you just let her have it. She needs it."

"Why, I think this should be reported," insisted Mother.

"Buy Ouida another sweater," said my father, and that was the end of it.

The daughters had a ten o'clock curfew when they were living in the Governor's Mansion. If Ouida sat too long on the front porch with her boy friend, George Nalle, her father would pound on the floor above the porch with his shoe, and she would quickly say goodnight and run inside. Dorrace remembers that her Daddy didn't dabble with his daughters' boy friends; he believed in tending to his business about their friends, so long as they came home in good time. But Governor Miriam did like to find out all about the boys. "Mother liked every boy who ever came to call," says Dorrace. "She was not like other people her age. All the young men talked to mother. She liked young people. She liked them more than people her own age."

A strange phenomenon seems to have come over Miriam Ferguson after she had been governor for a while; she did not worry about running again but seemed to relish the political encounters. "She learned a lot," says Dorrace. "She got to liking it very much." Many people gossiped that Governor Miriam did not even go down to her office, but her secretary, Gladys Little, remembers that she always got down to the Capitol very early in the morning. Two desks were set up in her office, one for Governor Miriam and one for her "advisor and confidant," as she referred to her husband. She liked to have him sitting beside her, she explained to everyone who questioned the placement of the desks, because "she needed a little help." The highlight of the business conducted in Miriam Ferguson's first term of office, as far as she was concerned, was passing the Amnesty Bill of 1925 which restored James Ferguson's full political rights.

Nola Wood, who served Governor Miriam as a secretary, speaks of the confusion of having two governors sitting side by side. She says:

Lots of times on the pardons and things—on the commissions—he'd write a memorandum on there: "Issue so and so. Issue so and so." In his handwriting. Why, I wouldn't no more write that up than a thing in the world. Send me to the penitentiary. I'd just roll them back out and say, "Have Governor Miriam write the memorandum on these," and he'd write it out in pencil. The Governor Miriam would write the same words on there—but in her handwriting. I went through mental agony working for them.

Miriam Ferguson had learned that she must have a thick skin and not let ugly remarks wound her, especially the many stories about the Fergusons selling prison pardons. Probably the most famous story concerned the father of a convict who went to visit the Fergusons' farm:

The prisoner's father was out in the fields walking along with Jim, but instead of talking about a possible pardon for the son, Jim kept pointing out the different cattle he had raised. Then Jim showed him a broken-down mule standing by the fence, which he said he would sell for $200.
The visitor was shocked, "Why, I can't think about that now," he said; "how is that going to help my son?"

"Well," Jim answered, "if you buy that mule from me, your son can ride home from prison on it." [11]

Many versions of this story travelled the miles across Texas; sometimes the animal was a dried-up cow, and sometimes it was a bull, but selling pardons was always the point. The rumor was founded, in part, upon the fact that the whole Ferguson family appeared to be fascinated by the plight of the state prisoners. During Miriam's term of office, the family went together to visit Huntsville. Dorrace describes the afternoon:

Daddy just couldn't resist prisoners. It was a kind of pastime or hobby with him. He liked to talk to them and eat with them and get up close to them and hear their stories. After my mother was in office, the whole family went down to the penitentiary. Then it had a high stone wall around it and in the center of the compounds was a big oak tree where they had set up tables and chairs where some of the prisoners were to come and tell the governor their stories. The first thing my mother would ask each one was, "Well, what did you do?" Finally, my father took her aside and suggested, "Miriam, wouldn't it be better if you asked them what they were charged with?" And my mother answered, "If they hadn't done something they wouldn't be here. Every one of them says he didn't do anything. If they're telling the truth the place is full of innocent people."

There are, in fact, so many stories that one imagines a picture of the Fergusons preoccupied with prison projects—studying their records at night, listening to convicts tell their stories in prison, or, as in this story that Dorrace tells, eating a picnic dinner with the prisoners at Camp Mabry:

Daddy had a group of model prisoners taken out to clean up the grounds. After the prisoners got there, he sent home the guard and told the men they were guarding each other. We went out every night and had supper with them. My father said he wasn't taking a risk; it was a sure thing. Those men weren't going to let one of their members run away and lose their chances for pardons.

In addition to Governor Miriam's family, her office staff was also accustomed to fraternization with prisoners. Ghent Sanderford, secretary to Miriam Ferguson in her first term of office, describes the governor's modest office staff in 1925:

We were just five of us. When Jim and Miriam were Governor at the same time, they got $4,000—that was the both of them together. I was executive secretary, and I got $3,000. Ernest Franklaw was the chief stenographer. Mrs. Wallace was the bookkeeper and made $150 per month, and Mrs. Guinn made $100 a month. Then there was a file clerk named Hugh Green. We were all used to the governor's waiting room, lined with chairs, always filled up with visitors, many of them relatives of prisoners who had come to plead their cases. [12]

In fact, Ghent Sanderford remembers, on at least two occasions, the prisoners themselves escaped from Huntsville so they could come visit the governor personally.

The first was a man who came in to express his gratitude to Governor Jim, and this is the story:

During World War I two soldier boys killed a man. One got a short term. The other got 99 years, and he was in prison and had been there a long time. The farm superintendent called Jim; he said, "This man is a good convict. His father is very low. He wants ten days to go see his father in Indiana before the old man dies." "My God, a 99 year man?" replies Jim. "I'll take responsibility on myself," says the superintendent. Well, the man was up there five or six days and his daddy died. The man called Jim direct and said his mother needed him. He asked for a ten day extension, and Jim said, "All right." So one day, what do you know? On the way back from his home to prison that fellow stops by the office. Says he wants to meet the Governor and to thank him for letting him go home.

The other visitor's story was even more surprising to Sanderford, who remembers very well one May afternoon in 1926 when a young man came walking into the governor's office; it was exactly four o'clock, and "he was just a little boy, oh, I say 'little,' he was twenty-two years old. . . ."

He closed the door about four o'clock. The office was crowded. I looked up to see this sneaky fellow come in. "Are you the governor's secretary?" he asked. I said I was. "Can I come in?" he asked. Can anybody hear us talking? I'm an escaped convict. I ran off last night so I could talk to the governor about a pardon."

"Just sit down," I told the young man, and he did.

I went into Jim's office, and he asked me what kind of people were waiting to see him. I said, why, office seekers, hangers on—and, an escaped convict.

"Well, sir," said Jim, "that last one's the one I want to talk to."

The young man went in, and the two of them talked and talked. The people outside Jim's office got restless. I went into his office and found him still talking to the convict. "Can't you close this out?" I asked him.

"Just a minute," said Jim. He was writing down a message on a card that said: "To any peace officer in the State of Texas: The bearer of this card is an escaped convict voluntarily returning to the penitentiary. Please do not arrest him. signed J. E. Ferguson."

Jim gave the card to the convict and started talking to him. "If they stop you, show them this card and they are likely to let you go on. When they get you back they're going to whip you. You take it and straighten your record, and on the fourteenth, I'll grant you a pardon."

On June 14th Jim said to me, "You remember that escaped convict? Now it's the 14th. I haven't heard from him. Look through your papers."

Well, I found that boy's pardon written in pencil like hundreds of other pardons Jim had ready. So many of them I just began to forward them when I

*found them, sent them on to the Pardon Board. I sent that boy's pardon to the
Board that day. "That's a hell of a nice thing to do," I told Jim.*

*But Jim wasn't satisfied. He wanted the boy to hear from him that very
day. "Go wire the warden," he told me. "I want the boy to know I didn't forget."*

Besides the family's concern for the forgotten man in Huntsville,
the Fergusons' connection with pardons was definitely the result of an
acute shortage of family funds. Jim Ferguson had realized early on that
they could not live on the governor's salary of $4,000. As Jim explained
to his friend, Austin lawyer Jerome Sneed, "Being governor has played
hell with my income. Anybody who has a business that amounts to
anything can't manage it and be governor at the same time."

Putting the motives and the rumors together, the question inevita-
bly arises, "How guilty were Miriam and her husband of taking bribes
from relatives of prisoners in exchange for their release?" Lawyer
Jerome Sneed blames the scandals on "friends of the Fergusons who
were worse than enemies," and Dorrace Ferguson Watt agrees:

*You know what started all the trouble, don't you? Our friends. They'd try to get
money out of the prisoner, and they'd say: "Give me $5,000 and I'll give half to
the governor. She is a good friend of mine."*

Ouida explains that the pardoning situation was in an acute position when her mother took office in 1925 after Governor Neff's administration. Afraid of bad publicity associated with the governor's pardoning powers, he had pardoned only ninety-two prisoners in his entire
term. True to her campaign promises and to her own conscience, Ouida
says, her mother issued a number of pardons, many of them months
past due. "The lies began to fly over the state, lies that said Jim Ferguson was selling pardons." But no one made any accusations in print,
Ouida insists, for fear her father would sue him.[13]

The fact that her boss was so tender-hearted is stressed by the
secretary to Governor Miriam, Gladys Little. Miss Little, described as "a
loyal little person," by Dorrace Ferguson Watt, saw the pardoning crisis
building up as a result of her employers' sympathy for people in trouble. She recalls a waiting room crowded with supplicants pleading for
their relatives' freedom, wanting to tell the governors their heartbreak-
ing cases. She remembers sentimental little gifts brought to Governor
Miriam by these visitors. One gift was a patchwork quilt sewn by the
mother of a condemned man, a quilt with an elaborate pattern centered
by a glittering Star of Hope. She remembers a gift from a convict who
desired only that the governor would grant him a furlough to spend
Christmas with his family. As an offering this convict had constructed a
wooden house, fashioned so that, when plugged into a wall outlet,
perforations in the wood lit up, forming the words "Home Sweet
Home." Gladys Little remembers the "pitiful cases," especially a 300-
pound woman who had shot and killed her unfaithful lover and had,
consequently, been sentenced to die in the chair.[14]

Nola Wood tells a different story. In a taped interview she describes the Fergusons' motives as the opposite of those described by Gladys Little. Nola Wood does not remember sentimental little gifts; she remembers gifts of money—cold cash. She recounts one occasion:

This fellow come in with a great roll of newspapers under his hat, and I had a big vault—vault big as these rooms here—where all the pardons and the commissions were filed. It was fire proof there. And then, he'd come in there with these men and in a big newspaper like this with the money all spread out, spread out on a big table like that—the money—and they'd pick it out whatever they wanted, or give him whatever change. Dollar bills. I've seen them pick them up and the man take them or the man would give him a roll of bills and they'd check them out and spread them out—fives and tens.

Nola Wood does not remember the fat woman who killed her lover in a fit of passion; she remembers the convicts who came into the office after they were released:

I saw the fellows who got paroles—the "big boys." They'd come to the office like anybody else did. They'd come back to my desk lots of times. Stood there while I'd write their pardons, pick them up, and go to the Governor to sign them. I lost a lot of sleep over them. The things I knew just wasn't right. They was just crooks. Looked as good as you and I do. But they was just thieves and crooks; I knew them through the records I had. A few of them I knew of. I'd hear about them, but I can't think of any one of them right now. Read about them in the paper or heard lawyers talking about them or something. I've seen money passed.

During the time she served the Fergusons by processing the pardons coming out of their office she worried about her own culpability in the procedure:

When I'd write these pardons I'd wonder, well, did they get $400 for this or $10,000 or a hundred? Boy, I've seen—I had five in my vault back there that these people would give them. I had a special spot in my vault back there where they kept track of all the records. They didn't keep any record of the cash money they were given. They'd just put it in a basket and mark it "Personal." I had a place where I kept her personal things—his—her personal things. . . .

Nola Wood must have made remarks about not feeling right about handling these pardons, because Jim Ferguson found out about her qualms of conscience. Jim went to Ghent Sanderford and demanded that she be removed from her position, and Ghent tells the story:

A lady named Mrs. Wood, she worked for the Secretary of State, had two or three children. She made out the pardons and proclamations, and she would pass by my apartment with papers under her arms. Word came that Mrs. Wood was disloyal. At first I paid no attention, because I thought the world of this

woman. Jim told me I'd have to fire her, and it went all over me. I stood up and got bossy.

"You're not going to?" Jim asked me.

"I didn't answer, and I saw his lips get thin and pale, and he asked me, "Who's the governor of this state?"

"Neither one of Us are!" I answered.

Too many stories were on the tongues of too many people. Besides the pardoning rumors, Miriam Ferguson was further humiliated by an investigation of the Highway Department which involved accusations against her husband for receiving kickbacks on contracts, bribing officials, profit-sharing and ownership of a company which did business with the state. Perhaps to defy her detractors in the last weeks of her administration Miriam Ferguson freed 33 rapists, 133 murderers, 124 robbers and 127 liquor violators.[15]

In the election of 1926, Dan Moody, Governor Miriam's former attorney general, defeated her in the primary by 2,000 votes, and he was re-elected by the people of Texas to serve a second term in 1928.

Once again in 1930 Miriam Ferguson ran for governor of Texas, because once again her husband had been legally barred from holding office when the Texas Supreme Court declared the Amnesty Bill of 1925 unconstitutional. This time Miriam's adversary was Ross Sterling, a businessman, whom the Fergusons labeled a wealthy "road hog" trying to get rich off building highways with state money for the trucking and bussing industries. "Ma" lost to Sterling 384,402 to 473,371.

When she ran against Ross Sterling in the election of 1932, however, two Depression years had taken their toll on Sterling's image. Jim promoted his wife's candidacy with a new slogan: "Two years ago you got the opportunity to get the best governor money could buy; this year you have an opportunity that patriotism can give you!" Then Jim added a line that had been a winner in past elections: "Don't worry, folks, I'll be on hand to help Mama. I'll be picking up chips and bringing in the water!"

Ross Sterling answered, not very gentlemanly, that he thought somebody "ought to shoot Ferguson in the foot, so as to end the threat he presented to Texas politics every two years." Miriam Ferguson defeated Sterling and then went on to defeat the Republican candidate, Orville Bullington.

Miriam Ferguson found the state of Texas in bad shape when she came into office in 1933. A deficit of fourteen million dollars had accumulated, and when the Security Trust Company of Austin was forced to close its doors, the state's cash deposits were wiped out. State warrants had to be discounted and the interest on state bonds was declared in default. Facing near bankruptcy, the legislature reduced the salaries of state employees and eliminated whole departments for the purpose of economy. To avoid even greater disaster, Miriam Ferguson ordered the banks of Texas to close for "Texas Independence Week" on March 3,

1933. The banks were allowed to reopen later under very strict regulations established by the Texas Legislature.

The bank crisis of 1933 is described by Mrs. Ferguson's executive secretary, Ghent Sanderford:

The governor did a very unusual thing when she closed the banks. She admitted she had no authority, but it still worked. Every bank except two or three obeyed her decree. The situation was bad; fine black land in Dallas County couldn't be mortgaged for $10 an acre. Nobody else besides her would have taken such a chance. Bankers came down here from Dallas and Houston, told of the deplorable condition; people were drawing money out of our banks by the multiplied thousands. The governor had no authority. Jim studied it, though. And he made out a proclamation for Mrs. Ferguson to sign. It read: "Close all banks in Texas indefinitely." You understand, this really was unusual. Roosevelt didn't close the US banks until three days later. We kept everything very secret, but Miriam Ferguson set the pattern. I asked Jim, after I read the proclamation, "By what authority?" I was thinking that most official documents read: "By the power vested in me by the State of Texas," but Governor Miriam was not vested with this authority. "Well," Jim says, "You can go in there to my desk and read the proclamation." I read it and it was prefaced by these words: "I, Governor Miriam Ferguson, by virtue of the authority assumed by me, do hereby order all the banks in the state of Texas closed indefinitely." And they did—they closed for three days.

Miriam Ferguson surprised everyone by saying that she would not seek re-election in 1934. Her family had occupied the Governor's mansion for almost seven years, she said, and she felt the Fergusons had "enough honor for one family." Her stern, Old Testament morality is attested to by the verse she marked in the Bible which she presented to her successor, James V. Allred, which read: "And the most proud shall stumble and fall and none shall raise him up; and I will kindle a fire in the cities, and it shall devour all round about him." Jeremiah 50:32

As Miriam had always insisted, the Fergusons had not gotten rich off the State of Texas. After their years in office, the family was beseiged with money troubles, losing their ranch in Bell County and being hounded by the Internal Revenue Service which demanded money for back taxes. Miriam ran for Governor again in 1940 but was defeated by W. Lee O'Daniel.

The question most often asked about Miriam Ferguson—"Was she a governor in her own right?"—keeps arising. Some of the people who knew the Fergusons say she was just a figurehead—a rubber stamp, repeating the ideas of her husband. Some say, though, that she was an unsilent silent partner.

Roberta Roidde, who lives on the Bosque County Ranch which was once owned by the Fergusons, remembers "Ma" Ferguson as a quiet, reserved woman whose ranch house boasted "a porchful of beautiful flowers." She remembers that, when the Fergusons decided to give up the dairy business and the ranch house, Mrs. Ferguson called all the neighbors on the telephone giving her flowers away to them. On the other hand, Mrs. Roidde remembers Mrs. Ferguson in a less generous situation: the Lady Governor had offered to pay an old lady who did fancy handwork for a piece of crochet, but after receiving the piece, she would never give the old lady her money.

Nola Wood, secretary to both Governor Jim and Governor Miriam, insists that Governor Miriam "didn't know a thing about being governor":

Governor Jim did all the work. She didn't know anymore about it than you do. She was in the office most of the time, but she didn't know what it was all about. Because she'd never been in business in her life. Never been in a business office. Just to go down to his office in the bank. She'd walk in there, and he'd maybe give her some money. That's all she knew. But she was a good person and raised her daughters like angels.

Nola Wood says that the impeachment had made James Ferguson very revengeful, but as for his wife:

Poor Governor Miriam. She didn't know what was going on. She took it like you would if you didn't know anything. She never did act like she was sad about anything or that there was anything going on. She was just an ignorant woman; you've seen housewives that just cook and wash dishes and sweep the floors. That's all Governor Miriam knew. She didn't know what all that office was about. She had no more idea than she could read a letter and understand it. She was ignorant. She knew how to raise her daughters and keep a good house and a clean house, but that's all the woman knew.

James Thomas De Shields concurs with Mrs. Wood, describing Miriam Ferguson as a "model mother and housewife." He says, gallantly, that she is "cultured, refined and witty and has a happy way of dispensing courtly etiquette when required in State occasions and as hostess to the people of Texas."

However, Few Brewster's memories of the lady-governor when she was a neighbor of his in Temple are not so "courtly." Those were the days when a vegetable man used to roll his cart down the street and sell his produce to the housewives. Judge Brewster remembers Mrs. Ferguson coming to the door and cupping her hands to her mouth and yelling out, "You got any muskmellons?" and the vegetable man yelling back, "We ain't got muskmellons, we got wattymellons," and her answering, "Don't need wattymelons."

Perhaps the answer to the question of Miriam Ferguson's real role in public office is that "Ma" and "Pa" were really "just plain folks." Perhaps Jim Ferguson used his wife as an alternate of himself to legally stand in for him when he was disqualified from holding office himself. However, one cannot accept this picture of "Ma" as an "ignorant housewife" without hearing arguments on the other side of the case. Both

Ferguson daughters insist that Miriam was the stronger personality of their two parents. Dorrace's words are: "At home my father was meek as a lamb," while Ouida remembers, during her mother's first term of office:

In those days of prohibition the penitentiary was overflowing with short-term liquor law violators. Since Daddy had never been a prohibitionist, he naturally did not consider these violations a serious offense. However, it was a question that gave Mama considerable concern. She and Daddy often had heated arguments over cases they took home for review in the evenings.[16]

And Nola Wood, who in her testimony vacillates between her opinion that Jim was a "sweet person, a real sweet person" and that he was a "crook," says this about Miriam:

Governor Miriam was sweet, too. But she was high tempered. And she'd let Jim have it once in a while. She wasn't scared of him. He was like a little kid been spanked when she got on a tear; then he'd start being good.

However, the most conclusive evidence of Governor Miriam's capacity for making her own decisions occurred after her husband's death on September 21, 1944. Jerome Sneed, a lawyer and close friend of the Fergusons, gives Miriam Ferguson credit for Lyndon Johnson's successful race for the United States Senate in 1948.[17]

Sneed explains the history of the Ferguson-Johnson relationship, and its connection with Coke Stevenson and Archie Parr. When James Ferguson was on trial for impeachment in 1917 by the Texas Senate, one of the very few who voted against impeachment on every count was Senator Archie Parr of Duval County, his staunch friend. When Miriam was elected Governor in 1924, Archie Parr was still his loyal friend and remained so for the rest of the Fergusons' career. Another friend of the Fergusons was Coke R. Stevenson, who, beginning in 1938, had sought state office five times; in five of these campaigns he had the support of both the Fergusons and Parr.

In 1941 another political figure entered into Jim Ferguson's circle of friends. He was young Lyndon Johnson who had just been defeated in his race for a seat in the US Senate by Governor W. Lee O'Daniel. After his defeat Johnson visited Ferguson, who officed across the hall from Sneed, and told him that he held Ferguson responsible for his loss of the election. Ferguson, Johnson believed, had placed ads in newspapers all over Texas in support of O'Daniel, not because he was O'Daniel's friend but because he wanted his friend Coke Stevenson, then Lieutenant Governor, to be able to fill the governorship vacated by the successful O'Daniel. Johnson told Ferguson that he could not feel hatred toward him because, in 1933, Mrs. Ferguson, as Governor, had given Lyndon Johnson's father a position that the family had sorely needed. Johnson hoped that Ferguson could see his way to support him in the future.

In the years that followed the friendship between Ferguson and Stevenson became strained, and the two parted ways. Jim Ferguson suffered a long illness, and in September of 1944 lay in his Austin home on Windsor Road, dying.

Jerome Sneed picks up the story four years later, in 1948, when O'Daniel has decided not to seek re-election. Stevenson, Johnson, and nine other candidates file to run for O'Daniel's place in the Senate. Sneed says, "Miriam Ferguson decided to throw her influence to Johnson."

And here is Dorrace Ferguson Watt's explanation for Mrs. Ferguson's decision:

My mother was very bitter against Coke Stevenson, about the way he had treated my father; for one thing he wouldn't even come to my father's funeral. Before that, as my father lay terminally ill, he asked my mother to call his old friend Coke and to ask him to come over. And what do you think that old snake-eyed thing said over the phone? He said, "I understand Jim's lost his mind." My mother said, "He hasn't lost his mind as much as you think!" And then my mother said to herself, "I'll cut his throat some day."

Sneed's story continues:

The returns of the Senate race came down to a photo finish and the results hung in the balance for many days. At one point Johnson led by 717 votes, and at one point Stevenson led by 316 votes. The votes from Duval County, which had in the past heavily supported Coke Stevenson, came in now in favor of Lyndon Johnson. It was not corruption, as E. E. Haley's book One Texan Looks at LBJ *had suggested, that won Johnson the election. It was Miriam Ferguson's contact with the Fergusons' old friend Archie Parr, informing him of Stevenson's ingratitude to the Fergusons who had befriended him for many years.*

Miriam Ferguson—on behalf of her helpmate and companion of forty-six years—her husband—had swung a senatorial election for the future president, Lyndon B. Johnson. She was, as she boasted, a housewife, a mother and a grandmother. She really was a farm girl, but she was also a person of sturdy—perhaps noble—pioneer stock, who did what she had to, rising to the occasion of her election as Governor of Texas.

NOTES

1. Ed Kilman, *Houston Post*, November 12, 1961.
2. Billy M. Jones, "Miriam Amanda Ferguson," in *Women of Texas* (Waco, Texas: Texian Press, 1977), p. 163.
3. Interview with Dr. A. A. Gruisendorf, San Marcos, Texas, September 14, 1972.
4. Gruisendorf.
5. Interview with Mrs. James Marian Hall, Houston, Texas, March, 1976.

6. Jones, 165.

7. Interview with Nola Wood, Austin, Texas, December 21, 1977.

8. Interview with Jerome Sneed, Austin, Texas, March, 1964.

9. Interview with Dorrace Ferguson Watt, Austin, Texas, April, 1964.

10. Rupert Norval Richardson, *Texas: The Lone Star State* (New York: Prentice Hall Inc., 1943), p. 427.

11. Interview with Floyd S. Nelson, 1936.

12. Interview with Ghent Sanderford in the Littlefield Building, Austin, Texas, August 29, 1967.

13. Ouida Ferguson Nalle, *The Fergusons of Texas or Two Governors for the Price of One: A Biography of James Edward and His Wife, Miriam Amanda Ferguson* (San Antonio: The Naylor Company, 1946), p. 189.

14. Ed Kilman, *Houston Post*, November 12, 1961.

15. Pamphlet: "Do Such Acts of Fergusonism Assure Your Home, Your Sister and Your Friends Safety?" n.d.

16. Nalle, p. 189.

17. Jerome Sneed, an unpublished tract titled, "Precinct #13 Jim Wells County." n.d.

Posing during a family reunion, 1933. The favorite photograph of her and Clyde.

The least favorite photograph, the fabled "cigar moll" snapshot. oval: rare studio portrait, probably as a teenager.

"TELL THEM I DON'T SMOKE CIGARS"
The Story of Bonnie Parker

John Neal Phillips and André L. Gorzell

The American Cafe, adjacent to the old Texas Hotel on Houston Street, was only a block from the Dallas County Courthouse, and not far from the main business district. Due to the location, business was fairly good, particularly for an establishment operating during the Great Depression years of 1930–32.

Among the employees of the cafe was a waitress of particular interest. Trim and petite, the young lady stood just under five feet and weighed less than one hundred pounds. A stylish arrangement of reddish-gold hair complimented her friendly blue eyes. Possessing a quick wit and attractive personality, she was easily one of the most refreshing features that the American Cafe had to offer. Courthouse employees, businessmen, and secretaries frequented the cafe, and many of the men liked to flirt with her. The young waitress was usually wise to these advances, however, and could turn them to her advantage in the way of tips. Nevertheless her popularity was genuine and lasting.

Prior to her job at the American Cafe, she worked at Marco's Cafe on Main Street, in downtown Dallas, two blocks east of the Dallas County Courthouse. At a time when unemployment and disillusionment were epidemic, the location of Marco's was often the scene of transient milling. Jobless street people, growing in numbers, would hang around the nearby railhead and its warehouses, hoping for a day

of work. Word began to spread of a tiny waitress at Marco's Cafe that sometimes forgot to ask for payment for food she'd served to certain unemployed visitors to the restaurant. As 1929 wore on the street wanderers became more numerous and so did the apparent hand-outs from Marco's seventeen-year-old, soft touch waitress.[1] The cafe owner begged the girl's mother to ask her daughter to slow up on the free meals, or he'd have to fire her. Finally, she ceased her one-woman bread line, but the careening economy sent Marco's Cafe into bankruptcy and it closed that same year. It was at this time that the young woman moved on to the American Cafe.

A lunchtime regular at the American Cafe was a young postal employee named Ted Hinton. More than anything else about the American Cafe, Ted remembered the charming waitress rushing orders from table to table, chatting, joking and just generally making the day more pleasant for the patrons of the restaurant. It was not long before Ted grew extremely fond of the young waitress.[2] She confided that "she wanted to be a singer . . . or maybe an actress or poet."[3] When she was younger she had taken elocution lessons. Her instructor thought the child very talented and had encouraged her to act in a few school plays. However, for the present she would have to contend with the reality of trying to make ends meet. There were more customers to serve and more tips to be made.

It wasn't long, though, before she resigned from her job at the American Cafe to go on the road with a close friend and companion.

A few months later, Ted was offered a new job working for Dallas County. In the months that followed he found himself thinking fondly of the engaging, strawberry blond waitress from the American Cafe. It would be nearly two years before the two would meet again.

Early on the morning of May 23, 1934, Ted—now Dallas County Deputy Sheriff Ted Hinton—along with five other officers unleashed the contents of nearly a dozen automatic rifles, shotguns, and pistols into a nearby tan 1934 Ford V-8 Sedan. The car lurched forward, rolling down the Louisiana country road and into a ditch. Hinton rushed to the passenger side of the car, still firing his .45 automatic. He threw open the door and there, falling into his arms, was the delicate, bullet-riddled body of the popular waitress from the American Cafe—twenty-three-year-old Bonnie Parker. Slumped over the steering wheel to her left was her constant companion of two years, Clyde Barrow. As he caught her falling body in his arms, Hinton held Bonnie close, trying to stand her up, then laying her gently back into the car. Her red dress was blotched with a darker red. Her stylish hat, apparently shot away, lay on the back seat. Her pretty face was stricken and streaked with blood. Hinton turned away, sickened by the sight of such a young, vivacious person so violently destroyed. Yet he was relieved to see the end of one of the most legendary outlaws ever to roam the Southwest.

Years later Hinton related this story to journalist, Larry Grove: "Ted, who was not emotional by nature, got quite emotional when he told me about opening that car door and Bonnie falling into his arms.

He was very fond of her."[4] Many people had mixed emotions about Bonnie Parker. Her public image was that of Clyde's cigar smoking "bandit moll,"[5] an image she detested. On the other hand, she was seen as an adventurer—a victim of the time—merely stealing from and wreaking havoc upon those that many people felt were the true Depression era villains: banks, policemen, and the politicians who controlled them. An alternate fascination, as well as horror, surrounded Bonnie Parker. To the few who actually knew her well, she was only a sweet young girl who happened to be very much in love with the wrong man—Clyde Barrow. All of these differing feelings, opinions and fallacies have combined to make Bonnie Parker one of the most appealing and notorious legends in Texas history.

"Clyde's name is up, Mama. He'll be killed sooner or later because he's never going to give up. I love him and I'm going to be with him till the end. When he dies I want to die anyway."[6] Bonnie spoke these words to her mother on the Wednesday after Mother's Day, 1933. A few months later in July, 1933, nearly one hundred Iowa police and National Guard seriously wounded Bonnie and Clyde. They became separated briefly. She and W. D. Jones, a third member of the Barrow gang, hid in the grass. They heard more gunfire. Silence. Bonnie thought Clyde was dead. "My heart turned to ice. Nothing else mattered—my wounds— my leg—death—nothing. They'd got Clyde." She told W. D. Jones, "I wish I had his gun, that's all." Jones said, "You couldn't do any good with it." Bonnie said, "I could do all the good I wanted to do with it—I could kill myself. He's finished and I don't want to live."[7] A few minutes later Clyde appeared. Quietly they hugged each other and then, with W. D. Jones, they proceeded to vanish from their pursuers.

Almost a year later, on May 6, 1934, Bonnie's total acceptance of her impending, and quite probably, violent death became more apparent. In conversing with her mother she began a sentence with, "Mama *when* they kill us don't let them take me to an undertaking parlor, will you? Bring me home. . . ." Mrs. Parker said that at that point Bonnie smiled a funny smile, "as if she were a million years old, as if she knew things no one could know for centuries."[8] During the previous two years, Bonnie and the Barrow gang had shot their way out of eleven gunfights resulting in the deaths of ten police officers and two civilians. She had sustained multiple gunshot wounds and in a near fatal car accident suffered severe burns, making her an invalid for months. Two of the gunfights were among the most massive assaults launched by police in United States history. In Platte City, Missouri, July 19, 1933, the police attempted to barricade Bonnie, Clyde Barrow, Buck and Blanche Barrow, as well as W. D. Jones, in a small motel court. Despite being completely surrounded by some twenty to twenty-five law enforcement officials, the five fugitives quickly shot their way to freedom. In the process a police armored car, positioned in front of the garage to block escape, was shot to pieces. Just four days later Bonnie and her companions were again surrounded, this time in a park near Dexter, Iowa. An estimated one hundred armed men, including Iowa State Police, the

National Guard, and local farmers, approached the quintet. Buck, already seriously wounded from the Platte City fight, was fatally shot; Blanche, also wounded, surrendered; and Bonnie, Clyde, and W. D. Jones escaped once again, on foot.[9] Both of their cars had been destroyed by gunfire and the bridge leading out of the area had been wrecked by authorities. It is small wonder that newspaper reports of the day began referring to Bonnie and Clyde as the "Phantom Pair."[10] Near panic seized the Southwest. By April 1934, escapes by the pair were so numerous and spectacular that highway motorists were warned to heed *any* call to pull over or risk being shot at immediately by police.[11] Pat and Alton Askins recall, as youths in southern Oklahoma, radio broadcasts urging citizens to remain indoors—Bonnie and Clyde were at large!

Reported sightings poured in from all over the country. Newspaper journalist, Larry Grove, recalls that on one single day three gas stations had reported being robbed by Bonnie and Clyde. One station was in Iowa, one in West Texas, and the third was near Tyler, in East Texas. Said Grove, "Even as fast as they drove there's no way in the world they could have been in three places at once."[12] Such was public paranoia surrounding the pair.

Bonnie's conviction to remain with the one she loved was strong indeed. She lived constantly in cars and slept only when Clyde was awake to keep watch. During the winter months, their families would give them blankets to keep the two from freezing on some back road. She never abandoned Clyde despite the possibility of clemency. Police had said that if she had turned herself in and testified against Clyde, she would have been set free. Evidently, even Clyde himself had asked her to do this but she refused. Her intense love and loyalty were her motivation.

Bonnie was born in Rowena, Texas (near San Angelo), on October 1, 1910. Her father was a bricklayer. She was the second of three children. When she was four years old her father died suddenly and shortly thereafter her mother moved the family to Cement City (now a part of Dallas). Her upbringing seems to have been typically middle class, with nothing to indicate a tendency toward crime. Unusually precocious, Bonnie had a flare for scholastics and things theatrical. While attending Bryan High School she became City-Wide Spelling Champion, and she had received private speech and drama lessons from an early age. During a grade school play, Bonnie was cast as a little black girl. When a little boy pulled off her wig, exposing her golden hair during the performance, she got so mad she began to cry. Her makeup began to streak and drip from her face. The audience began to chuckle. She liked that so much that she began performing a series of cartwheels and somersaults. The show broke up in a riot of laughter. Thus Bonnie demonstrated her ability to make the most out of a bad situation.[13]

On another occasion during a Sunday school class Bonnie once again demonstrated her wit and knack for creativity. Each child was called upon to sing a hymn. When it came to be Bonnie's turn she stood up and began singing, "He's a Devil in His Own Home Town." The class was very amused, even though it wasn't quite the hymn everyone expected.[14]

Bonnie was a very popular child. She always had a surplus of boyfriends. They would compete for her attention by constantly showering her with gifts, particularly candy. Bonnie's satchel was always full of chocolates. Her popularity extended beyond her schoolmates. County politicians took Bonnie to political rallies apparently feeling that her presence was an asset. In a later time in Bonnie's life, some of these same politicians sought to bring her in, dead or alive. Bonnie's temper and sense of justice showed itself from time to time. On one occasion, Bonnie noticed her pencils disappearing. Pencils were expensive and soon Bonnie's mother began to get angry with her daughter over the inordinate amount of pencils lost. Bonnie, by this time, had begun to suspect that two sisters in her class were taking her pencils. Bonnie set a trap for the girls and caught them in the act. After school she confronted them and not only fought them off but also chased their older brother away.[15] As quickly as it started, the mystery of the disappearing pencils stopped.

Bonnie had a particular fondness for children. One afternoon, Mrs. Parker arrived home to find the house filled with babies. Sitting amongst the wriggling, tiny bodies were Bonnie and her sister, Billie. Looking up, Bonnie and her sister announced, "We've had a party and invited all the children in the neighborhood." A few years later, Clyde Barrow told Bonnie's mother, "Holdups were things Bonnie never did get to really care for, but the kidnapping racket is where she'd really thrive," he said wryly, "if all the people we snatched were one year old or younger."[16]

Funds were low for Bonnie at Christmas time, 1933. She was able to send but a small parcel of toys to her nieces and nephews. While Bonnie was out driving with Clyde, she saw a toy car on the lawn of a local residence. The two turned back, picked up the toy car and drove off. After a while, she looked down and asked Clyde, "How do you reckon that little kid will feel when he finds his car gone?" Clyde said, "I guess he'll feel pretty bad. I'll bet he'll cry. Hell—we'll take it back." (And they did.)[17]

Ironically, Bonnie was not able to have children herself.[18] Bonnie was not pregnant when she was killed. Despite public romanticism, the autopsy performed on Bonnie after her death, proved that she was not pregnant. The rumor, however, remains.

The most prevailing view of Bonnie was that of a cigar smoking, gun toting moll. Perhaps more than any other myth this one persists. To Bonnie, it was the bane of her existence! The image lives with us today. It all started after a gunfight in Joplin, Missouri, on April 13, 1933. Several rolls of film had been confiscated and handed over to a local photographer to develop and print. He made two sets of prints, one set for himself, the other for the police, to whom he also handed over the negatives. The snapshots proved to be a revelation to the

police, primarily due to the fact that only a minute number of people had actually ever seen Bonnie and Clyde. The photos were distributed around the country to law enforcement agencies. In one picture, Bonnie was alone. She is in front of a Ford V-8 with one foot propped up on the bumper, hips thrust out helping to support a large pistol in her small hand. Her face was frozen in a scowl, with bright sunlight causing her to squint. In her mouth was a large black cigar. The picture quickly exploded into newspaper headlines across the country. Above all else, this one photograph caught the public's fancy. For her to take up a cigar repulsed some, fascinated others, and fed fuel to the fires of her legend. The person that the photograph annoyed the most was Bonnie herself.[19] She was appalled at the attention the media gave to such a seemingly minute detail. Bonnie claimed that she never smoked cigars.

Ever since the notorious photograph was first published, its origin has been in dispute. As was mentioned earlier, the photograph originated from a roll of film confiscated after the Joplin, Missouri, shoot out. The police handed the film over to a local photographer who developed and printed the rolls of film. Dallas County Deputy Sheriff Ted Hinton claimed that the first generation of the photograph was not at all remarkable. It showed Bonnie in the same pose, except that in her mouth was a rose instead of a cigar.[20] Hinton claims that the photographer actually drew a cigar in place of a rose, rephotographed the first generation photograph and released it.

The second version of the story is Bonnie's. She told her mother that she did pose with a cigar in her mouth, but it was really Buck's cigar. The incident, according to Bonnie, was a joke, and a private one at that![21] Bonnie, who saw her mother often, asked her mother to please tell reporters that she did *not* smoke cigars. In the months to come, many cars would be stolen and abandoned by Bonnie and Clyde. They all contained large collections of newspapers and detective magazines with pictures and stories of the pair, but Bonnie never grew accustomed to the image which she felt was so contrary to her true personality. Clyde went so far as to write a threatening letter to Amon Carter, owner of the *Fort Worth Star Telegram*, taking him up on his pledge of truth in printing. At that time the *Star Telegram* printed a message in every edition which, in effect, said that anyone dissatisfied with his portrayal in one of its news items could ask for a retraction. The newspaper persisted in referring to Bonnie as the woman who smoked big black cigars. Clyde tore out the "truth in printing" clause, circled it and wrote "Read This." The accompanying letter said that he (Clyde) and Bonnie knew where Carter lived and if this problem continued they were "coming after him." The letter went on, ". . . I stick by her and she sticks with me." The letter was authenticated by police signature files.[22]

Despite her media image, Bonnie was devoted to her family. She visited Dallas frequently at a substantial risk to herself. These regular visits were interrupted only once for a five-day period after November

23, 1933. Dallas County Sheriff's officers nearly trapped Bonnie and Clyde in a shoot-out on (the then unused) Texas Highway 183, near present-day Irving Mall, in Irving. Bonnie was furious about that particular gunfight. Not because she'd been caught in a trap, but because her mother, as well as Clyde's mother and sister, were parked only a few feet away and could have easily been hit. It was midnight, pitch black, and the officers involved said they had no idea there was another car on that road. They were having enough trouble seeing the fugitives' car and avoiding the wall of very effective gunfire pouring from it.[23]

Bonnie kept in touch with her mother through the mail when unable to actually visit. Sometimes it was necessary to drive hundreds of miles to mail a letter, to prevent authorities from discovering their actual whereabouts. Just as they were sure that the postmarks on letters to the family were being closely watched, Bonnie and Clyde were sure that phone calls between family members were being monitored. A family code was established centering around Bonnie's favorite dish, red beans. The Parker family would spot a person in a car driving past the house, throwing a soda pop bottle in the yard. Mrs. Parker would take the bottle into the house, after appearing to all the watchful neighbors to be quite displeased at the littering of her yard. Once inside, she would read the enclosed message which usually stated a time and place to meet. Mrs. Parker would call the Barrow family and ask if they would care to come over that evening, she was serving "red beans." Everyone would arrive prepared to venture to some lonely road, like Texas Highway 183, or some high spot overlooking the terrain, like Chalk Hill in far West Dallas.

Bonnie's passion for red beans was such that one afternoon when Bonnie and Clyde were traveling down a dusty farm road Bonnie caught a whiff of the delectable dish. They stopped at the little farm house, went to the door and offered the lady of the house one dollar for a jar of her red beans. The lady kept insisting that the two fugitives come in for supper! The two feared that they would be recognized by some other family member so they raised the price to two dollars. The kind lady finally gave in and handed over a jar of her red beans for two dollars. Bonnie said that the woman had the most quizzical look on her face as they drove off. She would never know who the admirers of her cooking had been that day.[24]

Bonnie often missed her mother. She often found herself two or three states away, heading in the opposite direction from Texas, when the urge would come over her. "Clyde, I want to see Mama," and instantly the car would be turned around and speeding toward Texas. Occasionally she would bring a gift. Just before Easter, 1934, Bonnie purchased a white rabbit for her mother. It was christened "Sonny Boy" and he lived in their car until a trip to Texas was possible. The scene inside the car must have been incredible. Lettuce, carrots, pistols, shotguns, ammunition, magazines, license plates, and makeup, all being used as a nest by "Sonny Boy" the rabbit. Clyde complained that the bunny smelled, so he decided to give it a bath. "Sonny Boy" didn't

respond well to the grooming and fell into a coma, evidently developing pneumonia. Bonnie began crying quietly as she rode along with her very sick rabbit. As time wore on and the condition of the rabbit worsened, Bonnie's despondency deepened. She pleaded tearfully for Clyde to stop and help revive "Sonny Boy." This he did, building a fire to warm him up. After a while the rabbit responded and soon it was active and alert. In time they were all on the road again, en route to Dallas.[25]

On April 1, 1934, they arrived on a high hill near Grapevine, Texas, northwest of Dallas. The hill overlooked the northern and southern approaches of Highway 114. It was perfect for a family gathering. They pulled the car some distance from the road up on a grassy slope. An outlaw companion, Henry Methvin, was sent into West Dallas to inform the Parker and Barrow families. An hour or two later the messenger/companion returned. The three fugitives and Sonny Boy relaxed and waited for the two families to arrive. The conflicting stories begin at this point. One source has it that Bonnie was sleeping in the car with Sonny Boy.[26] Another report claims that Bonnie was swaggering, swearing and drinking as well as wearing a man's clothes.[27] Clyde claimed that *he* was asleep in the car and that Bonnie, wearing a red dress, was by the roadside playing with Sonny Boy.[28] Bonnie saw two motorcycle police slow as they passed. She picked up Sonny Boy, eased back to the car and woke Clyde and Henry. The police officers, by this time, had turned around and were heading back up the road. As they turned toward the parked car a fusillade of gunfire ripped them to pieces. An eyewitness claims she saw a man and a woman dressed as a man walk over to the two officers.[29] Another eyewitness claims that a woman dressed as a man pumped more bullets into the officers.[30] Clyde claimed that it was he and Henry Methvin who walked over to the bodies. Still another version of the story claims that it was not Bonnie at all, but her sister Billie Mace who walked over to the bodies. (The witness, a farmer named Scheiffer, had never seen Billie Mace before but she would nonetheless be arrested for the crime, despite an airtight alibi. It would be weeks before she was finally exonerated.) Bonnie, Clyde, Henry, and Sonny Boy made a hasty exit and drove to Southern Oklahoma. Within a week, on April 6, a police constable was shot to death and a police chief was kidnapped outside of Commerce, Oklahoma. The assailants included a red-haired woman with a rabbit. Here, as before, Bonnie took no part in the shooting, according to Clyde. In fact, Clyde indicated on more than one occasion that, unless the situation absolutely called for it, Bonnie would not take up the gun. On one occasion this attitude could have led to their capture. It seemed to Bonnie that the whole town of Okebena, Minnesota, had turned out to block their escape after a successful bank robbery on May 16, 1933. In particular, one fiery old man was in the process of trying to ram their car with a railroad tie when Clyde calmly handed Bonnie a pistol and said, "Honey, shoot him before he wrecks us." She made no move at all to thwart the man's attempts. Clyde veered sharply to avoid being struck. "Why in the name of God didn't you shoot him?" Clyde exclaimed, "It's a wonder we weren't killed!" Bonnie smiled, saying, "Why, honey, I wasn't going to kill that nice old man. He was white headed."[31] Such was the paradox of Bonnie Parker. A paradox which was reflected by the public. A police officer of the day said that for every person working to bring her in there were two or three people working to keep her free.[32] Official opinion was reactionary. Politicians and police were clamoring to put an end to the fugitives that were making constant fools of them. Throughout the month of April, 1934, following the Grapevine and Commerce shootings, Bonnie's name appeared in newspaper headlines almost daily. A media frenzy climaxed on May 23, 1934, when her death brought a flood of adulation to the six officers involved in the ambush. Letters and telegrams poured in from all over the world offering congratulations. A Texas politician, congressman Robert Kleberg, introduced a resolution in Congress commending the State of Texas for ending the career of "public enemy number one."

Starting in the mid-thirties, a series of movies began appearing that were loosely based on the famous Texas bandits. The earliest starred Henry Fonda and Sylvia Sydney as two bank robbing lovers who die in a hail of gunfire while whispering, "thank you . . . thank you for loving me." Clearly the sentiment is with the outlaws; however, beyond Hollywood fantasy, such a sentiment had some basis in reality. Even those directly involved with Bonnie Parker have had similar feelings. Mrs. Ted Hinton has stated that her late husband "thought the world of Bonnie" despite the fact that Ted was one of the six men who ultimately killed her. She also said that research on Bonnie Parker would reveal "a good, well-bred little girl with a good education. She just happened to fall in love with the wrong man." This feeling even extended to some of their victims, the most notable of whom was Police Chief Percy Boyd of Commerce, Oklahoma. After being wounded during a shoot out with Bonnie and Clyde, in which a fellow officer was killed, Boyd was herded into the fugitives' car and kidnapped. Not having bothered with introductions, Boyd at first didn't realize who his fast shooting, hard driving assailants were. Finally he recognized them and said, "I don't mean to be nosey but aren't you Clyde Barrow and Bonnie Parker?" "Yes," they replied. Boyd said they slowly began to strike up a conversation and soon were carrying on as if there had never been a shootout and a killing. Boyd added that he felt a warmth and attractiveness in Bonnie. He came to like his captors very much and apparently they liked him as well. He remembered seeing the white rabbit that Bonnie was going to give to her mother. Bonnie told Boyd all about her family and the two exchanged family photos. For fourteen hours the bandits and the peace officer laughed, joked, and enjoyed one another's company. Bonnie asked Boyd if he would deliver the rabbit to her mother if anything happened to her while he was in the car. He agreed. Bonnie dressed Boyd's wound and gave him a new shirt. When he was released in Kansas, Clyde gave him bus fare to get home. Boyd asked Bonnie if there was anything she would like him to tell the newspapers.

Clyde gunned the engine as Bonnie thought of a statement. Her face brightened with a smile, and as she and Clyde pulled away she said, "Tell them I don't smoke cigars."[33]

NOTES

1. Emma Krause Parker and Nellie Barrow Cowan, *Fugitives* (Dallas: Ranger Press, 1934), p. 47.

2. Larry Grove, interview April 2, 1980; Mrs. Ted Hinton, interview April 15, 1980; John W. "Preacher" Hays, interview April 20, 1980.

3. Ted Hinton, *Ambush, the Real Story of Bonnie and Clyde* (Austin: Shoal Creek Publishers, Inc., 1979), p. 8.

4. Larry Grove, interview April 2, 1980.

5. Quoted in several magazines and newspapers including *The Daily Times Herald*, Dallas, Nov. 23, 1933.

6. *Fugitives*, p. 164.

7. *Ibid.*, p. 196. (Bonnie and Clyde had a serious accident near Wellington, Texas, on June 10, 1933. A bridge was out and Clyde drove straight into a ravine. The car caught fire, burning Bonnie all over, especially her leg.)

8. *Ibid.*, p. 239.

9. Actually Parker, Barrow, and Jones were also wounded. In addition, Bonnie still could not walk because of the severe burns she'd received five weeks earlier in the Wellington auto accident. The trio swam a river and stole a farmer's car on the other side of the destroyed bridge.

10. *The Daily Times Herald*, Dallas, April 7, 1934.

11. *The Daily Times Herald*, Dallas, April 2, 1934.

12. Larry Grove, interview April 2, 1980.

13. *Fugitives*, p. 38.

14. *Ibid.*, p. 35.

15. *Ibid.*, p. 43.

16. *Ibid.*, p. 54–55.

17. *Ibid.*, p. 210.

18. L. J. Hinton, interview May 5, 1980. Mr. Hinton's father, Ted Hinton, saw the autopsy report on Bonnie Parker. She had had an operation which prevented conception. The autopsy also showed no pregnancy.

19. *Ambush*, p. 47.

20. *Ibid.*, p. 39.

21. *Fugitives*, pp. 150–159.

22. Webb Maddox, *The Black Sheep* (Quanah, Texas: Nortex Press, 1975), p. 32.

23. *Ambush*, p. 105; L. J. Hinton, interview May 5, 1980: Mr. Hinton's father said that when Bonnie (She was driving.) began to turn around and pull along side her relatives' car, her headlights blinded him and the other officers involved. They began firing wildly in the direction of the lights.

24. *Fugitives*, p. 159.

25. *Ibid.*, p. 229.

26. *Ambush*, p. 137.

27. John H. Jenkins and H. Gordon Frost, *I'm Frank Hamer* (Austin: Pemberton Press, 1968), p. 220.

28. *Fugitives*, pp. 229–230.

29. *The Daily Times Herald*, Dallas, April 1, 1934.

30. Jenkins, *I'm Frank Hamer*, pp. 220.

31. *Fugitives*, p. 164.

32. *Ambush*, p. xiii; L. J. Hinton, interview May 5, 1980; John W. "Preacher" Hays (former Dallas Deputy Sheriff), interview April 20, 1980.

33. *Fugitives*, p. 240.

GLAMOR GIRL CALLED ELECTRA

Frank X. Tolbert

Electra Waggoner Biggs, the world famous sculptor, should raise a statue in Electra on the town square for her remarkable aunt, Electra Waggoner Wharton Bailey Gilmore. Or perhaps the statue should be in the 4700 block of Preston Road in Dallas where Electra One made life exciting in the early years of this century.

Anyway, Electra town (pop. about 4,000) was named for the first Electra Waggoner.

Her father, W. T. Waggoner, owned a ranch of more than 500,000 acres which encompassed a supply village for the Comanche Indians from just across the Red River in Indian Territory. It was first called Beaver by Chief Quanah Parker of the Comanches, and then Waggoner for the cattle king. In 1902 the townspeople petitioned to have the post office's title changed to Electra in honor of the beautiful and popular cowgirl.

Electra was well educated—and willful. While on a world tour with her parents, she annoyed them by such an action as having a butterfly design tattoed on one of her shapely legs when they were in China. She was given a big ranch in Wilbarger County for a birthday present. She called the ranch Zacaweista, the Indian name for the tall grass that grew there.

By 1918 the Waggoner cattle kingdom was well planted in producing petroleum wells, as the half million acres in six counties still is today.

The first Electra was one of the first girls in Dallas to have a complete trousseau from Paris, which she bought before she was married to a Philadelphia socialite, A. B. Wharton. She was also Neiman-Marcus' first customer to buy $20,000 worth of clothes in a single day. Mrs. Carrie Neiman told me Electra came back the next day and got about $20,000 worth of other things she'd forgotten. And these were 1907 dollars, real dollars.

If you want to see where Electra lived in Dallas, drive by and take a look at 4700 Preston Road, an estate backing on Turtle Creek. Life then at 4700 Preston Road was just one big exciting party. Guests included socialites such as Ann Morgan, daughter of old J. P. Morgan, and politicians of the likes of Theodore Roosevelt, and New York matinee idols such as Lou Telegen and Carlyle Blackwell.

One of the most successful house parties started at 4700 Preston Road and wound up two hundred miles to the west at Zacaweista. On the ranch, the timing was just right for Electra's guests, mostly from the East, to watch an oil well gush with such savage force that it blew off the crownblock of the derrick.

Carrie Neiman told me that almost every day when Electra was in Dallas, Neiman's had orders to send out a large stock of dresses for the gorgeous cowgirl's selection. The dresses would have to arrive in the original packages from Paris or New York, for she refused to consider a dress that anyone had tried on.

Her dressing room was like a Neiman-Marcus stockroom. One long closet was hung with fur coats. There were usually 350 pairs of shoes in her shoe cabinet, and she had a new pair of shoes delivered daily either from Neiman's or from New York.

Electra One paid only about $200,000 for that great estate on Preston Road. You probably couldn't buy the gatehouse for that now. After buying the house only a year after it was built, she caused $100,000 worth of remodeling. And she furnished the place with $500,000 in art objects collected from throughout the world, including Persian rugs that cost $42,000.

On a hill in the eastern reaches of Decatur, Texas, there is a big house which looks like a Spanish castle. Electra One's father was building that house when she was born on the ranch near Decatur in 1882. She was named for a grandfather, Electius Halsell.

Electra One died Thanksgiving day, 1925, in New York City. She was only forty-three. Yet no one could say she hadn't lived life to the fullest.

Electra Two, Mrs. Biggs, the sculptor, now lives on and owns Electra One's beloved birthday present, Zacaweista Ranch.

Reprinted from the *Dallas Morning News,* Saturday, May 3, 1980.

THE BABE

Mary Kay Knief

Texas Foundation for Women's Resources

Babe Didrikson Zaharias is honored in at least ten halls of fame, she won eighty-two golf tournaments, and she was an Olympic track star, a superior basketball player, a topnotch baseball player, and an excellent bowler.

These general statistics give all the necessary support to the Babe Didrikson Zaharias legend. But this legend, like all legends, consists of much gilding. She was not a football player or a boxer, although she was always willing to pose for pictures with stars of those sports. She *was* better at kicking extra points than her high school friend assigned the task, but league rules kept her from playing. Both Babe and her sister Lillie denied that Babe ever played football other than touch-tag games as a kid. In the sports she did participate in, however, she excelled.

One book on "superstars" described Babe thus:

Babe Didrikson Zaharias tried almost every sport and succeeded at everything she tried. She led the Dallas Cyclones to three AAU national championships in women's basketball and scored 106 points in one game. She pitched for the House of David touring baseball team and once struck out Joe DiMaggio. She made a cross-country billiards tour and several tours with a pro basketball team. Handball, swimming, diving, lacrosse, football, even boxing—she did it all. Her best were track and field and golf.[1]

Even Babe didn't remember the encounter with DiMaggio that way. She remembered being booked into big-league ball parks to give golfing demonstrations before the games. Once at Yankee stadium, after completing the golf demonstration, she tried playing third base in infield practice and then started pitching. She went to the dugout and persuaded a shy Joe DiMaggio to come out and let her pitch to him.

All I was afraid of was that I might hit him with a pitch, or that he might hit me with a batted ball. "Whatever you do, please don't line one back at me!" I said to him just before I went to the mound. I did hit him right in the ribs with one pitch, although I don't think it hurt him. But I guess he was being careful about his batting. He skied a few, and then finally took a big swing and missed and sat down.[2]

Her goal, even before becoming a teenager, was to be the greatest athlete who ever lived. If she took up a sport and then was not allowed to play it competitively—which is what happened in tennis when she was declared a professional before ever competing in the game—she would not play that game again. She wanted to be in a position to compete and to win.

This love of competition drove her. And prior to her marriage to George Zaharias, a successful wrestler and promoter, the need for money drove her. She provided much of the support for her parents from her work and winnings.

And, of course, that drive paid off. In addition to all the events she won, she was named the Associated Press Woman Athlete of the year in 1932, 1945–47, 1950 and 1954 and the AP Greatest Woman Athlete of the Half Century 1900–1950. The male winner of this last award was Jim Thorpe.

The Babe was a tough kid who grew up in a neighborhood of tough kids. She learned to hurdle hedges as she ran down the street, and there is a story that she persuaded neighbors with nonconforming hedges to trim theirs to a level to match others on the block. Her hurdling style was affected by the natural width of the hedges throughout the time she competed in this sport.

She came from an athletic family, the sixth of seven children. Mildred Ella Didriksen (for her, it later became Didrikson) was born June 26, 1911, in Port Arthur. Actually, the date of Babe's birth is at question. Although all sources seem to agree it was June 26, the year is disputed. In her autobiography, Babe claims to have been born in 1914, and the official Texas historical marker at the entrance to her burial plot says she was born in 1914. In her application for the Olympics in 1932, she claimed 1913. In the early 1950's, she said she had been born in 1915, and once, in applying for a visa, she even declared 1919 as the year of her birth. Although there is no birth certificate on file at the Jefferson County courthouse, according to Johnson and Williamson in *"Whatta-Gal": The Babe Didrikson Story*, Babe's sister Lillie did have a baptismal certificate listing the date as 1911. Lillie said, "I went to a lot of trouble to get it right on the gravestone." The stone, only a few feet from the 1914 dated historical marker, says Babe was born in 1911.[3]

What difference does it make? Not much. But it does mean that instead of being a teenager, eighteen years old, when she became the world's sweetheart at the 1932 Olympics, she was, indeed, an adult of twenty-one.

Her father Ole had emigrated from Norway to Port Arthur in 1905 and had worked for three years before sending for his wife and three children. The family, ever growing, lived in a house Ole had built on Seventh Street until, on the day the seventh child was born, August 16, 1915, a hurricane hit the Gulf Coast, and the family watched their home fill up with water. Everything was lost, so they moved to Beaumont. The trolley line ran down the center of their street, freight trains rolled on the tracks at one end of the street, and the town's largest industrial complex was at the other.

Although the father never was able to earn a real living, this family was imbued with competitiveness. Babe said of her mother:

You could tell by the way she handled herself that she was a natural athlete. . . . I think that as far as athletics are concerned, I probably took after my mother. I understand she was considered the finest woman ice skater and skier around her part of Norway.[4]

Babe's brother Ole played on one of the first professional football teams in Texas. Louis was a champion boxer in the Texas National Guard. Arthur started out to be a professional baseball player but had to quit because of eye trouble. And it was sister Lillie with whom Babe always worked out as a youngster.

At first she was kept off the girls' high school basketball team because she was too small, but after practicing with the boys' coach, she did make the team. It was during a game with a Houston team that she was picked by Colonel M. J. McCombs to play with the Employers Casualty Company's Golden Cyclones of Dallas. Employers Casualty then gave her a job which she was able to come back to whenever she needed it. She left high school February 17, 1930, to join the team and scored fourteen points in a 48–18 victory the next night. On the train to Dallas she wore a dress she had made and won a blue ribbon for at the State Fair.

Despite the fact she was a seamstress, she was far from feminine. Chopped off hair and a lack of money for or interest in clothes, plus her athletic build, made her appear very mannish. When she was playing golf, Babe was five feet, seven inches tall and weighed 160 pounds. It wasn't until a friend took Babe under her wing after Babe became a golfer that she took on a softer appearance. She later declared she loved to be surrounded by feminine things in her home.

Nineteen months after leaving Beaumont and after competing in basketball and track and field for the Golden Cyclones, Babe was called the "ace of the local Golden Cyclones" by the *Dallas Morning News*, which also said she probably was "the world's outstanding all round feminine athlete."[5]

As a child she was known as "Baby" in her family and even at school, but it was when she began hitting home runs that she was nicknamed "Babe" after Babe Ruth. She credited the other kids in the neighborhood with giving her the name. Years later she played golf with Babe Ruth for a cancer benefit a few months before he died of cancer and a few years before she did.

The names "Super Athlete" and "Wonder Girl" came into use after she competed as a one-girl track team in the combined 1932 national amateur athletic track meet for women and Olympic tryouts in Evanston, Illinois. She scored thirty points while the twenty-two girl team from Illinois Women's Athletic Club came in second with a score of twenty-two.

Without returning home, Babe and the other women athletes went to Los Angeles for the 1932 Olympics. It was this setting, with nearby Hollywood and the hoopla and ballyhoo that attended events that included "stars," that set off the Olympics and helped create legends. Babe garnered more nicknames, including "Whatta-Gal," "Texas Tornado," and "The Terrific Tomboy."

At that time, there were only five Olympic events for women and no one could enter more than three.

On her first throw of the javelin at the Olympics, Babe broke the world record by more than eleven feet with a throw of 143 feet, 4 inches. Afterward she said her hand had slipped on the javelin during the throw which did not have the classic high arc typical of the event but skimmed the ground. Years later she said she had not warmed up properly that day and that she tore a cartilage in her right shoulder when her hand slipped.

In the eighty-meter hurdles, Babe and Evelyne Hall each won their heats in world record times. In the finals, both were timed at 11.7 seconds, another world record, and Evelyne had a welt on her neck from the tape. But Babe had thrown up her arm as she finished, something she had told Evelyne was the smart thing to do, and Babe was declared the winner after the judges huddled to make a decision. Forty-three years later, Evelyne Hall still believed she had been the winner that afternoon.

In the high jump, Babe and her chief competitor, Jean Shiley, cleared the bar at 5 feet, 5¼ inches. When the bar was raised to 5 feet, 6¼ inches, Babe sailed over with more than an inch to spare, but after she was in the pit, her foot hit a stanchion, knocking the bar off. The judge ruled a miss and Jean Shiley missed, too. The bar was moved back to 5 feet, 5¼ inches. Both women made it, but the judges ruled Babe had made an illegal jump by diving over the bar. This rule no longer exists, but at the time, the Western roll, where the jumper's head clears the bar before the rest of her body was not allowed. Jean Shiley was awarded first, the gold, and Babe was second. Babe felt cheated this time, both on the 5 feet, 6¼ inches jump and then at 5 feet, 5¼ inches using a jump she said she had used earlier that afternoon in competitions across the country.

Babe's return to Dallas was that of a hero. Ten thousand people were waiting at Love Field; the police department band played "Hail to the Chief"; she rode in the fire chief's open, red limousine; there were roses and thrown confetti. The people loved her; they needed heroes.

But her Olympic teammates did not love her; they hated her. They felt that she was too boastful, too arrogant, too full of practical jokes. They had prayed for Jean Shiley to beat her.

Writer Grantland Rice, her number one fan, described her after the Olympics:

She is an incredible human being. She is beyond all belief until you see her perform. Then you finally understand that you are looking at the most flawless section of muscle harmony, of complete mental and physical coordination the world has ever known. This may seem to be a wild statement, yet it happens to be 100 per cent true. There is only one Babe Didrikson and there has never been another in her class—even close to her class.[6]

Two years later she was pitching for the House of David baseball team, known as the boys with the whiskers. It was a real comedown for Babe. She would pitch a few innings before turning the job over to the regular pitcher. She didn't travel with the team. She would pitch, then get in her car and drive to the next town.

Early in 1933 she was given star billing in an RKO vaudeville show. She sang, ran on a treadmill, hit plastic golf balls into the audience, and played the harmonica—an eighteen minute show. She appeared for a week in Chicago and could have traveled with the show but decided she wanted to be outside and to play golf.

Babe had decided after the 1932 Olympics that she would become a champion golfer. The day after the high jump fiasco, Babe played golf with Grantland Rice, Westbrook Pegler, Paul Gallico, and Braven Dyer, all sports writers. Babe declared in her autobiography that she had never played golf before that day. She said she told Colonel McCombs ". . . how silly I thought it was for people to hit a little white ball and then chase it." And supposedly, on this day she had to have the club pro show her how to hold the club, and she did not know about teeing up the ball. However these stories got started, she had played golf in high school and in Dallas, and this was at least her eleventh match.[7]

Beatrice Lytle, Babe's high school physical education teacher, called Babe "the most teachable person" she had ever known. She was the person who first taught Babe to play golf, and she remembered that to be around 1927:

Those stories about her driving the ball two hundred and fifty yards the first time she swung a club or about shooting in the nineties her first round—they were just stories, they are not true. She could outdrive me after a while, it is true, but she never did beat me on the Beaumont course.[8]

Despite that, Beatrice Lytle kept the first set of golf clubs Babe ever used for their "historical value." Babe's score that day after the 1932 Olympics was ninety-five, according to Johnson and Williamson.[9] In 1955, Babe said: "A majority of my drives that day were between 240 and 260 yards. Of course, I had some bad shots in between. I've read since that my score for the round was eighty-six. Actually I think it was around 100."[10]

Babe was always one to practice, practice, practice. She practiced so much for her first tournament, the Texas State Women's Golf Championship in 1935, that her hands bled, but she won the championship. In her autobiography, Babe said, "I've always had the confidence that I was capable of winning out."[11]

The U. S. Golf Association declared her ineligible for women's amateur golf in 1935 but reinstated her in 1943. Her championships included the U.S. Amateur and Trans Mississippi Amateur in 1946; the North and South and the British Women's Amateur in 1947 (She was the first American to win.); the U. S. Women's Open in 1948, 1950, 1954; the Western Open in 1940, 1944, 1945, and 1950. And these are only some of the eighty-two golf tournaments she won. In the mid-1940's, she had a seventeen-tournament winning streak.

In 1949 there was a total of $15,000 in prize money for women golfers and that was from one company. In the first five years, the total Ladies Professional Golf Association prize money multiplied fifteen fold to $225,000. (Babe was a charter member of the LPGA.) In 1949 Babe was the leading money-winner with $4,300. In 1950 she again was the leader, with $13,550, and in 1951 she won $15,087, more than had been available two years before.[12]

Babe was a woman competing in sports when that was not considered by many to be the thing for women to do. Golf *was* more acceptable than most other sports, except, perhaps, croquet, because of its country club roots. Johnson and Williamson said, "Yet her era was unsympathetic to women and, as a female athlete, she was seen by many as a freak. She was insulted, ignored, laughed at."[13]

A campaign against women's sports was begun in 1923 by Lou Hoover, wife of Herbert Hoover, then Secretary of Commerce. The group was called the Women's Division of the National Amateur Athletic Federation. Their original plan was to eliminate elitism and see that every young woman had a team to play on and was not qualified only to be a spectator. But the idea became corrupted, trying to prevent any woman rising out of the "team-for-everyone-and-everyone-on-a-team" mode (They took a stand against women going to the 1932 Olympics.), disdaining businesses and churches that sponsored teams, and believing that exercising women should not be seen.[14]

So, while women had begun to become more involved in sports during the first part of the century, this open-mindedness was reversing when Babe was reaching an age at which she could compete. Had it not been for the Women's Division, women's sports probably would have grown throughout the century and purses might have equaled those in men's sports. Instead, women's sports just began in the 1970's to reach the level of popularity they had before the Women's Division's campaign, and the purses are still growing, still not matching those of the men.

Babe, herself, was testimony to some of the Women's Division's worst fears: ". . . Babe's association with those bands of vagabond ballplayers and the tough veneer she offered the world did nothing to advance her reputation as a respectable—or even an acceptable—model for young women of the day."[15] Babe said she had an advantage over other women athletes because she grew up competing against boys. She said girls need to get "used to being smashed around."[16]

Babe was not intellectually sharp, and in high school she did almost nothing but sports—volleyball, tennis, golf, baseball, basketball, swimming. Ruth Scurlock, an English teacher when Babe was in school and wife of the Beaumont paper's sports editor, said of Babe's high school days, "Her very excellence at sports made her unacceptable to other girls. She was an alien in her own land, believe me."[17]

One of the boys from the neighborhood reported that he got to know Babe on the sandlots, and she was the only girl there. She wasn't the last player picked for a team though, and she got to play shortstop or third base.

Once in high school a big football player stepped up to her, stuck out his chin, and said he doubted she could hurt him no matter what she tried. She swung once and he dropped to the floor, senseless—and he bragged for years about being hit by this famous woman athlete.

Someone more sensitive to people's reactions might have quit, but Babe had drive and she was tough. She also had a sense of humor. She loved to entertain. Although she only spent a week on the RKO circuit, she always was an entertainer. She loved the press, mugged for photos, and played to the gallery. Once, after a winning round at the British Women's Amateur in 1947, barefoot and wearing a kilt, she did a Texas-style highland fling on the clubhouse lawn. It was also supposedly at this tournament that, in response to a dignified man who asked her how she could drive the ball nearly 300 yards, she responded, "I just take off my girdle and beat the ball, sir."[18] Babe later claimed in her autobiography that this comment originated once when she was on stage with the chanteuse Hildegarde, who said, "Babe, I can't understand why I don't hit a golf ball as far as you do. It seems to me I swing my club the same way." And Babe replied, "Hildegarde, it's not enough just to swing at the ball. You've got to loosen your girdle and really let the ball have it!"[19]

But having a sense of humor and being tough could not prevent what was to happen to Babe. In April 1953 she found out she had cancer of the lower intestine and had to have a colostomy. She wondered what she had done to deserve this. She had been active in the fight against cancer, participating in American Cancer Society benefits. The year after her surgery, she went to the White House to join Dwight and Mamie Eisenhower in opening the 1954 annual Cancer Crusade.

And she came back in golf. Three and one-half months after the colostomy, she played in the 1953 Tam O'Shanter "All-American Championship." The first day she shot eighty-two, the next day eighty-five. On the third day, when she was doing so poorly that she broke down and cried, her husband and friends tried to get her to quit and go back to the club house. "I don't pick up the ball!" she said and continued to play.[20]

The next year she won the National Women's Open, taking it by twelve strokes, as well as winning the Serbin Open, the Sarasota Open, the National Capital Open, and the All American Open. In addition, in 1954 she won the Vare Trophy, which was named for Glenna Collette Vare and awarded annually to the holder of the lowest stroke average in the LPGA. Babe's stroke average that year was 75.48.

But in 1955 the cancer returned, and she was in and out of John Sealy Hospital in Galveston. She kept her golf clubs in the hospital room with her. Betty Dodd, Babe's close friend and protégé, said:

Her muscle structure was unbelievable. Her will to live was so great she just wasted away to nothing; it was a very slow death. She had so much muscle, such vitality and was in such good shape, it took time to wear her down.[21]

Even in death she was legendary. She died September 27, 1956.

NOTES

1. Frank Litsky, *Superstars* (Secaucus, N.J.: Derbibooks, Inc., 1975), p. 350.
2. Babe Didrikson Zaharias (as told to Harry Paxton), *This Life I've Led: My Autobiography* (New York: A. S. Barnes and Co., 1955), p. 181.
3. William Oscar Johnson and Nancy P. Williamson, *"Whatta-Gal": The Babe Didrikson Story* (Boston-Toronto: A Sports Illustrated Book, Little, Brown and Co., 1975, 1977), p. 35.
4. Zaharias, p. 9.
5. Johnson and Williamson, p. 73.
6. *Ibid.*, p. 111.
7. *Ibid.*, p. 137.
8. *Ibid.*, p. 59.
9. *Ibid.*, p. 137.
10. Zaharias, p. 61.
11. *Ibid.*, p. 47.
12. *Ibid.*, p. 190.
13. Johnson and Williamson, p. 20.
14. *Ibid.*, pp. 29–32.
15. *Ibid.*, p. 132.
16. *Ibid.*, p. 51.
17. *Ibid.*, p. 55.
18. *Ibid.*, p. 178.
19. Zaharias, p. 46.
20. *Ibid.*, p. 6.
21. Johnson and Williamson, p. 20.

MODERN TIMES

Janis Joplin.

JANIS
And the Austin Scene

Stanley G. Alexander

Janis Joplin's palpable accomplishments were small as such things go: four record albums and, by Port Arthur and Austin standards, at least, a lot of money, but what she left behind, more than anything else, was an image that is so immediately striking and so ultimately elusive as to be legendary in a sense that excludes stardom and press agentry. One pattern of legend features non-conformity, rejection and pain, hatred and punishment, departure and suffering, solitude and growth, accomplishment and triumphant return. Not only is Janis's life story redolent of features such as these, but it is also related to, indeed immersed in, the larger myth-story of youth society and youth culture in her time, the 1960s. This young Texas woman, rather average and unprepossessing in appearance (although rock reporters would, some of them, make a sort of goddess of her, later), became a symbol and a legend. By an alchemy that is both familiar and mysterious, she conveyed to thousands upon thousands of the westworld young an image which served to isolate and express what they themselves recognized as authentic: the tricky and well-nigh indescribable essences of their time.

Janis was born in Port Arthur on January 19, 1943.[1] Her father, Seth Joplin, was a longtime resident of the Gulf town, a cannery and refinery worker, and an operating engineer. Her mother, Dorothy, was a sturdy middle-class housewife during the family's early years and later was registrar of a local business college. A younger sister is named Laura and a brother, Michael. I never heard Janis say anything specifically

about her family, although she was always knocking Port Arthur.
Nothing that I've heard or read about her family or the city serves to
anticipate what Janis was like. In fact, little in her childhood seems to
indicate the precociousness so often reported of legendary figures, but
with puberty and adolescence, this changed in a significant way. She
felt herself to be different, different from her family and from her peers.
The story of the ugly duckling is suggested again and again by the facts
of her early life and, of course, by the manner of much of the telling in
the biographies and adoring obituaries. It is perhaps too easy, but I find
this analogy compelling. Janis began to separate herself from her family.
Whereas she had been a charming and loving daughter who had obvious intellectual ability and a flair for the aesthetic, she became the
wayward child.

Up to the age of twelve or thirteen Janis was interested and active
in painting. She was ambitious and productive, given the limitations of
her background and talent, but the intenseness of her disappointments
before giving up the art, this intense, almost violent reaction seems
now a certain prefiguration of the emotional power Janis would discover in singing and in the specifically sexual frustrations represented
in the blues lyrics she sang. When she didn't win the school competitions and when others gained recognition, one friend especially, that
she didn't, she stopped painting. By the time she was in Port Arthur
High School, she was no longer the quiet, almost withdrawn child who
had tried to please parents and teachers, but a fledged misfit who
already sought the identity of outsider, even outcast.

Her father once said that Janis was at age fourteen the first revolu-
tionary Port Arthur had seen. At first the word sounds terribly mistaken, overblown: she was a rather unattractive girl whose non-
conformist and vaguely anti-social gestures estranged her classmates,
most of them, a girl of "nice" family who unaccountably had the worst
people as friends and who yet cared enough to suffer from the predictable retaliatory blows and gestures.

Janis in Port Arthur was a child of the Fifties, when the staple of
popular magazine and newspaper journalism was Youth Problems,
with emphasis on drinks, drugs, delinquency, sex, and crime. *Teenager*
almost became a permanently dirty word, as did *juvenile*. Informed by
such images as those projected by James Dean, Janis early thought of
herself and her raunchy Port Arthur and Austin friends as beatniks. It
was the only name she knew, the only identity, which would counter
and offer insult to the patterns and probities of life in Port Arthur that
she so despised. Janis and her friends and a lot of people like them who
would become associates and fans—these were folks cut loose from
their hometowns, adrift and moving their not-so-slow thighs to San
Francisco to be hippies and freaks and rock musicians.

But up to—in fact, during—the time when I knew her as, like me,
a singer looking for an audience in Austin, she was still, despite the
virulence of her rebellion, inside the parameters of the middle-class life.
She was going to college, first at Lamar State in Beaumont, then at The

University of Texas, and then again, still later, during a season of disappointment and aimlessness when she had come home from San Francisco (about 1964), back at Lamar. That I knew her at all is a mini-lesson in the vagaries of history. Julie Paul was driving north on Rio Grande Street, bored as hell in her still almost new TR-3, when she saw Janis and Powell St. John and Lanny Wiggins walking along with musical instruments (Janis with autoharp!). Julie asked where they were going; they said to pick at a party. Julie went to their party with them and on the next Saturday night brought them to Kenneth Threadgill's old converted filling station-beer joint, where Bill Malone, Ed Melon, Willie Benson, and I had the best gig-for-drinks that ever was.

Imperceptibly at first, but then more and more dramatically, the music and the whole Threadgill's phenomenon began to change. Janis and The Waller Creek Boys were at about the same level of accomplishment as we were: Powell was a good, but not yet hugely competent harmonica player; Lanny was a novice, actually, on both banjo and guitar; and neither one could or would sing very much. Janis was still carrying around her autoharp and singing imitatively the repertory of such as Baez and Judy Collins as she'd begun to do in the coffee houses near Lamar State College in Beaumont. Her range and power were just coming into play with songs like Bessie Smith's old "Black Mountain Blues" and a piece or two she did in conscious imitation of Odetta, who did an Austin concert in about 1960. Their most popular piece at Threadgill's, and very deservedly so, was "Silver Threads and Golden Needles," which, if you heard it now, would make you forget all about Linda Ronstadt and even the original by Buffalo Springfield.

Threadgill's was perfect for such novices as we all were, especially at first, when families and friends, old fans of Kenneth's, and his neighborhood Saturday night crowd were our main audience. But with Janis's performances the crowds began to grow tremendously. This was not simply the so-called Ghetto bunch, friends with and strongly identified with Janis and anticipating the freaky decade to follow. Now there was a large sprinkling of ordinary university students, younger Austinites, Threadgill's old fans and our new ones, and, by 1961, even fraternity and sorority types. There was an excitement that was new, that would now perhaps be identified by the word *energy*, and most of this was focused on Janis. The old filling station/beer joint soon was too small for the tremendous crowds. The musicians moved to the back rooms to wait their turns at the mikes and sound system Threadgill had installed, losing the status of customers and not quite gaining that of pros. Finally only a few people sat in chairs. Most stood or sat on tables or on the big window ledges. Sometimes it was hard to keep a beer high going, so many customers had to be served, and Bud, Kenneth's son-in-law and Saturday night bartender, simply opened beer bottles which were passed out over the heads of the packed crowd and accepted the money when it was passed back.

This went on for about a year, until Janis left to go back to San Francisco. Her close Ghetto friend Winn Pratt was dead now from his unbelievable car plunge into Lake Austin from a crest of Mount Bonnell, and people were drifting off to other places, usually on the west coast, some of them already having real trouble with the drugs they graduated to from mushrooms and cactus. Julie went off to Sacramento to attend the state college there. Teaching in Denton, I would only get news of Janis infrequently while on trips back to Austin. She was singing in bars in San Francisco; she was sort of down and out; she was in a band and getting a following; she was in Austin again briefly, because jobs were scarce or dope was a problem. Then she was out there again and from Julie Paul we learned that she was suddenly (1965–66) making it big. She was in a band called Big Brother and the Holding Company, and some people, recalling her general lack of sexual preference, mistakenly thought that she was big brother. Now you could learn about Janis from the magazines and television and your daily newspaper, and the old Austin crowd felt itself a part of those big events—but only briefly. It soon became plain that Janis was of that larger world out there. Reminiscing in 1968 with a writer for *Ramparts*, she had long since dropped the Austin identity she once had for us:

> *I went to California at a very young and fucked-up stage, about eighteen. I used to sing in a little bar outside of Austin, Texas, called Threadgill's. Fantastic bar. All kinds of hillbillies come in every Saturday night, and everybody brings their guitars and sits around a big wooden table and drinks free beer and plays. I sang Rosie Maddox songs. But I didn't really sing hard until I got with this band.*[2]

So, virtually nothing of Austin was taken into the Janis legend, a fact which may suggest how much the legend belongs actually to the rock ethos of California and New York and the dominant publishing and media concentrations in those locales. Some of the Austin bunch had been involved in getting Janis back out to California to join Big Brother and the Holding Company, specifically, Chet Helms, the main organizer of the band, and Travis Rivers, the stud sent to bring her back out, she remarked sometime later. Then, she was with—for several years actually living with—the band that was soon the number three San Francisco group behind Grace Slick and the Jefferson Airplane and the Grateful Dead. At a time when the San Francisco sound publicized by Ralph J. Gleason and *Rolling Stone* was becoming super-big, Janis naturally enough lost touch with Austin. On the other hand, she seems to have responded many times to old friends' messages, some requests for aid, and so on. She was sentimental about Austin, especially Threadgill, who always loved her and showed her a kind of hick-genteel admiration and grace that she never asked for or got from anyone else, barring possibly the kid from Maine that she talked some about marrying at a time just before the end.

The big break came for Big Brother and the Holding Company in June, 1967, when they were invited to play at the Monterey Pop Festival. During the Haight-Ashbury and North Beach years of playing mostly in the Bay area, they had been part of a striking and historically important development in rock, beating their way up through the competition to be one of the top three bands in the region. These groups, Big Brother, the musically fecund Grateful Dead, and The Jefferson Airplane, were at the top of the heap, the very top spot being generally accorded to the Airplane because of the popularity of Grace Slick. All three were at Monterey where the really big festival happening was brought about for the first time.

The First International Pop Festival, it was called, and it established a new American way to get happy. The crowds were there, 50,000 strong, in all the Love Generation chic regalia of beads and jeans, granny gowns, and colorful headbands. The entertainment was grand; Otis Redding was featured and Janis's intense admiration of him brought her to the very foot of the stage to get the full experience of his marvelous presence. The new fad of destructive performance was underway as The Who wrecked virtually all their instruments, Jimi Hendryx perhaps taking the prize by burning his guitar on stage. The Dead were well received, as were the Airplane despite a bad set. Redding beautifully worked the crowd into a unit of communal pleasure, and Hendryx was exciting and brilliant in his innovation. But it was Janis who blew everyone else away, including, as later events would show, her own band. Big Brother was the hit of the festival and Janis was the focus, not only of the crowd's loving response, but of a tidal wave of journalistic and popular acclaim. She was translated overnight into super-stardom such as only a few have enjoyed in this century of super-stars.

The magic that from now on would emerge between Janis and the crowds she sang to was tested again just weeks later at the Monterey Jazz Festival. Here the crowd was different, dominated by Blacks and others who came for the strong blues offering, an informed, aesthetically intense crowd not likely to be pleased by mere hype. Big Brother's afternoon on stage also scheduled such guests as B. B. King, Clara Ward, T-Bone Walker, and Big Joe Turner, a chastening array of talents given the special nature of the festival crowd. There were all of these downhome and traditional blues performers, one of Janis's biographers explains,

. . . and there was Janis, a freaky white chick from Texas who screeched and wailed and jumped and carried on. But she was funky enough so they could dig her. By the end of the first song, the Monterey County Fairgrounds arena was packed with people writhing and twisting along in huge chains. It was unbelievable.[3]

From now on the skyrocket-rollercoaster path of infinitely marketable popularity would have Janis in its very nosecone. Big Brother had already been recorded by Mainstream, a speculative outfit that got promising performers on contract and on tape but didn't do anything, really, until something big happened as at Monterey with this band. The result was *Big Brother and the Holding Company*, a very poor but commercially successful record of the band's accomplishments. Another result was a new management contract with Albert Grossman and a recording contract with Columbia Records. With people like Bob Dylan under his charge, Grossman knew what he had, knew what he wanted, knew what he could get for it.

The rest of the story is played out far from Texas, and, for that matter, far from the San Francisco where Janis matured and perfected the blues-mama personna she had begun to affect in Austin. A lot of her life now was lived in New York and on the interminable and exhausting eastern and northern tours booked by Grossman. By the time of the New York concerts and during the recording of *Cheap Thrills*, an unrecognized premonition of the band's fate was already being mentioned by critics. On the one hand these writers were perceiving the end of something special and regional in the music itself, the ending of the San Francisco phase. On the other, the perception was growing that Big Brother represented a mismatch, that Janis was too far superior to the musicians. More and more occasions of dissatisfaction and outright quarreling were marring their relationship and even some performances. Janis sensed that something was happening, too: "San Francisco's different," she told Nat Henthoff. "I don't mean it's perfect, but the rock bands there didn't start because they wanted to make it. They dug getting stoned and playing for people dancing."[4] By the time *Cheap Thrills* hit the stores, charts, and million-dollar and Gold Record marks —all virtually at the same time—Janis had decided to leave Big Brother in San Francisco and start looking for another band. The band was a casualty of Janis's growing professionalism, her need to feel that the huge crowds and all the buyers of records were hearing her at her very best. Likely Grossman was involved, too, in a long-term plan and the ultimate big bucks.

Rock music was now solidly a national pop phenomenon, and Janis was the greatest thing in pop music. In the great American mixmaster of dynamic culture the predictable concatenation had occurred once more: the cultish out-group thing is co-opted by everybody else. The outside becomes the inside, all the old bets are off, and the revolution becomes the quite-popular-thank-you established center. And, like always, a large segment of the population is proudly avantgarde and, simultaneously, hugely mainstream. Rock music is making it everywhere. Woodstock has happened. The *Kosmic Blues* album was a huge commercial success but got many poor reviews and a vast chorus of people saying, "Let's wait and see." This led to another band change and the creation of the Full-tilt Boogie Band that played for the last tour and the last album, *Pearl,* a title which picked up Janis's San Francisco nickname. She was in Los Angeles, doing the last work on the album when she died so suddenly on October 4, 1970.

My first reaction to Janis's death was anger, that she'd ultimately had so little control over her life. I had been put off by what I saw of her at the Threadgill memorial mini-fest she'd attended three months before. I had hoped to see the old Janis and all I could see was the projected blues mama, complete with gown, hat, and boa. I saw her as having been swallowed by her legend, by the image she'd created. Since then I've thought a lot about the image and what she herself may have meant by it, and what she thought about it.

What, for example, did she herself think about the blues mama image she cultivated as early as the Austin days? It is really no inconsiderable thing that she managed it at all, a white woman singing blues and making it stick, shouting, moaning, groaning, sweating, grimacing, tensing and moving her body in ways both crudely suggestive and inexplicably erratic. Part of the image was also the costume of long gown, Nineties hat or headpiece, and boa. Boa!! This part of the image had history and lore, and hence it was one for which some responses were already predictable. The image goes back to the "new freedom" of the era of the Nineties and the kind of woman who was then thought to be free and easy: the buxom, heavy-breasted dancehall "girl." It is fascinating that just a short time before her death Janis attended a cocktail party-press occasion given for Mae West in connection with the film of Gore Vidal's *Myra Breckinridge*. So here is the newly arrived star who sings the blues and many times affects a full-blown sort of Sophie Tucker apparatus, spinning something of herself off the West legend. She wouldn't have missed it, she told a reporter, because West was the "Queen Momma." Yet, despite the power and vitality of the image, in a peculiar sense it was overmastered by the way she sang and performed and by her own response to the pathos in the blues message. Janis was not in performance or in person a Sophie Tucker or a Mae West. Instead of their worldly wise eroticism Janis shows a terrible passion that seems to come from disappointment and despair for which love itself is no cure.

The last time many of the old Austin crowd saw Janis was in July of 1970, about three months before her death. Julie had called in May or June, letting me know about the memorial celebration planned for Kenneth Threadgill. I was seeing him occasionally in Austin while he still had the beer joint open, and we would swap information about who'd seen or heard of whom among the old group, with Janis's successes always a staple of the exchange. Julie said on the phone that, no, nothing was wrong with the old boy; his friends just wanted to get something going, have a get-together for all the habitues and sons-of-habitues who'd enjoyed his place over the years. And, oh yes, wow, Janis was to be there. She was to fly in from Hawaii, in fact, from where she's been resting from a lot of hard work. No one else that I've read, by the way, mentions this interlude, and I am coming to doubt if it was authentic information although it was repeated around the picnic grounds the evening of the celebration.

I wanted to go, was quite excited about it, to tell the truth. I'd seen Janis just for a minute on the Drag one bright Austin day when I'd come down from Stephenville. We didn't really talk then, and now I looked forward to seeing and hearing her. At about dusk, Shiva's Headband, Spenser Perskin's immortal Austin country rock group started the entertainment with a good, solid set. Toward the end of the set, when Spenser's wild fiddle had everything going fine, the word came rustling through the crowd: "Janis! Janis is here." And the laid-back picnic atmosphere yielded to an electric sort of excitement that lasted all night. Everyone was up, high with the prospect of seeing and hearing the fantastic lady who had made it so superbig. Everybody except maybe Janis herself.

I went around backstage after a while, hoping to see her. And so I did, finding her seated with others I didn't know on the hood of a pick-up truck nosed in toward the shed-structure backing the stage. She recognized me, but didn't so much greet me as slide down onto her feet and lean breathily against me, murmering something I couldn't hear distinctly. Then she turned to greet someone else and we didn't exchange a word. Unless my impression is wrong Lanny didn't even see her face to face during the evening. Suzanna, a Nacogdoches friend, had stationed herself near the Joplin group. She told us delightedly later that at one point Janis had some sort of disagreement with one of her companions and suddenly with both hands lowered her dress top and flourished a naked breast in the man's surprised face.

She sang at about mid-point in the evening. She was shaky, some said from a recent illness, some—Julie maybe—explaining that she'd been trying to cure a habit. Whatever she was taking that night didn't help, I think, but her voice was still strong, still had that quality that could make you break out with a case of shingles after a few bars. The two songs were a sort of Alpha and Omega offering from early and late: "Down On Me" from the first album and "Bobbie McGhee" from the last, *Pearl*. The twelve or fifteen hundred people gave her long applause and tried their best to get her back, but she was tired, she said, and wanted to hear Mr. Threadgill sing before she had to leave and catch her plane. On the way to and from the airport, Julie said, Janis talked a little about her life, the new album then being recorded, the touring and hard work. "It's not easy being Janis Joplin," she said.

This wasn't Janis's last visit to Texas, however. She came back once more about a month later to attend the archetypal and now-famous Tenth Anniversary Reunion of the Thomas Jefferson High School graduating class of 1960. The occasion is famed because it sheds some light on Janis's complicated character and her response to a career now more outrageous than even she could have imagined. Her appearance at the reunion was deliberately campy and outrageous. Clad in jarring purple and white satin, with pink and blue feathers flowing down from her head of wild, abundant hair, she wore sandals and a small trinket shop of rings and bracelets on fingers and arms. John Heath, a Nacogdoches attorney who grew up in Port Arthur a year behind Janis, had a friend at the reunion who said, as others have, that Janis was very wasted on this occasion and in Heath's words "People cut her a lot of slack or she would have been arrested."

Nobody's report suggests that the superstar Janis Joplin had much fun at her high school reunion, even though she was ooohed and aaahed over a lot by people who, ten years before, wouldn't have spoken to her. Her father didn't understand why she came back for it. "It was so out of character for her. Maybe the ten years made her a little nostalgic." But Janis's own words, spoken to a reporter, tell the real reasons and tell also how fame and fortune may actually never fully cure the wounds of adolescence: "Just to jam it up their asses. I'm going down there with my fur hat and my feathers and see all those kids who are still working in gas stations and driving dry cleaning trucks while I'm making $50,000 a night."[5] It wasn't easy being Janis Joplin.

NOTES

1. Insofar as published materials were used to form a background for the present study these were consulted on a few points having to do with chronology and with events which occurred in other places after the time when I knew Janis in Austin. Some of the works which should be mentioned in this regard are Myra Friedman's *Buried Alive: The Biography of Janis Joplin* (New York: William Morrow and Company, 1973); Jonathan Eisen, *The Age of Rock: Sounds of The American Cultural Revolution* (New York: Random House, 1969); and Steve Chapple and Reebee Garafalo, *Rock 'N' Roll Is Here to Pay: The History and Politics of the Music Industry* (Chicago: Nelson-Hall, 1977). Quotations were all taken from the useful, almost documentary collection of materials published by Deborah Landau under the title *Janis Joplin: Her Life and Times* (New York: Paperback Library, 1971).

2. Landau, p. 31.

3. Ibid., pp. 59–60.

4. Ibid., p. 64.

5. Ibid., p. 27.

1980–1981 Dallas Cowboy Cheerleaders.

LEGENDS IN THEIR OWN TIME
The Dallas Cowboy Cheerleaders

James Ward Lee

No one but the most conservative and exacting folklorist will enter a cavil when the Dallas Cowboy Cheerleaders are called legendary. The phenomenon of the Cheerleaders is not a prose narrative—one requirement for a legend—but the folk history of these young women is spawning songs, tales, and movies not only in Texas but all across the nation. That the Cowboy Cheerleaders set off the wave of professional cheerleading is undeniable; that the young women who made up the group were of legendary proportions is evident; and that vigorous and lively tales about the Cheerleaders began to circulate among the folk and the medium of the folk—TV—is beyond question. Therefore, to set the Dallas Cowboy Cheerleaders up against some of America's legendary heroines—Gypsy Rose Lee, Mae West, Marilyn Monroe, Ma Barker, Miss Bonnie Parker, and Ms. Gloria Steinem—does not seem a departure from the proper study of folklore and popular culture.

That the Dallas Cowboy Cheerleaders caught the fancy of the American public in the mid-seventies is mildly amazing. What is totally startling is that the Dallas Football Team has cheerleaders at all, for the Dallas Cowboys are to NFL Football what the FBI was to law enforcement during the regime of John Edgar Hoover. Thomas Landry, who—as the sportscasters can't resist saying twice in every game—is the only coach the Cowboys have ever had, shares the late Mr. Hoover's sense of humor and grave demeanor. The management of the Dallas team is part H. Ross Perot and part Billy Graham; in fact, if football players could take the field in white shirts and ties, carrying New Testaments, they would certainly be made to do so. That this computerized, Americanized organization of Bible-thumpers should suddenly in the early seventies field a team of half-clad, nubile pom-pom girls is as much an anomaly as if the legendary Rev. Dr. W. A. Criswell were to leave home, hearth, and church and propose marriage to the legendary Candy Barr.

But General Manager Texas E. Schramm did indeed unveil, so to speak and as it were, his newly done-up cheerleaders during a playoff game in 1975. Super Bowl X (1976), however, marked the official and total American debut of these legendary women before 50,000,000 television viewers. After that, the fatty tissue was in the fire: other cheerleader corps sprang up around the NFL; *Playboy* Magazine rushed to judgment and showed nude and semi-nude[1] pictures of various NFL cheerleaders—not "official" Cowboy Cheerleaders of course; talk shows ensued; firings of the photographees ensued; the legal profession became involved; girlie magazine publishers mumbled about the First Amendment to the Constitution of the United States of America; *Playboy* published a second cheerleader layout;[2] and enterprizing producers got out three television shows about the Cowboy Cheerleaders for the mass audience and an X-film for the dirty raincoat set.

If the foregoing paragraph makes it seem that the professional cheerleading phenomenon occurred in an instant, the paragraph is not misleading. It seemed that one day there were no cheerleaders for NFL teams and that the next day every team had a corps of pom pom wavers. The Dallas Cowboys deserve the credit—or the ignominy—for this sudden explosion. Following hard upon Dallas's cheerleaders were the San Diego Chargerettes, the Chicago Honey Bears, the Denver Pony Express, the New Orleans Angels (earlier the Bonnes Aimees), the Cincinnati Ben-Gals, the Buffalo Jills (as if Buffalo Bills were not a silly enough name), and, worst of all, the L.A. Rams' Embraceable Ewes. Even the staid Miami Dolphins formed a group, abandoned their ichthyological motif in favor of the name Starbrites, and hired June Taylor to choreograph their dance routines.

If the Cowboys were in the process of becoming America's Team, its cheerleaders were quick to become America's pep squad. Contrary to all we have come to expect from the television networks, the first big cheerleader special was made in Dallas and not in New York or Los Angeles. ABC forsook the Embraceable Ewes and produced a singing, dancing embarrassment called "The Thirty-Six Most Beautiful Girls in Texas." The show was mostly a series of production numbers built around Hal Linden and Charles Nelson Reilly, but ABC apparently liked what it saw well enough to come out the following year with a television movie, "The Dallas Cowboy Cheerleaders," with plots, subplots, character development, heartaches, and a happy ending. It was incredibly bad—stupid, tasteless, amateurish—and naturally it became "the second highest-rated made-for-TV movie in history. . . ."[3] After the initial showing and the obligatory re-run, ABC produced a sequel with the imaginative title "Dallas Cowboy Cheerleaders II." In the sequel, John Davidson replaced New York Yankee shortstop Bucky Dent as the male sex symbol, and, for some unaccountable reason, Duane Thomas, who never fitted into the Dallas Cowboy mold and was sent away, was hired as a male love interest. In both movies, professional actresses replaced cheerleaders in main roles, but no one was supposed to notice. "Cheerleaders II" ranked only 31 in the week's Nielson ratings, which may signal the end of the cheerleader boom or the emergence of taste in America. Or, more probably, the decline may be attributed to the over-abundance of T/A shows now fouling the airwaves. Incidentally, the Cowboy front office will allow its highly protected but unpaid cheerleaders to appear on such TV shows as "Love Boat," but it will not allow them to compete in trashsport jiggle shows against other cheerleaders.

It may appear to the reader that the concept of NFL Cheerleaders originated with Tex Schramm and that Mr. Schramm's idea sprang full blown like Venus on the famed abalone shell. Actually, the idea of some sort of cheerleaders goes well back into the history of the NFL. The usual practice had been to bring in various groups of high school cheerleaders and high school bands to provide some color. In fact, Dallas had a cheering corps from the start of the franchise in 1961. Ms. Dee Brock organized a group of male and female cheerleaders from various Dallas high schools, outfitted them in modest outfits, and acted as their leader from 1961 until 1974. The group went by various names—one was the Belles and their Beaux—until they were called, finally and simply, the Dallas Cowboy Cheerleaders. The number varied, and as the number of high schools increased in Dallas, the practice of taking one boy and one girl from each school created a too-large squad. The number finally stabilized at about ten, and the methods of choosing cheerleaders changed gradually until it became somewhat similar to the present method of holding open tryouts.

One of the problems with regular cheerleaders is that pro-football fans can't be organized and led in cheers. If one remembers seeing games before the "new-style" cheerleaders, one can see in his mind's eye a small group of frustrated high school girls jumping about and waving their arms before thousands of bored blue collar workers more interested in beer than in bellowing. *Playboy* gives the credit to Tex Schramm for conceiving of the new wave of pom pom wavers.[4] It may be true, as Jim Henderson of the Dallas *Times Herald* says, that "They say Tex' idea of a good time is tying his shoes,"[5] but if he did indeed invent the new cheerleaders he had his wits about him that day. Schramm is quoted in *Playboy* as saying, "It all started six years ago . . . when we reevaluated our fans' response to the kind of cheerleaders we'd had here from the outset . . . we changed our approach . . . and decided to make our cheerleaders more or less atmosphere producers."[6]

Schramm certainly produced the atmosphere at the new Texas Stadium in Irving, Texas. The cheerleaders appeared in revealing new uniforms designed by Paula Van Wagoner; the press of her professional career caused Dee Brock to be replaced by Suzanne Mitchell as duenna and Texie Waterman as choreographer; the stadium with the hole in the top suddenly became the Mother Church of Professional Cheerleading; and the Dallas Cowboys were quickly becoming America's Team.

A sensible person looking at all the hoopla surrounding America's Pep Squad could not but be puzzled. The folklorist or popular culturist is never supposed to be amazed at the goings-on of the folk and is supposed to be able to explain the various phenomena he is considering in dispassionate terms. But the case of the Dallas Cowboy Cheerleaders, their national popularity, the near hysteria of various NFL owners over the *Playboy* nudie photos of cheerleaders, the Cowboys organization's near paranoia over the treatment of the "Thirty-Six Most Beautiful etc." puzzles even the most detached mind and stultifies even the strongest will. The overriding question of "who really cares?" gets lost in the maze of facts which followed the first euphoric revelation of the professional cheerleaders.

What is needed here—and will be provided—is recapitulation. The cheerleaders were re-formed, as Mr. Schramm said, to break in the new stadium, and they appeared during a playoff game in 1975 and in Superbowl X in 1976. The notion of scantily clad young women above high school age doing quasi-dance routines while waving pom poms caught on. *Playboy* ran two picture layouts of various cheerleaders and caused a furor among NFL owners—even to the extent of having one or two pep squads disbanded. The news media began making fun of the moss-back nature of the owners, and the networks stepped up their exposure (pun intended) of the many NFL cheering groups. Even though none of the "official" Cowboy Cheerleaders appeared nude in the first *Playboy* issue, the Cowboys did not escape the first wave of adverse publicity, for as part of the first *Playboy* layout, there appeared, as an allied story, a feature on the Dallas Cowgirls, Inc., a group of former "official" cheerleaders who had formed a rump organization to capitalize on the popularity of the Dallas Cowboy Cheerleaders.[7]

It was at about the time of the first *Playboy* issue that things began to go wrong for the Cowboys. The Cowgirls, Inc. had produced a poster in competition with the "officials," and the Cowboy organization sued. A porn film maker did a movie called "Debbie Does Dallas" and the organization sued. Later, a male gate crasher dressed in a cheerleader uniform and a wig jumped in among the cheerleaders—the Cowboys sued. Ms. Suzanne Mitchell saw someone selling a desk at the Big D Bazaar with a decoupage of a cheerleader on it, and she threatened to sue. The sober, high-nosed attitude and litigious nature of Schramm and Co. must have created real joy among the legal profession. Their attitudes gave the newspaper people material for many acerb comments on slow news days. Jim Henderson's article entitled "Going Up Against the Organization" appeared on Christmas Day, 1979—a slow news day—and raked the Cowboys over the embers. He ran through a number of their legal jokes, including the one about the go-go dancer who billed herself as a former cheerleader. Henderson says, ". . . The Organization sent hit men to enjoin her from using the sacred colors to market her skin show." He concludes by commenting that the Cowboys can and will sue anybody into the headlines: "If you ever decide to break into show business, go out to Texas Stadium, wear a stingy-brim hat and scowl through the highlights. Chances are you'll get busted for impersonating Landry and your career will be on its way."[8]

Why Dallas didn't sue ABC over the third Cheerleader production is hard to determine. That made-for-TV movie pictured Ms. Suzanne Mitchell in a most unflattering light. Ms. Mitchell was played by actress Laraine Stephens as cold, heartless, stupid, and downright mean. If Ms. Mitchell were as cold and as hard as ABC made her seem, it is hard to believe that hundreds of aspiring actresses and models would pour into Dallas each spring to try and become one of "The Thirty-Six etc."

But come they do. From all over Texas. Girls from Longview and Plainview; from Clute and Clyde and Claude; from Fort Davis and Fort Stockton and Fort Worth; from San Antonio, San Augustine, San Saba, and San Angelo; from Hico and Waco and Chico—and would come from Groucho and Harpo if we had named our towns properly. The aspirants come from all sorts and conditions of women. There are nurses and teachers, carhops and costume designers and coeds, former drum majorettes and superannuated high school cheerleaders. All are drawn to Dallas, which is to cheerleading what Milwaukee is to beer, Nashville is to hillbilly music, and Bogota is to controlled substances.

The only entrance requirements are a pure heart, a firm body, a mastery of the dreaded pom pom, and the ability to move sinuously to the stirring strains of the national anthem of all cheerleading, the soundtrack from "Saturday Night Fever." Tryouts go on for weeks. Ms. Suzanne Mitchell, Texie Waterman (who played herself in both movies), disc jockey Ron Chapman, and even Imperial Potentate Texas E. Schramm sweat and swink, weep and fast, over the selections. When the final cuts are made and all but thirty-six hearts broken for a se'ennight or two, the new corps is formed and the next season is underway.

All this "post-haste and romage in the land" leads thirty-six young women toward a job which pays $15 a week. In the early days the girls made little more than the stipulated $15, but in recent years they have made a great deal more on various promotions. Ms. Tina Jimenez, who was a member of the squad in 1976, but who was cut in 1977 "for no good reason,"[9] and helped to form the "Cowgirls, Inc." to get in on some of the aftermath of the cheerleader craze, claims that the Cowboys Organization took all the proceeds from the "official" poster "to pay for Tony Dorsett's entire multimillion-dollar contract," but made the cheerleaders buy their own boots and "pay for the special nail polish they wanted us to use."[10] That the Cowboys are not a free-spending organization is well known; in fact, the cheerleaders have had to find their own sponsors for trips to the Super Bowl on several occasions. A press release given me by an anonymous informant tells that Dallas businessman Paul McGuire paid the whole tab for the cheerleaders trip to Super Bowl V in Miami. For Super Bowl VI in New Orleans, it took the efforts of the Sunrise Optimist Club of Dallas and Vickery and Co., a carpet distributing company, to get the girls to the big game. The cost of the trip to New Orleans was $1,300. These trips were made in the days when Dallas still used high school cheerleaders, but Ms. Jimenez claims that in the semi-pro days "a local radio station and Dr. Pepper" paid for a Super Bowl trip.

Nowadays, it appears that being a Cowboy Cheerleader pays well—both for the thirty-six and for the Organization. The girls perform on TV, at state fairs and ribbon cuttings, and at certain other carefully selected events. The cheerleaders group was incorporated in 1978[12] and has worked out a system for all promotions. No fewer than two girls can attend a function; no appearances are made where liquor is served; and any request for the presence of the cheerleaders is carefully screened. The fees are large—all Ms. Suzanne Mitchell will say is "It's a lot" and declined comment that for big attractions the fee is $2,000 per day per cheerleader.[13]

Ms. Mitchell is vice-president and director of the Dallas Cowboy Cheerleaders, Inc., whose talents are represented by New York's William Morris Agency, but "nothing is accepted for them without the okay of the Cowboy management in general and Miss Mitchell in particular."[14]

The talents of these young women have paid off almost as handsomely as Ms. Tina Jimenez has suggested. One estimate is that the "official" poster sold 700,000 copies at prices ranging between $1.99 and $2.50 each. If all the money for that poster went to the Cowboys, as has been suggested, the proceeds should go a long way to paying Dorsett's large salary. It appears that the Cheerleaders now share in the proceeds of public appearances and other activities in a way that causes cheerleading to be a modestly lucrative business. The present arrangement works as follows:

> . . . *each girl gets a flat negotiated fee, with transportation, hotel and food also paid. Of that total cumulative fee, the Dallas Cowboys get a cut of not quite one-third, and the Cheerleaders get one-half of the remainder. The other half, Miss Mitchell explained, goes into a pool and is split between all 36 Cheerleaders at the end of the year.*[16]

It seems that the press coverage of the NFL cheerleaders is not as great as it once was, and it is possible that the fad will go the way of the famous hula hoop of the fifties. Once the personal appearance money begins to become diminished, the Cowboy front office is not likely to do much in the way of subsidizing the squad. But it is quite clear that no matter what the pay is, young ladies will keep rushing to Dallas every spring to try out. At present, 2000 girls appear to try and become one of the "36 et ceteras." And many of them see the year or so, as Ms. Jiminez did, as "steppingstones to stardom."[17] It may be that stardom will not come from these small but publicized beginnings, but the group will live in legend alongside the sturdy pioneer women who helped conquer Texas, the valiant maggies who helped conquer A&M, and the famous ladies of La Grange who helped conquer boredom for thousands of undergraduates and even some of Texas' finest lawmakers.

NOTES

1. Robert Blair Kaiser, "Pro Football's Main Attractions," *Playboy*, 25 (December 1978), 152–60, 380–82. Much of the documentation of this essay comes from various news sources, but some comes from informants who cannot be named because of their connections with the Dallas Cowboy Football Team. No one connected with the Cowboys will speak for publication without the consent of the team's front office. Some useful informants could not be used because the Cowboys required approval of the text as a condition for cooperation I was told.

2. Walter L. Lowe and Dan Sheridan, "What Do You Say to a Naked Cheerleader? Goodbye!" *Playboy*, 26 (March 1979), 143–51, 173.

3. Bob Brock, "Cheerleaders Return to the Ratings Bowl, Dallas *Times Herald*, Jan. 13, 1980, Sec. H, p. 1.

4. Kaiser, p. 155.

5. "Going Up Against the Organization," Dallas *Times-Herald*, Dec. 25, 1979, Sec. E, p. 1.

6. Kaiser, p. 155.

7. "Texas Cowgirls, Inc." *Playboy*, 25 (December 1978), 162–63, 380.

8. Henderson, Sec. E, p. 1.

9. "Texas Cowgirls, Inc." p. 162.

10. *Ibid.*, p. 380.

11. *Ibid.*

12. Paul Rosenfield, "The Cheerleaders' Sideline," Dallas *Times-Herald*, Nov. 22, 1979, Sec. K, pp. 1, 15, 17.

13. *Ibid.*, pp. 1, 15.

14. *Ibid.*, p. 15.

15. Ruth Eyre, "Topless Cheerleader Poster a Sellout: Judge Temporarily Halts Distribution," Dallas *Times-Herald*, Dec. 23, 1978, Sec. B, pp. 1–3.

16. Rosenfield, "The Cheerleaders' Sideline," p. 17.

17. "Texas Cowgirls, Inc." p. 162.

Same old song, new words.

HONKY TONK ANGELS

Sue Simmons McGinity

I didn't know God made honky tonk angels
I might have known you'd never make a wife
You gave up the only one that ever loved you
And went back to the wild side of life.

My fascination with the wild side of life and those mysterious beings commonly known as honky tonk angels and honky tonk queens began when I was a growing youngster deep in the heart of rural Texas. When my parents and I made our weekly shopping trek to the county seat, I was intrigued with the sounds, aromas, and figures that flowed from the maws of the twentieth-century variant of the old-time saloon or tavern. Within the four walls of the honky tonk were dim-lit bars and dance floors where displaced and laboring menfolk, along with an occasional feminine counterpart, sought refuge from their daily toil and the heartbreaks of reality. By World War II years, when I became acquainted with this social institution, the musical sounds of old-time string bands had been replaced by those emanating from a money-hungry machine known as the jukebox. While the honky tonk patron passively sipped his beer, raised hell with a fellow customer, or two-stepped across the wooden floor with a honky tonk angel, he could listen to the mournful voice of Ernest Tubb, who repeatedly complained about "walking the floor" over a lost love. A little later, he could empathize with Hank Williams, Sr., who seemed to continually have the "honky tonk blues," or some similar malady.

Although the honky tonk angel, with her heavy makeup, tightly curled hair, and even tighter dress was obviously not in the same hierarchy as the celestial ones I had learned about at mother's knee or in Sunday School, she was far more interesting to me. Publicly damned or praised, or both, she was a popular figure in a large percentage of country-western lyrics and in barrooms and honky tonks where she worked or "hung out." Her dualistic image gained national recognition in the early fifties, when song writers and performers began to debate the question of her origin and maker. Hank Thompson proclaimed in the still-popular "Wild Side of Life," that he didn't know that it was God who made her, while in a song entitled "It Wasn't God Who Made Honky Tonk Angels," Kitty Wells contended the distaff point of view—that there was always a man to blame for her existence.

While this controversy swept the nation's air waves via radio, phonograph, and jukebox, in my home county, God, together with the Southern Baptists, voted the county seat "dry." Not only was the honky tonk angel soon dethroned in my personal milieu, but following the untimely death of the greatest honky tonk singer of them all, Hank Williams, the nation and I began to move our feet and bodies to the beat of popular music heavily influenced by rock 'n roll. Jukeboxes pounded out "Blue Suede Shoes" and country pop fare by singers like Jim Reeves, whose lyrics retained the honky tonk flavor, but whose instrumentation and vocalization style did not.

Even though the honky tonk queen was never completely deposed from her barstool throne in country music or real life, she temporarily took a public back seat to the teeny-bopper heroes. However, the people who fed the music machines, paid the cover charges, and bought recordings demanded cheatin' songs, where the honky tonk angel still reigned. By the 1960's, with the revival of the honky tonk songs, she was permanently settled in the public spotlight once more.

The oxymoronic terms *honky tonk angel* and *honky tonk queen*, both well worn in country music lyrics, carry dual connotations, while they also acknowledge the twofold nature of the honky tonk woman. Regardless of whether the lyrics glorify or condemn her, however, they always define her in her relationship to a male or males. That is, she is limited to several roles, or their variants. From one viewpoint, she is described somewhat like a goddess, but in spite of her sometime extreme exaltation, her feet of clay are revealed. In no song are the two sides of this figure so well developed as in "The Queen of the Silver Dollar," first popularized about a decade ago by Doyle Holley and later by Dave and Sugar. The lyrics cleverly sustain irony and a royalty metaphor throughout. By means of a cross town bus, this queen travels each night to her "smokey kingdom." As she enters to the music of an "old piano minstrel," she claims her only symbols of royalty—her barstool throne and wine glass scepter. "Jesters" compete for the favors of the pathetic figure, who wears a "stained and slightly torn" satin dress, "scuffed and worn" shoes, and jewels that are only rhinestones. Her duality is reinforced and given an additional facet of meaning in the final stanza, as the male singer-narrator confesses his own role in her life:

> *The Queen of the Silver Dollar*
> *Is not as haughty as she seems;*
> *She was once an ordinary girl with ordinary dreams;*
> *But I found her and I won her,*
> *And I brought her to this world;*
> *I'm the man who made a Queen of a simple country girl.*

Repeatedly, such lyrics point out that the honky tonk angel's fall was not her own doing, but that of a male or males. Moreover, from the male point of view, she can be redeemed through him or another male. Like Milton's Lucifer and company, she exists in a hell-like milieu, but retains remnants of her "angelic" nature. These factors help assuage the guilt-stricken conscience of the male. If an angel can fall, not only is he, much like Adam, also allowed to do so, but his exoneration will be even greater if he is instrumental in saving a fallen angel from destruction. In many songs, the male speaker vows to himself and to the deposed one, that *he* is her *only* salvation. In "Neon Rose," sung by Mel Tillis, for example, the "blue, blue rose that grows 'neath the neon sun," is described as a "sunshine lady, maybe just a little bit shady," who will some day have the opportunity, with the aid of the male, of course, to go where "real flowers grow." However, until such time, he implies, she must content herself with being *his* "precious neon rose."

More often than not, the lyrics treat the honky tonk angel as a victim, who was once an innocent *country* girl with old-fashioned virtues. With the troubles she has suffered, however, an angel would turn to sin. A Bicentennial year hit for Wayne Kemp, "Waitin' On the Tables," tells the story of just such a martyr.

> *She cried the night he left her,*
> *But she's gonna make it now;*
> *She's just trying to make a living*
> *The best way she knows how;*
> *All the dirty jokes from barroom folks,*
> *She ain't got time to learn;*
> *She's just waitin' on the tables;*
> *Waitin' for the tables to turn.*

In short, the victimized woman talks, laughs, flirts, and follows the crowd, while her male creator ashamedly looks on. Conway Twitty, popular honky tonk genre singer since about the mid-sixties, speaks for such a blameworthy male in a recently popular song, "The Image of Me." Warning the listener not to be fooled by the happy persona of a particular honky tonk angel, he discloses the male's role in her creation:

> *I met her in a little country town.*
> *She was simple and old-fashioned in some ways;*
> *But she loved me until I dragged her down,*
> *Then she just gave up and drifted away.*

A similarly sad and tragic story is told in "That Girl Who Waits on Tables," a hit in the early seventies by award-winning musician Ronnie Millsap. As the lyricist-speaker watches the victim serving drinks and dancing with other men, who lustfully admire her, he recalls:

> *That girl who waits on tables used to wait for me at home,*
> *And she waited 'til all her love was gone;*
> *I'm too late, but I still worship the floor she's dancing on;*
> *That girl who waits on tables used to wait for me at home.*

In other lyrics, the spokesman collectively accepts the guilt for the angel's fall. "It's men like me that are to blame," he may confess. More common, however, is the male who watches his one-man woman as she only plays the role of a honky tonk angel for "big tips." In some songs, under the watchful eye of her lover, the honky tonk working girl smiles and shakes her "pretty hips" at other men. However, as Barbara Mandrell's and David Houston's duo, "After Closing Time," reveals, when the barroom lights are turned off, the temptress turns on her man, who comforts himself and exonerates her as he brags, "she'll be mine after closing time."

Few traditional country music lyrics that portray the honky tonk angel as victim are sung by or from the female viewpoint. However, one of the all-time greats, Kitty Wells' "It Wasn't God Who Made Honky Tonk Angels," though penned by a male, points an accusing finger at "married men" who "think they're still single." A more recent, though never-so-popular ballad, features a soliloquy addressed to her sweetheart's mother. Admitting various indiscretions, she acknowledges, through songster Leona Williams "Yes ma'am, he found me in a honky tonk," and "I've seen the other side of town where good girls shouldn't go." However, as she vows her love, she reminds mom, that "some one like your lovin' son helped to show me how."

From still another perspective, the honky tonk angel in relation to the males in her life, is pictured as a maternal being. Although the active honky tonk angel is no one's real mother in traditional country lyrics, she can and does serve as a mother substitute. In such portraits, her celestial qualities are less obvious, but her goodness is extolled. Regardless of her specific role as friend, lover, guide, comforter, and at times, even wife, in this capacity she is loving, nurturing, and helpful to the men in her life. A classic example is "Country Bumpkin," popularized in the early seventies by vocalist Cal Smith. It narrates the account of a country male on whom one could "almost smell the barnyard," and a "barroom girl with wise and knowing eyes." In spite of her initial repulsion and ridicule of the country-boy-come-to-town, they are soon married, and within the proper time, behold, "that same woman's face was wrapped up in a raptured look of love and tenderness," as she admired her "boy child" or newly arrived "country bumpkin." Concluding with her death scene, the lyrics reiterate her farewell to her husband and son, "So long, country bumpkins, . . . I've seen some sights, and life's been somethin'/ See you later, country bumpkins."

However, the honky tonk angel does not necessarily become wife and mother to be helpful. In "Bartender's Blues," George Jones sings the plight of a depressed male "standing at the edge of the sea," yearning for "a honky tonk angel to hold me tight to keep me from slippin' away." Elevated to a virtual saviour figure, the "blue ribbon angel" in Nick Nixon's "It's Only a Barroom," is defended by the male spokesman as "one of a kind/And not just a tramp that I found." Moreover, when he reaches her Kingdom, he'll "be in seventh heaven."

"Honky Tonk Angel," popular now and in recent years on labels bearing a wide range of artists' names, including that of Elvis Presley and Conway Twitty, succinctly expresses the friendship role of the loving honky tonk woman. A combination plea and accusation by a dejected husband/lover who bemoans the lack of love at home, it seems to address his former sweetheart:

> So, tell me if you think it's over,
> And I'll leave it up to you how it ends,
> 'Cause if you don't want the love I can give you,
> There's a honky tonk angel who'll take me back in.

Ironically, the speaker says that the honky tonk angel is an old friend who is waiting and will be happy just holding his hand, and he, hers.

As a comforter and "rock" or "fount" of inspiration, the maternal figure may serve as a spiritual guide to the loser on the barstool. In a 1977 hit by the popular Oakridge Boys, a tambourine-playing girl nightly fills the request of a lonely and down-on-his-luck cowboy, who requests a benediction at the "Y'all Come Back Saloon," the title of the song as well as the establishment, where an empathy seems to prevail between the singer and the cowboy, who share "faded love" and "faded memories."

"Rosie Bokay," a barmaid in a song by the same title, befriends the male who spends his nights atop barstool mountain. Although the male spokesman, vocalist Charlie Walker, makes no attempt to describe Rosie as an admirable woman, he clearly expresses his need for her and her fulfillment of his wants. He says in part:

> She pours me my label and sits at my table,
> And hums me a honky tonk song;
> * * *
> If not for the long nights I spend with Rosie,
> My days would be cloudy and gray;

and repeatedly expresses his need for her "to love my troubles away."

Still another relationship to man is shown through the songs depicting the seductive, good-time gal of the honky tonks. Because of her questionable reputation, she is the most colorful and best-known honky tonk figure. However, she is not all bad by any means. Her type encompasses several categories, but both good and bad traits seem to be present in all. From one viewpoint, she is a professional; the honky tonk is her life and she knows how to live in it. She is universal, as the traveling man says via Freddie Weller in "Liquor, Love and Life," another Bicentennial year production. The devil-may-care spokesman meets her wherever he goes:

> Out in Tuscon, Arizona, met an angel named Ramona,
> Smart, the best I've ever seen;
> Well, she worked at the Devil's Inn,
> Filled me with head-cracker gin,
> And danced into my world just like a dream.

Reminiscent of Merle Haggard's popular country classic, "Swinging Doors," a more recent song entitled "Cold Beer Signs and Country Songs," by Johnny Bush, partially recounts the story of a man who has been banished by his sweetheart, or wife. Explaining that the honky tonk is where he feels at home, he enjoys bathing himself in "neon lights, party dolls, and wine." In closing, he explains, "tonight it's who I'll go home with not who I'll go home to."

The angels in Red Steagall's "Party Dolls and Wine," Johnny Bush's "Champagne Ladies and Blue Ribbon Babies," as well as Jim Edd Brown's "Barroom Pals and Good-time Gals," are cut from the same cloth as the infamous honky tonk woman in the fifties classic, "The Wild Side of Life." Because she chose to share "beers, smiles and tears" with other honky tonkers in crowded back street bars filled with loud, country music, and thick smoke, "she'll never make a wife for a home lovin' man." This everybody's-baby-every-night type is clearly delineated in "God Only Knows Who'll Take Her Home." Not only does she paint her face and wear tight dresses, but the lyrics also infer that her dance card reveals a fickle nature; in the words of vocalist Red Steagall:

> The first dance of the night is mine,
> She'll do the fast two step with John,
> Watch her glide across the floor with Billy Joe;
> Next slow dance she'll give to Don,
> Kentucky waltz belongs to Tom,
> And, then, God only knows who'll take her home.

But lest she be judged too harshly, the final lines tell the listener that "she wasn't always like she is today/She had dreams and she had plans/To give her love to just one man."

A virtual country classic popularized by David Houston in the mid-sixties and sung by many other artists, is "Almost Persuaded," which pictures a drinking girl with "ruby red lips, coal black hair and eyes that would tempt any man." As this barroom seductress whispers "I need you/Take me away from here and be my man," the alert male sees the reflection of his wedding band in her tempting eyes, and in the nick of time escapes her snare. But even in these lyrics, she is not condemned; he simply remembers the one waiting at home.

The epitome of the seductive female as honky tonk siren is characterized in such songs as two made popular several years ago by singer Connie Cato. In "Superkitten," the feminine speaker warns "Mama Cat" to keep Tom inside while she is on the make. Haughtily confident, she growls:

> *Superkitten is on the prowl tonight*
> *With all her claws in sight,*
> *In a low-cut dress with rhinestone sets*
> *To glow in the neon lights.*

Moreover, she cautions, "I've combed my fur/And tuned my purr."

From the third person, admonishing viewpoint, the seductress in "Superskirt" retains many of the same characteristics as superkitten. The same feminine songster puts males, as well as other women, on alert:

> *She comes on like a rose in June,*
> *But really she's a Jezebel;*
> *She'll lead you on with sweet perfume,*
> *But you'll be sorry you fell.*

In hundreds of traditional country songs, similar to those used as examples, the honky tonk woman is directly or circuitously delineated. For the past four decades, regardless of time, these songs have consistently given her certain characteristics. First, she is eternally feminine—bearing the most admired and at the same time, some of the weakest traits of her sex. As such a figure, she is naturally defined in her relationship to males. Rarely do the lyrics dwell on her association with other women. While she acts as friend, comforter, or guide to the men in her life, she may also tempt or encourage them to drink, gamble, commit adultery, and lead a degenerate life, but her good qualities usually far outweigh the bad. She is frequently pictured as victim of life's hardships. More often than not, she has failed in some way, usually with the aid of the male, who takes credit for her creation and resultant downfall. Very seldom, however, does she overtly seek revenge. Instead, the barroom is her temporary stage and its inhabitants, only her fellow players. With their aid, she expects to go on to better things. Physically she is attractive and ageless. She is a WASP, "P"

meaning puritanical, even though, in this instance, she breaks most of the commandments. Ironically, in spite of the emphasis on traditional feminine traits, hers is a more realistic image than that of many other women in song and literature. She is not completely idealized or absurdly elevated, nor is she unequivocably damned. Rather, according to country music lyrics, the honky tonk woman is a queen without a crown, an angel without a halo.

> *It wasn't God who made honky tonk angels*
> *As you said in the words of your song*
> *Too many times married men think they're still single*
> *That has caused many a good girl to go wrong.*

The songs quoted at the beginning and end of "Honky Tonk Angels" are "The Wild Side of Life," by William Warren and Arlie A. Carter and "It Wasn't God Who Made Honky Tonk Angels," by J. D. Miller.

WOMAN AS VICTIM
In Modern Folklore

Ann Carpenter

How are women pictured in modern American folk legends, such as the urban belief tales and the traveling anecdote? For one thing, women are not pictured in modern legend as they were in legends set in the past. In narratives told as true or as containing truth in the pioneer past at least, there were narratives about active, heroic women to parallel our tales of folk heroes. Perhaps no women won the heroic stature of John Henry or Davy Crockett, but we have had legends of the pioneer wife who saved her husband's life by removing an Indian arrow from his chest with her trusty butcher knife—of historical figures like Kate Shelley, the fifteen-year-old girl who crossed the Des Moines River railroad bridge during a raging storm in 1881 to warn an approaching passenger train of a wreck ahead. Few such legends of admiration are related about modern American women.

In fact, the modern historical figures who seemingly might have become centers of admiring legends are instead made objects of laughter in modern jokes. For example, a typical joke concerns one time that Eleanor Roosevelt was accompanying her husband on a campaign trip and was confronted with a drunk man at a train stop. "You're the ugliest woman I ever saw," the drunk stuttered. "Is that so?" said Mrs. Roosevelt, "well, you're the drunkest man I ever saw." "Yes," the drunk agreed, "but I'll be all right in the morning." Jacqueline Kennedy Onassis appears most notably in a popular item in contemporary graffiti

which reads: "Jackie Onassis picks her nose." Some jokes about Lady Bird Johnson are not repeatable in mixed company.

How then are women pictured in modern folktales, in narratives given contemporary American settings? Most of the female images are the traditional stereotypes: woman as wife, mother, sex object, seductress, witch, old maid, loathly lady, and other types. One traditional characteristic, however, dominates the portrayal of women in modern legend: that is the view of woman as *victim*. The victimized female suffers in modern stories from physical pain, horrible fright, loss of a child or loved one. Many times she dies. She is innocent—undeserving of the suffering. She suffers alone. The cause of her suffering is some concealed danger in the environment that she cannot avoid. She does not act heroically; rather, she passively endures her suffering.

The plot, for example, is the same in dozens of urban belief tales related by teenagers. A madman (usually escaped from an asylum) hides himself and produces a threat to the woman; she may or may not escape death, but she does suffer. In one popular story, a girl is alone in her room one night while her roommate goes to do the washing. The girl is too terrified to investigate the mysterious moans and scratchings she hears, and next morning she discovers the body of her roommate, who has been brutally murdered (usually her legs cut off and lips sewn shut) and has died just outside the door. In another urban belief tale, a baby sitter keeps getting phone calls from a man who says he is murdering one by one the children with whom she is sitting. She feels secure since she knows the children are upstairs asleep. The operator finally traces the calls to the upstairs extension just as the madman murders the last child and starts down stairs after the babysitter. The plot is similar in the story about the woman who assures herself that nothing is wrong during the night by the companionship of her dog who sleeps beside her bed and licks her hand when she is scared. One morning she wakes up to find everyone in the house (including the dog) murdered and a note pinned to her pillow, reading "Humans can lick, too." Or the murderer-madman might be hiding in the back seat of the woman's car without her knowledge. She narrowly escapes when a truck driver forces her to pull into a service station. Or the madman may be roving lover's lane with a hook. One of the newest versions of the plot concerns a record called "The Roller Coaster." According to the story, while the song was being recorded, an art director (obviously mad) was posing a girl for the record cover. He covered her nude body with honey for the picture. When the honey would not come off, she became upset, and he murdered her. Her dying scream can be heard on the recording.

Most local legends and traveling anecdotes in modern America have the same female protagonist who is frightened, harmed, or killed, but the cause of her suffering is some other concealed danger rather than a madman. For instance, the popular legend sometimes called "The Department Store Snakes Story" is almost always told about a woman. I have found few variants about a male victim compared to hundreds told about a female. In this story the woman is trying on or handling merchandise in a discount store when she is bitten by a snake that was hatched out in the merchandise on its way to America from some foreign port. As a result she dies or loses a limb or at least spends a lot of time in intensive care. Likewise it is usually a woman who is injured in the contaminated food legend. For example, a pregnant woman eats a rat concealed in a bucket of Kentucky fried chicken and loses her unborn child or is paralyzed or dies as a consequence. Dozens of other hidden danger legends have women dying from LSD hidden in their drinks, from black widow spiders concealed in artificial flowers, or from roaches that nest in a girl's highly ratted hairdo and finally eat through to her brain.

The death of the victimized female is usually gruesome. She dies by horrifying means: her throat is cut, her lips are sewn together, she eats a rat. A number of modern legends concern women buried alive. In one text, a girl injured in a car wreck was declared dead by the justice of the peace and buried. Noises coming from her grave brought an investigation in which she was found alive, but she had pulled out her hair and bloodied her hands trying to escape; she died shortly thereafter. Another gory legend concerns bumping sounds heard by motorists on a large city street. Supposedly a young girl was killed by a hit-and-run driver, and the sound is her body bumping the fender. Or some say her arm was cut off and is thumping against doors of passing cars.

Even traditional female stereotypes are many times given added characterization as victims when they appear in modern legend. One example is the traditional loathly lady, the hideous woman who threatens a man. In traditional stories, she is sometimes transformed into a beautiful girl after a man embraces her or accepts her, as she does in Chaucer's "The Wife of Bath's Tale." The transformation does not often appear in modern legend, but modern loathly ladies retain three characteristics: hideous appearance, dangerous power, and frightening confrontations with men. The modern victim angle is added as the motivation of the frightening appearance or vicious attitude. The legends say that in the past the loathly lady has been the innocent victim of some horrifying accident or crime. For example, tire testers near Marfa report seeing a terrifying woman who seeks to lure them off the highway to their deaths. Her motivation? She has been a victim, for she and her husband died in a wreck with a tire tester. Headless women roam around Garden City and Sweetwater seeking revenge for their deaths—and possibly new heads to replace lost ones.

Loathly ladies are often turned into eternal wanderers because of something terrible that has happened to them. Bloody Mary haunts Winkler County with the cry, "Give me my baby," as she searches for her murdered child. Women who lost a child in a car wreck on a bridge are said to return to the area to search for their children in similar tales set in Winters and Stephenville. Even in modern retellings of the "La Llorona" (The Crier) legends of Mexican-Americans, the victimized angle appears. The Crier's children drown, and she is unable to find rest

until she locates their bodies for burial. Her cries are heard around rivers, lakes, and streams, and she may grab people, thinking they are her children. In many instances, informants go to great lengths to picture The Crier as a victim. Some say her husband left her, she was unable to feed her children, and so in a fit of madness and despair, she drowned them.

Other genres of modern folklore reflect a preoccupation with victimized females, although perhaps not as frequently as legends are concerned with them. Consider the most popular jump rope rhyme in elementary playgrounds:

> *Cinderella, dressed in yellow,*
> *Went upstairs to kiss her fellow;*
> *Made a mistake and kissed a snake.*
> *How many doctors did it take? One, two, three, four, . . .*

In parodies of standard songs, school children gleefully turn female teachers into victims. To the tune of "Battle Hymn of the Republic," they sing

> *Glory, Glory Halleluyah,*
> *Teacher hit me with a ruler;*
> *Met her at the door*
> *And shot her with a German .44.*

Or they sing:

> *On top of old Smoky*
> *All covered with sand,*
> *I shot my poor teacher*
> *With a green rubber band.*
> *I shot her with pleasure, I shot her with pride;*
> *I couldn't have missed her, she was forty feet wide.*

Or they may sing, "Row, row, row your boat gently down the stream./ Throw your teacher overboard, and listen to her scream."

As in these parodies, the female victim becomes the source of laughter in modern jokes if people believe she is somehow deserving of the discomfort or suffering. Apparently modern Americans believe she deserves to suffer if she is ugly or old, or if she is a wife, a schoolteacher, an old maid, or a mother-in-law. There are hundreds of examples, such as a comic ballad entitled "The Old Maid Song," which I collected from an informant living near San Antonio. The old maid in the song is a robbery victim. The burglar is hidden in her house (like the madman in so many urban belief stories). Furthermore, the old maid is victimized in being partially dismantled during the song. Her ugliness and status as "old maid" are the hearer's rationale for finding the situation comic:

I'll sing you a song of a burglar man
Going to rob a house.
He looked all around and then crept in
As quietly as a mouse.

About nine o'clock an old maid came in,
Being so very tired, she said.
She looked all around, but she forgot
To look under the bed.

Then she pulled out her old false eye,
The hair off the top of her head.
That burglar man had forty-one fits
As he came from under the bed.

She did not scream or holler at all
But stood there as meek as a lamb.
She said, "Oh Lord, my prayer is answered.
At last I have found me a man."

Then from a drawer a revolver she drew
Saying to this burglar man,
"Young man, if you don't marry me,
I'll blow off the top of your head."

That burglar man looked all around
But seeing no place to scoot,
He looked at that old maid standing there,
And said, "Lady, for the Lord's sake, shoot!"

It is difficult to understand why there has been little or no study of woman's image in modern folklore. Perhaps the multitude of madmen, snakes, contaminated food, and spiders plus the vision of mutilated limbs and suffering bodies have been just too revolting. Nevertheless, if we were not so close to these stories in time and place, we would probably be compelled to find out the reasons for their existence. If we encountered a Pacific island civilization that always pictured elephants being tortured, we would want to understand why the culture felt the need to abuse that animal in their stories. Understanding our own culture's obsession with picturing women as a victim should occupy us no less. Much more research is needed to uncover why we almost always picture our victims as being female instead of male. Moreover, we need more study to learn why we so frequently add the victimized aspect to every female image. The answers to these questions are likely to be complex and contradictory.

The image of woman as victimized female may perform sociological functions. The image may both reflect our culture's vision of femininity and influence females to pattern themselves after that cultural ideal.

Just as parents in our society typically discourage girls from fighting and other self-defense measures as being unladylike, heroines of children's literature, fairy tales, as well as many folk narratives provide passive models for girls to emulate. The horrors inflicted on passive heroines also serve as part of female training in fear, in the same way as parents' warnings of potential harm and dangers may mold girls to fear and avoid pain. Since we teach boys to be aggressive, to ignore pain, and to be brave (all opposite directions from those frequently given girls), males cannot be equally substituted as focal characters in most victim stories.

That the stories may reflect some very real fears should not be overlooked. The urban belief tales of teenagers, for example, should be more carefully studied as reflections of fears on entering the adult world and its unknown dangers, fears of sexual maturity, and fears of physical harm. The image of woman throughout modern folklore may reflect a preoccupation with this fear of physical harm. With hundreds of thousands of women being attacked every year, these narratives warn women about actual dangers lurking in deserted buildings, in unlocked cars, or lover's lanes, and even in their own homes.

Victimized female narratives may have psychological functions. The movement for women's equal rights has produced fear, hostility, doubts, and confusion among both men and women. This confusion may be reflected in the folklore. Perhaps we fear that woman is a victim of discriminatory laws, stubborn prejudices, and impossible expectations just as surely as she is a victim of madmen, snakes, and contaminated food. The victimized female of legend cannot avoid her suffering and usually cannot overcome it, perhaps reflecting cultural doubts about how to solve the dilemmas faced by modern woman. In the legends we may be transferring to the female story victim our guilty feelings about women and our misgivings about what woman's position should be. As the victim suffers or dies, we may feel a release of our pent-up emotions. We may have projected our negative feelings to an innocent but inferior victim to achieve purification. The victimized female—following the pattern of the innocent wrongly abused—in this way may be functioning as a scapegoat for modern America.

MRS. BAILEY AND THE BEARS

Margaret L. Hewett

The Baileys was born and raised at Big Sandy in Polk County, Bemie Bailey told me this. he is 84 years old.

He said during the Cival War, his Dady was a Cournal, while he was gone off to war his wife was staying, by herself with three small children, they raised the corn and fattened their Hogs, their selves, many nights she had to take a pine torch and go to the Hog pen and run the bears off, they got so bad she had to turn the Hogs out, so they could bunch together in order to fight the Bears off.

She killed a Hog and cooked the fat out, they did not have any floor in the House: it was all dirt, one night she heard something scratching, she got up and found a Bear was digging under the wall right where she had her grease barrel sitting she was afraid to move it back, for fear the bear would get into the cabin and kill one of her children, so she already had a little fire in the fire place, she got her old iron tea kettle, and filling it with grease she had it boiling, by the time the Bear had dug enough to stick his head through, she poured the hot grease on his nose and eyes, he let out a roar and jerked his head back, but he like to have torn the cabin down, he went so crazy, he screamed and beat the walls for an hour they didnot get any more sleep that night.

From *Tales from the Big Thicket*, University of Texas Press.

CONTRIBUTORS

Francis Edward Abernethy is Professor of English at Stephen F. Austin State University and Secretary-Editor of the Texas Folklore Society.

Stanley G. Alexander is guitar picker and country singer, author of *George Sessions Perry* in the Southwest Writers Series, and Professor of English at Stephen F. Austin State University.

Audray Bateman is the Curator of the Austin-Travis County Collection in the Austin Public Library. She is a member of the advisory board of the Texas Foundation for Women's Resources, writes a weekly column called "Waterloo Scrapbook" for the *Austin American-Statesman*, and published *An Austin Album* in 1978.

James W. Byrd is Professor of Literature and Languages at East Texas State University where he founded and directs the J. Mason Brewer Folklore Symposium annually. A past president of the Texas Folklore Society, he is a book reviewer and publishes articles regularly on Black literature and folklore.

Ann Carpenter of San Angelo, a regular contributor to the PTFS, has recently retired as Associate Professor of English at Angelo State University to write, paint, work in the family business, and watch her daughters grow.

Diane H. Corbin is a weaver of fine cloths, a Ph.D. in French, and a teacher of English at Stephen F. Austin State University.

H. Gordon Frost of El Paso is a professional writer who is presently teaching in high school and writing the definitive study of prostitution in the farthest part of West Texas. It will be called *Gentleman's Club*. Look for it at your favorite bookstore.

André Gorzell is a Dallas artist and writer currently formalizing the story line and illustrations for a series of children's books.

Martha Hartzog works as a writer for the Southwest Educational Development Laboratory, has published articles and a book on rare books, and is a researcher for the Women in Texas History Project.

Margaret Hewett is the finest story teller in Moss Hill in the Big Thicket.

Dan Kilgore is a Certified Public Accountant and weekend historian in Corpus Christi. He is a past president of the Texas State Historical Association.

Mary Kay Knief has her own communications consulting business in Austin, specializing in writing magazine articles, editing newsletters and magazines, designing brochures, and currently doing research for the Women in Texas History Project for the Texas Foundation for Women's Resources.

James Ward Lee, past president and twenty-two year member and jovial soul of the Texas Folklore Society, is Professor of English at North Texas State University.

Sue Simmons McGinity, Professor of English at Tarleton State University, is a traditional country music lover, picker, and singer.

Jack Maguire, executive director of The University of Texas Institute of Texan Cultures in San Antonio, has been writing about Texas for more than forty years. He is the author of three books and more than 400 magazine articles. His syndicated column, "Talk of Texas," has been appearing in state newspapers each week since 1962.

Mary Elizabeth Nye is an art dealer in Dallas, a long-time member and devoted listener at Texas Folklore Society meetings, and a very cultured and sophisticated lady.

Pamela Lynn Palmer is an amateur detective, historian, treasure hunter, genealogist, translator of French and Spanish, and rummager of old trunks. She's the Special Collections Assistant at the Steen Library,

Stephen F. Austin State University. A poet with two collections and a third in the works, this article is her debut in prose.

Maisie Paulissen teaches literature and film in The University of Houston. She has studied at the Folger Shakespeare Library, written for *American Imago*, and addressed the Fourth Annual Conference of Film and Literature.

John Neal Phillips is a free-lance artist, photographer, and film maker in Dallas.

Mary Beth Rogers, owner of MB Rogers Associates, an Austin-based public relations firm, is the director of the Women in Texas History Project of the Texas Foundation for Women's Resources. Mrs. Rogers is the author of several publications, including *The Story of Texas Public Lands—A Unique Heritage.*

Sherry A. Smith is researcher with the Women in Texas History Project, working with the Texas Foundation for Women's Resources.

Frank X. Tolbert is one of Texas' leading journalists and one of its most famous authors. His "Tolbert's Texas" must go back to when the *Dallas Morning News* laid the chunk and his *Informal History of Texas, Day at San Jacinto, Staked Plains*, etc. are all good beginnings in a study of Texas History. He's a big one!

Martha Anne Turner, former Professor of English at Sam Houston State University, is a prolific writer who averages two books a year in addition to her contributions to magazines and journals.

Marylyn Underwood is an English instructor at Victoria College in Victoria, Texas. She is a long-time area historian who has published several articles in history and folklore as well as in religion.

Frieda Werden is an Austin poet, researcher for the Women in Texas History Project, and the producer of a radio series for KUT entitled "Women of Action."

John O. West, president of the Texas Folklore Society 1968–69, founded *The American Folklore Newsletter* and edited it with his wife, Lucy, for the first seven years. A native of El Paso, he teaches English and folklore there at the University of Texas, as well as collecting Southwestern lore (especially Mexican) in the area.

Ruthe Winegarten is Research Director of "Women in Texas History— The Difference They Made," a project which created a statewide traveling exhibit on the contributions of Texas women to the development of that state. She is editor of the *Texas Women's History Project Bibliography* and author of "I Am Annie Mae; the Oral History of a Black Texas Woman" (Winter, 1980, *Chrysalis*).

ILLUSTRATIONS

Page 8 & 9/*The Lady in Blue*/reproduced from an early 17th century woodcut of María de Agreda.

15/*Angelina*/"Angelina", painting by Ancel Nunn reproduced courtesy of Claude Smitheart/Lufkin, Texas.

20/*Emily Morgan*/music courtesy of the Robbins Music Corporation.

& 21/wood engraving of rose.

30/*La Llorona*/wood engravings of flood & murder scene by José Posada.

& 31/woodcut of woman by Manuel Manilla.

38/*Belle Starr*/photograph from *Bella Starr: or the Bandit Queen*, 1889, Richard K. Fox *Police Gazette* publication. Courtesy Steck-Vaughn from the Steck/1960 facsimile edition.

& 39/photograph courtesy Hale Photo Supply, Oklahoma City, Oklahoma.

50 & 51/*Chipita Rodriguez*/wood engravings of accused woman & ghost by José Posada.

57/*The Capitol's Lady*/photograph courtesy Austin-Travis Country Collection, Austin Public Library.

59/*Sally Skull*/photograph of historical marker, Refugio County.

72 & 73/*Sophia Porter*/Photographs courtesy *The Denison Herald*. Portrait is in the Sherman, Texas Historical Museum.

79/*Elise Amalie Tvede Waerenskjold*/1895, from a calling card. Courtesy Mrs. William Warenskjold, Cleburn, Texas. From The Institute of Texan Cultures.

84/*Adah Isaacs Menken*/Mazeppa playbill from the Gabrielle Enthoven Collection, Victoria and Albert Museum. Signed theatrical photograph reproduced with permission.

& 85/"Tied to the Fiery Steed" frontispiece of "The Mazeppa Galop", one of many tributes to Menken's London boom.

94 & 95/*Elisabet Ney*/Liendo Plantation photo by Frank X. Tolbert, *Dallas Morning News.* Original portrait in her studio (Provincial Museum, Hanover, Germany). Photograph courtesy Texas State Archives.

106 & 107/*Mollie Bailey*/photographs courtesy Western History Collections, University of Oklahoma Library.

115/*Martha McWhirter*/courtesy Dayton Kelly, Salado, Texas. From the Institute of Texan Cultures.

123/*Aunt Dicy*/Mrs. Murla McGraw Gardner, 77, lives in the area of Kilgore and Longview. She had her Garret snuff ("Four star; it takes the strongest for me") on the bench, with a dip brush made from a twig of the proper tree. Photo by Bill McRae.

132 & 133/*El Paso Madams*/calling cards and photographs from Alice Abbott's photo album from the collection of H. Gordon Frost.

144 & 145/*"Ma" Ferguson*/photographs courtesy Texas Collection, Houston Public Library.

163/*Bonnie Parker*/Photographs courtesy of Archives and Research Center for Texas and Dallas History, Dallas Public Library. Bonnie with Clyde courtesy of L.J. Hinton.

173/*Electra Waggoner*/courtesy of Waggoner Estate.

175 /*Babe Zaharias*/photograph courtesy Institute of Texan Cultures, San Antonio Light Collection. Other photographs courtesy Babe Zaharias Foundation, Beaumont.

184/*Janis Joplin*/photograph by David Gahr from *Buried Alive: The Biography of Janis Joplin,* by Myra Friedman (Morrow, August 1973).

& 185/Photograph by Herb Greene from <u>The Rolling Stone Illustrated History of Rock and Roll</u> edited by Jim Miller (Random House, 1976)

194/*Dallas Cowboy Cheerleaders*/Photograph of 1980–81 Dallas Cowboy Cheerleaders courtesy Dallas Cowboy Cheerleaders to the Texas Foundation for Women's Resources.

& 195/Photograph courtesy the Nacogdoches Daily Sentinel.

203/*Honky Tonk Angels*/Line art originally published in 1870 & 1927. Modern photograph by Frank Habich.

211/*Woman as Victim*/Cynthia Ann Parker and her daughter. Courtesy Institute of Texan Cultures.

217/*Mrs. Bailey and the Bears*/Photograph of Sarah Elizabeth (Sally) Bolton courtesy F.E. Abernethy.

INDEX